— *A Maverick Publication* —

OREGON'S BIG COUNTRY

A PORTRAIT OF
SOUTHEASTERN OREGON
by Raymond R. Hatton

ISBN: 0-89288-128-3   PB
ISBN: 0-89288-129-1   HB

(COVER) **Spring comes to the Adel Country, east of Lakeview. Fault block mountains enclose a green, irrigated basin. This scene is typical of many areas of Oregon's Big Country.** Photo by Barry Peril, Bend.

Published by
MAVERICK PUBLICATIONS
P.O. Box 5007 • Bend, Oregon 97708

TABLE OF CONTENTS

ACKNOWLEDGEMENTS

The completion of the manuscript as presented here would not have been possible without the assistance of many. I would like to thank Stuart G. Garrett, M.D., and Dr. Bruce Nolf, Distinguished Professor of Geology at Central Oregon Community College, for their respective summations of the Plant Life and the Geology of *OREGON'S BIG COUNTRY*. Several people — I call them authorities — have provided information. At the risk of oversights, I thank the following: "Bud" Parks (Fort Rock), Lena Meyers (Silver Lake), Marvin Kaschke (Hart Mountain), Jon Scharff (Malheur Refuge and Steens), Pauline Braymen (Harney Basin) and Ross Butler (Treasure Valley) for their reading and critique of the parts of the manuscript on their local areas. Marcus Haines (Burns) and Bob Kindschy (Vale) willingly assisted me in my research. Individuals who helped with the photographs included Marcus Haines (Burns), Bob Kindschy (Vale), Barry Peril, Charles A. Blakeslee, Dr. Stuart G. Garrett (Bend), Ron Cornmesser (Ontario), Dr. Pat McDowell and Tim Townsend (Eugene). Their help is greatly appreciated.

Caryn Throop and Bob Boyd of the High Desert Museum assisted me with the historic aspects of the P Ranch and buckaroos, respectively. Librarians in Burns, Lakeview, and Ontario kindly assisted me in my research. There have been ranchers, residents and store owners living in small isolated settlements throughout the region who have shared their stories and opinions of their own "neck of the woods" ..er, make that desert.

I owe many thanks to Peter Hawkins who skillfully edited the entire manuscript and took time to discuss many different aspects of *OREGON'S BIG COUNTRY*.

Thanks are expressed to Lyn Jensen who designed the layout of *OREGON'S BIG COUNTRY* and to Ken Asher, Publisher, Maverick Publications, Bend, for creating the book from its manuscript form.

Finally, I owe a big thanks to my wife, Sylvia, for her patience and persistence in typing into the word processor the whole manuscript. Those familiar with my writing, must know what a task that was!

RAYMOND R. HATTON

FOREWORD

This is a glimpse at Oregon's Big Country, the sparsely populated chunk of territory that makes up Southeastern Oregon. In general, the region is that which lies south of Highway 20 (Bend-Ontario highway) and east of Highway 31 (La Pine-Valley Falls). This region, part of which is loosely called Oregon High Desert Country, contains some of the least known sections of Oregon. Historical data for *OREGON'S BIG COUNTRY* came largely from newspapers, especially microfilm of Burns and Lakeview weekly papers since the late nineteenth century. Field notes and interviews in the region provided important information. It is my hope that the unique character of the High Desert Country has been captured in *OREGON'S BIG COUNTRY*.

Typical landscape along Highway 20 between Vale and Juntura. The highway follows the Malheur River for many miles. Arable land as shown here is at a premium. Oregon Economic Development photo, Salem.

INTRODUCTION

My first introduction to Oregon's Big Country was in the 1950s while traveling northward on Highway 395 between Lakeview and Riley. I can still remember the towering ramparts of Abert Rim, but what impressed me most was the vastness of the desert. The year before, I had moved to Idaho from England — more specifically from the urban, industrial Midlands, a landscape of belching factories, unused polluted canals and rows of brick houses: relics of the Industrial Revolution.

Somewhere near Wagontire, I stopped the car, got out and surveyed the desert. The highway along which I had just traveled, and that ahead towards Riley, stretched like an endless ribbon, finally merging with the distant hills. The sun beat down unmercifully. So vast was the overwhelming space that I took the occasion to photograph the scene, later to show relatives and friends in England what the wide open spaces of America were like. However, at that time the desert landscape meant nothing to me.

Several years later I moved to Bend. I repeatedly ventured into the High Desert, learning in time to read its landscape. Powerful forces of nature, occurring in a time framework not measurable on a human scale, have tilted the land as if a giant were playing with building blocks. The shorelines of once vast lakes are clearly discernible around many desert basins. Here and there, etched into the hillsides, are small, cave-like recessions carved by wind-driven waves on the former lakes.

I close my eyes and listen. The wind, the seemingly ever-present desert wind subsides. I "see" and "hear" a small band of scantily-clad Indians, spears in hand, search for their next meal. They trail along a lake shore, their excited voices gradually dissolving into the returning desert wind.

Suddenly, along the trail ahead, clouds of alkali dust swirl into the air. A small procession of wagons, pulled by lumbering oxen, emerge from the dust cloud. The somber members of the migrant train, some riding on the wagons, some on horseback, some walking, all looking tired and gaunt, wearily make their way westward across what to them must seem like an interminable wasteland. The eerie creak, creak of the wagon wheels becomes more and more faint until the only sound heard is the rustling of the wind in the sage.

Yet another dust cloud, a far wider one, appears on the desert plain. Cries and shouts in Spanish and English echo across the lands. A cattle drive! ... hundreds of cattle, pushing, shoving, and bawling, driven by vaqueros and buckaroos, head for a distant waterhole, then far beyond to the California trailhead.

I search the desert for one more glimpse of history. Against the rimrock an abandoned shack, its siding and shakes weather-beaten by the scorching desert sun, sandblasted by the unrelenting winds, and partially vandalized by desert intruders, silently stands, testimony to the hardy souls who tried to take the desert. Suddenly, joyous shouts break the silence. Two young children, neatly dressed, hair combed, emerge from the homestead, wave 'bye to their forlorn-looking mother and skip gaily along a desert trail. Little do the children know that their school will soon close its doors for the last time. They and mother will soon move to the big city, perhaps Bend where papa holds down a job in the lumber mill.

The stage with its fault-block mountains, alkali flats, sage-studded plains awaits the next act. Soon, man with electricity, wheel lines and mechanized equipment will enter the scene.

As the afternoon sun gives way to evening, the rimrocks cast long shadows across the desert, which is now tinged by ochres, tans, and various shades of red. The day ends in a blaze of color as the western sky catches fire: one last chance to bring color and mystique to the High Desert.

These desert lands that I fleetingly glimpsed and almost rejected back in 1957 now take on meaning. Yet still the space and loneliness is overpowering. Miles and miles of sage and sand, contained by the abrupt edges of fault scarps or in some instances by jagged lava flows, are for the most part devoid of habitation. The small, isolated settlements such as Fields, Brothers, Frenchglen, and Riley become important hubs of activity, far beyond what their size would indi-

cate. Burns, Ontario and Lakeview, with traffic lights (well, there is one blinking light in Lakeview) and supermarkets and a downtown, become ''big cities.'' Klamath Falls, Ontario, and Bend, on the periphery of the High Desert, seem like metropolises.

This book focuses on Oregon's Big Country, a vast, sparsely populated region of Southeastern Oregon. It is in many ways still a frontier land, where the stereotypes of the American West — wide-open spaces, cattle drives and buckaroos — are very much a part of the landscape.

Highway 31 winds past ranches and homesteads established adjacent to Summer Lake in the late nineteenth century. Winter Rim, named by explorer John C. Fremont, overlooks the Summer Lake Basin. Oregon Economic Development Photo, Salem.

THE REGION

Oregon's Big Country, a vast semi-arid chunk of real estate, makes up Oregon's southeastern quarter. This geographical region, which extends from the edge of the pine forests of Central Oregon to the Idaho and the Nevada borders, at first glance (and for some, their second or third glance!), is largely desolate and windswept. Rugged fault block mountains enclose miles and miles of sagebrush plains, alkali flats, and in many places, surprisingly large lakes. To many, the landscapes of this section of Oregon are overwhelming, even frightening.

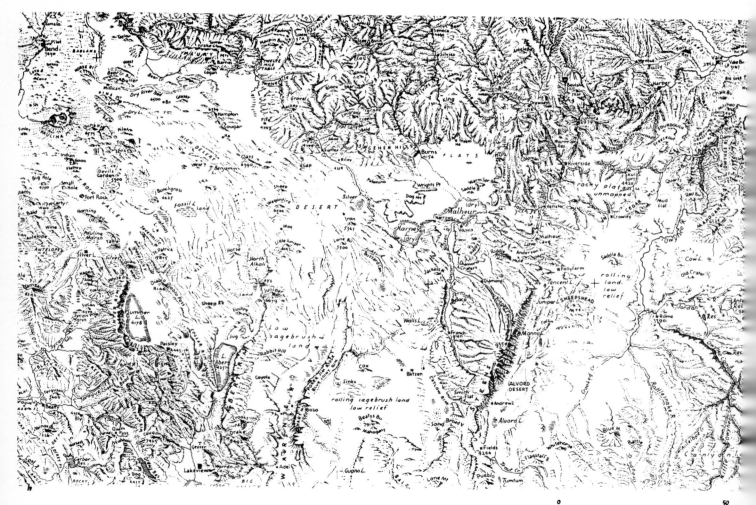

The main landforms of Southeastern Oregon are identified on this reproduction of part of Erwin Raisz's "Landforms of Oregon" map. The area shown, over one-third of the area of Oregon, contains only 0.02 percent of Oregon's population (Bend area excepted). Map from the *Atlas of Oregon*, permission of Dr. William Loy, University of Oregon.

Compared to the lush, green Willamette Valley, much of Southeastern Oregon seems barren and repulsive. Indeed, the history of the white settlement of Oregon indicates that people largely shunned Southeastern Oregon until late in the nineteenth century. Some of the first to describe the region were explorers — Peter Skene Ogden, 1825-26; John C. Fremont, 1843-44. Wagon trains, such as the Meek and Applegate parties, bravely ventured across the poorly-mapped desert lands. Marauding bands of Indians repeatedly attacked isolated ranchers, small immigrant groups, overland stages and miners passing through the region. The first "settlements" in Oregon's Big Country were military camps — Harney, Warner, for example — intended to bring peace to the region.

The 1863 Surveyor General's Office map of Oregon showed that while the Willamette Valley had been surveyed and settled (cities such as Portland, Salem, Oregon City, and Eugene had been established), there was no surveying, nor were there towns of any kind in Southeastern Oregon. Following this tumultuous period of history, large tracts of land were granted to companies who were supposedly required to open up the sparsely-settled parts of Oregon by constructing wagon roads. The Oregon Central Military Wagon Road Company, authorized in 1864, was to have surveyed and built roads from Eugene across the Willamette Pass and the southern part of Oregon to the Idaho border. The company was granted alternate, odd numbered square-mile sections in a band three miles (5 km.) wide — some 800,000 acres (328,000 ha.) of land. Road building was accomplished in certain areas but in 1873, the company's lands were transferred to the Pacific Land Company, a large San

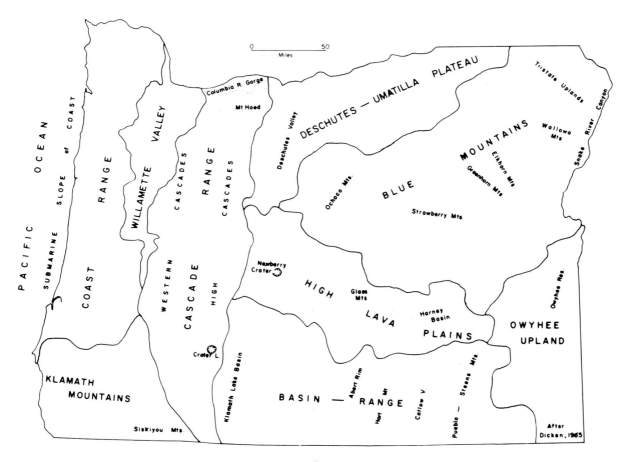

The geomorphic divisions of Oregon as outlined by Dicken. This book focuses on the High Lava Plains, Basin-Range Province, and the Owyhee Uplands. In this volume, the Klamath Lake Basin is not discussed; the Harney Basin has been included with the Basin and Range Province as its history and economic development is closely related to the Blitzen Valley, Catlow Valley, and Steens Mountain. Source: Dicken (1945).

Francisco-based cattle company. In the 1870s and 1880s, land bordering lakes in the Warner Valley and in the Harney Basin were designated swamp lands. Nearly a half million acres (205,000 ha.) of "swamp lands" were granted by the state of Oregon to one individual.

By 1885, Southeastern Oregon was crisscrossed by wagon trails, some becoming the forerunner of today's highways, others simply cutting across the desert where today the lands are uninhabited. The 1885 Corps of Engineers map of Oregon filled up large unsurveyed or uninhabited areas of Southeastern Oregon with names such as "Great Sandy Desert", "Sage Plains", "Alkali Desert", "Barren Valley". By this time, the railroad had come to the Willamette Valley, which had been completely settled.

By the 1880s, the cattle industry had expanded rapidly throughout large areas of Southeastern Oregon. However, a succession of severe winters (discussed in a separate section) decimated the herds. Later, sheepherders, many of them Irish or Basques, drove huge flocks of sheep over the range lands, at times in conflict with the cattlemen.

Early in the twentieth century, encouraged by the passage of the 1909 Revised Homestead Act and by promotional literature, hundreds of settlers flocked to the desert lands, expecting to find the advertised "rich, volcanic soils" and a climate "suitable for crops of all kinds." The homestead boom lasted about ten years. Climatic factors (especially drought and summer frosts), predators, and isolation combined to force out

Southeastern Oregon as mapped in 1885. Of particular note are the number of military camps scattered throughout the region and the extent of wagon roads, some of which closely approximate the location of existing roads. Other wagon roads were along routes that are no longer used for travel. The accuracy (or inaccuracy) of physical landmarks was a reflection of the lack of knowledge of the region as a whole in the 1880s. Map: Office of the Chief Engineers U.S. Army.

most of the homesteaders. The desert once again became almost exclusively livestock country. The 1921 Oregon State Highway Commission map reflected the impact of the homestead era. Dozens of communities that had been established between 1910 and 1916 briefly flourished and were then abandoned. There were, for example, twelve such places (Fremont, Loma Vista, Cliff, Fleetwood, Wastina, Buffalo, Woodrow, Sink, Arrow, Connley, Lake, and Viewpoint) in the Fort Rock Basin alone. Drought years, coupled with the Depression of the 1930s, led to a U. S. government takeover of large sections of the desert lands. Today, the Bureau of Land Management has jurisdiction over 71 per cent of Malheur County, 63 per cent of Harney County, and 49 per cent of Lake County.

The arrival of the railroads to Burns and Hines and to Lakeview opened up the way for these cities to utilize the large stands of ponderosa pine that cloak the mountains north of Burns and west and east of Lakeview. Today, the industrial landscapes of Lakeview and Hines include mill operations. In Malheur County, the Owyhee Project brought water and prosperity to the Treasure Valley. The arrival of cheap electricity in Harney and Lake Counties in the 1950s and 1960s made it possible to pump the ground water that lies beneath the old lake basins to the surface and to use it for irrigating acres of alfalfa. Thus large sections of the desert have bloomed.

However, as a whole, the scenery of Oregon's Big Country is mostly a product of the natural, not the cultural landscape. It is this natural environment that fascinates the "desert rats", those individuals who return and return again to the region. They will know the out-of-the-way places, will point out the wildlife: "Look, soaring ahead, an eagle... " "There... an antelope. No, two, three... more." "See that abandoned cabin over by the rimrock." "What a life those homesteaders must have had."

Yes, Oregon's Big Country is a region full of surprises. The scenic geology, the varied and abundant wildlife, the fickleness of the desert climate, the unbelievable expanses of sage, the open vistas, the solitude, the recreational opportunities all help create an aura of excitement and mystique about the region. Even some of the names of obscure places — Skull Creek, Deadman's Bedground, Devil's Canyon (Harney County), Jug Mountain, Poverty Flat, Lone

Grave Butte (Lake County), Starvation Spring, Defeat Butte (Malheur County), create curiosity. The region includes the better known Steens, Hart Mountain, Fort Rock, Malheur Wildlife Refuge, and Owyhee Reservoir. However, the region abounds in places virtually unknown to most Oregonians, including the Pueblos, Poker Jim Ridge, the Trout Creek Mountains, and the Sheepshead Mountains.

New discoveries are still being reported in the region. In the summer of 1986, Oregon State University anthropologist Roberta Hall led an expedition to the High Desert to check out the report of a "small pile of rocks that had been meticulously and mysteriously stacked in two long rows." The rock stacks or cairns, located on top of a sagebrush-covered plateau, stretched for over a mile (1.6 km.). A circle of stones resembled an ancient amphitheater and prompted the scientist and others to speculate whether the cairns had been used for astronomical purposes or for directing game to help in hunting. At the site was evidence that Indians had fashioned arrowheads and other tools there, perhaps as long ago as 9,000 years.

What other mysteries of the desert lands remain to be discovered? For example, at the turn of the century, in *An Illustrated History of Baker, Grant, Malheur and Harney Counties* (1902), D. M. Rosendale, a mining engineer, reported:

"I had occasion to visit Harney County last week and have every reason to believe that I discovered traces of cliff dwellers. I was alone on horseback, traveling through the southeastern portion of Harney County, when I made the discovery.

"The spot was a peculiar one. Cliffs of black basaltic formation, without a vestige of vegetation, rose abruptly from the desert and formed a narrow defile. After passing through the defile and leading my worn-out horse, I proceeded to scale a hill for the purpose of getting my bearings, as I had evidently lost them for the past six hours. Turning on one point of the hillside, which was half filled with sand-blown crevices, a strange sight was presented to me. There before me were about sixty-five cliff dwellers' habitations, deserted, of course, but in a fair state of preservation. The clear and unclouded sky was looking upon a picture of queer and very strangely formed small buildings, roofless, bound together with no material whatsoever, but hewn

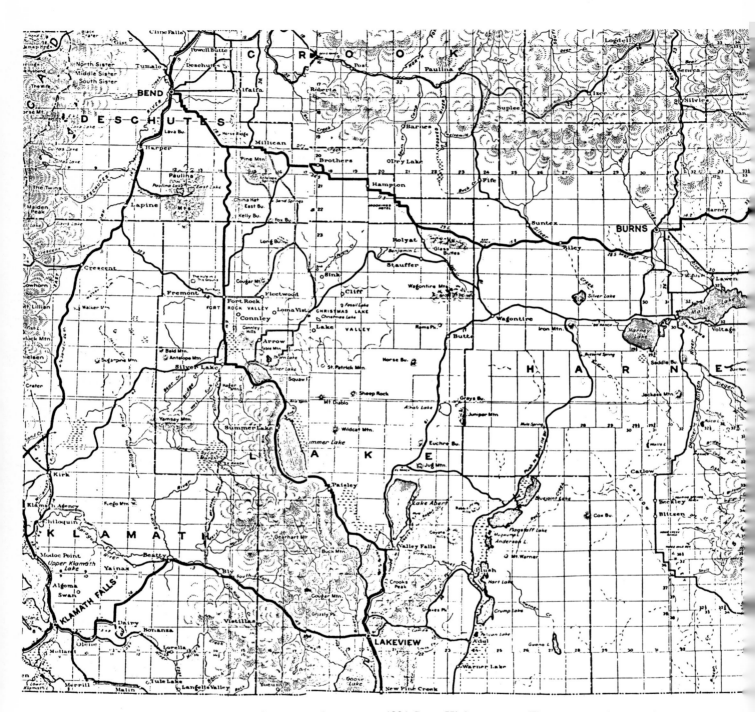

Southeastern Oregon as shown on a 1921 State Highway map. The map reveals several interesting features. Note the zigzag alignment of the Bend-Burns highway. The main Lakeview-Burns highway passed west of both Lake Abert and Alkali Lake then joined the Bend-Burns highway about 20 miles (32 km.) west of Riley. The names of several homestead communities are shown in the Fort Rock-Christmas Lake Valley, Catlow Valley and Alvord Valley (then known as the Wildhorse Valley).

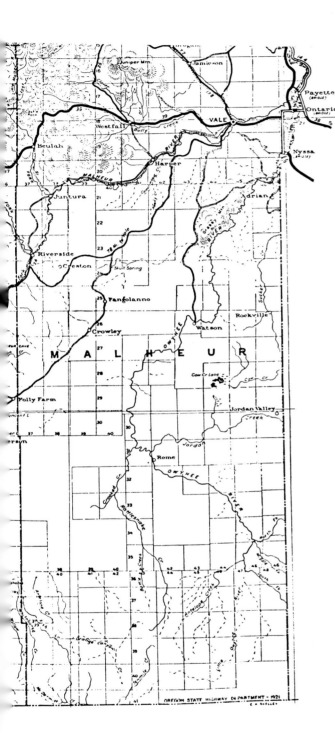

with all the skill of the ancient craftsmen.

"In the middle of the place was an upright stone, resembling the famous altar stones of the ancient Aztecs of old Mexico. Most probably on this stone the bloody rites of human sacrifice were once performed by an extinct race. As I was already much delayed in my journey, time did not permit a thorough examination of the locality, nor an exploration of the caves; yet I am thoroughly convinced that the caves served at one time as the habitations of what are commonly known as cliff dwellers.

"The interior of southeastern Oregon affords a great field for the mineralogist, the explorer, the entomologist, and the admirer of grand and weird scenery....

"So isolated is the Harney Country of Oregon from all the usual courses of travel, and so non-communicative have been the stockmen and prospectors who alone have penetrated to its most remote regions, that its topography, its mineral wealth and its scientific wonders are comparatively unknown to the general public...."[1]

And then there is the legendary "Blue Bucket gold" found and then lost by the Meek wagon train![2] Such intrigue!

The Geography of Space

If you take Massachusetts, Connecticut, Rhode Island, New Jersey, and Delaware and place these states in Southeastern Oregon, you would still have over 5,000 square miles (13,000 km²) left over. You would also have increased the population of the sprawling Southeastern Oregon region by over 44,000 per cent! Southeastern Oregon (Lake, Harney, and Malheur Counties and the desert area of Deschutes County) represents 39 per cent of Oregon's area, but contains less than 0.02 per cent of the state's population.

The late Reub Long, a lifelong rancher from northern Lake County, measured Oregon's High Desert country in terms of "looks". It is perhaps a half-dozen "looks" from the top of Pilot Butte, Bend's volcanic landmark, across the desert plains and fault block mountains to Idaho's western border. One enrollee at the Civilian Conservation Corps camp on the western flank of windswept Hart Mountain in the 1930s aptly summed his feelings: "The country is all right, but there's too much of it.''

Residents of Oregon's vast desert lands take the task of bridging their geography in stride. On major shopping excursions, residents of Christmas Valley are likely to go to Bend, a 100-mile (160 km.) drive each way. Several years ago, one woman regularly drove 150 miles (240 km.), mostly over dirt roads from the isolated Whitehorse Ranch, to attend the monthly Cow Belles meeting in Burns. Christmas Valley students who attend Paisley High School endure a two-hour bus ride each direction. By the time they have earned their high school diploma, they will have logged 96,000 miles (153,600 km.) in the yellow bus. Crane High School, 28 miles (45 km.) east of Burns, is one of the few public boarding schools in the United States. The students don't even go home after the last bell of the day. Because of the distances to their homes, mostly far-flung ranches, students live in the school's dormitory.

Mail carriers in rural areas of Harney County log over 200,000 miles (320,000 km.) a year servicing about 200 mail boxes. One route, from Princeton to Whitehorse Ranch, is 290 miles (464 km.). And it isn't freeway. Neither snow, nor sleet, nor high winds that scream down the sharp east face of the Steens, nor washed-out roads, nor mud, nor dust, nor flying gravel prevent mail deliveries to lonely ranches. Mail deliveries from Lakeview to the northern parts of Lake County — Paisley, Summer Lake, and Silver Lake — are made six days a week and accumulate an annual mileage of over 62,000 miles (99,200 km.).

The Harney County telephone exchange may possibly be one of the largest in the United States, encompassing 5,200 square miles (13,520 km²). A single repair job in the south end of Harney County may necessitate a day's work, considering the travel time. Said one repairman, ''The work is lonely, driving five, six, even eight hours and not see another human being. It sure gives you time to think. And you get the job done right the first time.''[3]

If vast distances create problems today, imagine what it was like 70, 80, or 100 years ago. In 1917, the journey by stage from Portland to Lakeview via Bend took four days. However, it was only a three-day journey by rail if one traveled the Portland-San Francisco-Reno-Lakeview rail lines![4] When the La Pine basketball team played at Silver Lake in March 1917, the team not only lost 30-3 but endured two days of

rough travel — 50 miles (80 km.) via Fremont each way.

In 1914, Anne Monroe, a correspondent for the *Oregonian*, journeyed from Portland to report on an Oregon Agricultural College ''short course'' given in Burns. In traveling from Bend to Burns, Monroe wrote: ''You travel mile after mile over a vast flat country whose encircling hills maddeningly recede — you never gain on them. You're traveling mile after mile under the same blue sky, over the same level land, and never getting anywhere. All day you just see country and still more country, till your eyes ache with country. The ''short course'' drew nearly 200 men and almost as many women from a radius of 150 miles [240 km.] in the dead of winter through snow and against biting winds. They traveled day and night with teams, farm wagons or on horseback from way down in the Catlow Valley, 100 miles [160 km.] to the south where 300 families, many in tents, are homesteading and from the Wildhorse Ranch (Alvord Basin) 125 miles [200 km.] southeast of Burns....''[5]

Those who travel the back roads of Oregon's Big Country (most of the roads in the region *are* back roads!) can readily appreciate the concept of space. One sunny but cool January I traveled from the Alvord Basin over Long Hollow, through the Catlow Valley, then on past Frenchglen to Burns. During the 130-mile (208 km.) journey, I saw one other human, a solitary rancher tending to his late afternoon chores in the shadow of Catlow Rim. On two occasions, both in summer, I've negotiated the dirt road that connects the Hart Mountain Refuge with Frenchglen. The first time on the lonely road, I encountered one vehicle. The next trip, rush hour, no doubt, I met two pickups.

The question of space for a visitor is, at worst, a temporarily unnerving situation. For new residents of the remote ranches or small settlements, especially if they have just come from a sizeable urban area, the isolation and distances to cities such as Ontario, Burns, or Lakeview can create problems. In the mid-1980s, the Education Service District of Harney County included ten one-room schools. According to the district superintendent, Jim Courtney, a major reason for the 50 per cent teacher turnover each year is the rural isolation. Special assistance is given by two traveling consultants of the Educational Service District to help teachers prepare for the multigrade teaching situation. Periodically, students and the teacher from one school gather at another school to socialize.

It is ironic, almost contradictory to say that during the few weeks that the Steens Mountain loop road is open, 19,000 people visit the mountain, and that, during the course of a year, thousands of hunters, sightseers, photographers, and naturalists drive the winding grade to the Hart Mountain Refuge. The Malheur Refuge south of Burns receives thousands of visitors a year. Yet, so vast is the High Desert country, the sense of space is a predominate aspect of the geography of Southeastern Oregon.

The Geological Base
by Bruce Nolf

The bedrock of Southeastern Oregon is mostly volcanic in origin, or derived as sediment from volcanic sources. These rocks are geologically young, almost all less than 30 million years old (late Cenozoic) in age. Several volcanoes in the region have been active within the last few tens of thousands of years, and deposition of sediments in basins is an ongoing process. Deformation of these rocks is also young, and is primarily extensional in nature. Faulting is the dominant structural feature of rocks exposed in this region, with vertical offsets ranging up to thousands of feet. Because displacement is recent, scarps produced by faulting are commonly steep and relatively little modified by erosion.

The physical landscape of Southeastern Oregon, therefore, is in large part the direct result of recent and, in many cases, continuing geologic processes: faulting, volcanism, erosion of volcanoes and uplifted crustal blocks, and deposition of sediment in local enclosed basins. As a rough generalization, a visitor may assume that linear escarpments are likely to mark fault scarps, that shield-, cone-, or dome-shaped rises are likely to

In Southeastern Oregon, extension, or tectonic stretching, has created a series of normal faults with uplift of a bedrock block on one side and downdrop on the other. The resulting landscape has a rectilinear, blocky appearance. The uplifted blocks (horsts) form upland plateaus, while large downdropped blocks form basins (grabens). This aerial view shows Silver Lake, which is located in a graben connected to the Fort Rock basin. The saddle in the middle is Picture Rock Pass. In the far distance, to the south, is the graben in which Summer Lake is located. Photo by Tim Townsend, Eugene.

be volcanoes, and that flat basin floors are sites of sedimentation.

Southeastern Oregon has been subdivided into three provinces, the Basin-Range, the High Lava Plains, and the Owyhee Uplands. To the west the region is bounded by the young volcanoes of the High Cascades, and to the north by various uplifted ranges of older rock, comprising collectively the Blue Mountain Province. The Basin-Range is characterized by recent large-scale block faulting that has produced a series of north-south-trending mountain ranges, separated by broad, sediment-filled basins. Drainage is principally interior. The High Lava Plains Province is characterized by very youthful volcanism along a wide northwest-southeast-trending fault zone, the Brothers Fault Zone. This fault zone is marked by numerous closely-spaced faults with relatively small (tens of feet) vertical displacement. The Owyhee Uplands is less conspicuously faulted and is deeply dissected by streams draining outward into the Snake River. Fluvial erosion is therefore a more conspicuous element of the Owyhee landscape than in most other areas in Southeastern Oregon.

BEDROCK AND THE LANDSCAPE

Despite volcanic origins, much of the bedrock of Southeastern Oregon is notably layered, and at first glance much of the terrain resembles that underlain by sedimentary rocks. Although the rocks are diverse, principal types include basalts, tuffs, and non-marine sediments derived by erosion of volcanic materials. The nature of these various bedrock types controls much of the small-scale topography. In general, resistant units form ledges or cliffs, and softer units tend to erode to more gentle slopes. Individual volcanic centers dot the landscape, typically forming topographic highs.

Basalts: As shown dramatically by television coverage of Hawaiian eruptions, flows of basaltic lava are typically quite fluid when erupted. Such lavas may spread rapidly over large areas, solidifying in layers representing successive outpourings of lava. Individual flows may range from less than a foot to tens of feet in thickness, the thickness depending upon the slope, the volume and fluidity of the flow, and the degree of ponding at the site of solidification. Horizontal flows may attain considerable thickness where pooled in a closed basin, as in a basin bounded by

fault scarps or by volcanoes. Solidified basalt flows are commonly characterized by vertical fractures, typically a foot or so apart, giving a unit a distinctly columnar appearance. This fracturing accommodates the considerable post-solidification contraction that occurs as the basalt cools from temperatures of solidification (roughly 1,800 F. or 1,000 C.) down to ordinary surface temperatures. This contraction is analogous to the contraction of wet mud as it dries, forming mudcracks with a polygonal pattern. Fracturing of this type in volcanic rocks is referred to as columnar or polygonal jointing.

Basalt is generally a strong rock, quite resistant to mechanical weathering and erosion. It therefore tends to stand out in positive relief in terrain subjected to considerable erosion, or to uphold relatively steep slopes or cliffs where dissected by stream valleys or faults. Principal failure on steep slopes is along vertical contractional fractures and horizontal flow contacts, so that a face cut in basalt tends to be somewhat step-like in profile. The "risers" in such a profile are the fractures formed by contraction when the lava cooled, and the "treads" are the boundaries between successive flows. Particularly notable cliffs of this type, comprised principally of dark, layered basalt flows, are those on the east side of Steens Mountain, the west side of Poker Jim Ridge, the sides of Hart Mountain, Catlow Rim, Guano Rim, and the east and west sides of the Warner block. Abert Rim, a part of the escarpment on the west side of the Warner block, is especially well known because it rises steeply above Highway 395 and is viewed by travelers on that route.

Erosion of softer materials (typically sediments or soft ash) from around masses of basalt or other resistant volcanic rock may eventually leave the basalt standing above the surrounding landscape. At several sites in Southeastern Oregon, volcanic flows have filled valleys previously cut by streams into soft bedrock. Subsequent erosion of the softer material may ultimately leave the volcanic valley-fill perched above the surrounding landscape, showing the route of the older drainage system, often as a long, somewhat sinuous ridge. Wrights Point (south of Burns), Railroad Point (west of Denio), and numerous low ridges on the surface of the westward-tilted Steens block are well-known results of this process, commonly referred to as topographic inversion. Wrights Point and Railroad Point are capped by basalt, and the ridges on the Steens by resistant welded tuff.

Basalt flows commonly issue from cinder cones and spatter cones, or from fissures. The most diverse collection of basaltic vent structures in North America occurs at the Diamond Craters field in the Harney Basin.

Tuffs: Volcanism in Southeastern Oregon has been punctuated by explosive eruptions of large amounts of fragmented volcanic material (tephra). Explosion clouds commonly reach heights of several miles, and the material falling from such clouds (airfall tephra) may blanket large areas with layers of unconsolidated ash. Such deposits are typically light in color and soft, offering little resistance to erosion. Exposures tend to be poor, except in road cuts or at other freshly cut sites. Natural slopes are usually relatively gentle.

Large eruption clouds may also give rise to high-speed flows of incandescent ash, depositing extensive sheets of hot ash which are thickest in valleys, basins, and other low spots, and thin or missing on the tops of mountains. If the ash is still hot enough on deposition, the heat of the ash may be enough to weld together individual particles, forming a unit which is quite resistant to erosion. These welded tuffs may be several feet to tens of feet or more thick. At a distance, such units may resemble layers of resistant basalt, but texturally they are quite different indeed, being comprised of fragments of volcanic material, either pumiceous or welded into a dense glassy rock.

Volumes of some individual ash flow deposits in Southeastern Oregon are in the range of tens of cubic miles, dwarfing in size any known historical event on earth. Material is sometimes erupted so rapidly that the magma chamber at the source collapses inward, forming a large depression known as a caldera. Harney Basin is centered on such a feature, which was the source for ash flows covering much of eastern Oregon, flowing over the Strawberry and Aldrich Mountains to deposit a conspicuous unit in the John Day Valley.

Sediments: Closed basins, sometimes dry and sometimes occupied by lakes, have been a feature of Southeastern Oregon geology through much of Cenozoic time. At times of explosive volcanic eruptions, tephra fell directly into these basins, and more was swept by erosional processes off surrounding highlands and into the basins. Weathering and erosion of bedrock adjacent to these basins also contributed to their filling. In general, a material was deposited near the basin edges, commonly in the form of alluvial fans, and finer sediment and evaporites were deposited in the centers of the basins. Environments were entirely non-marine, but the waters of some lakes have been quite alkaline at times, largely due to evaporation out of closed basins. Fossils are mostly plant material and the remains of vertebrate animals.

Subsequent compaction and cementation has lithified these sediments somewhat, but thicknesses of accumulation, and therefore depths of burial, have generally not been great enough to produce strongly lithified sedimentary rocks. Hence these units tend to be nonresistant to erosion, underlying relatively gentle slopes. Where these beds occur on high escarpments, they facilitate considerable landsliding, as at Winter Rim and much of the west face of the Warner block.

Climate of the Region

It is midwinter, and brisk, biting winds howl across the frozen lands of Southeastern Oregon. The thermometer reads around 24 degrees F. (-4.4 degrees C.), but it feels much colder. Thick clouds scud across the skies, periodically bringing flurries of snow and burying the tops of the barren buttes that brood over the desert. On the range, cattle put their backs to the icy blast, but there is little or no shelter. The landscape, at least that which is visible, is a drab, seemingly lifeless gray. As darkness descends, a visitor to these wind-swept lands cries for shelter, warmth, refuge — survival. The only echo is the shrieking desert wind. It offers no protection, no hope of warmth. This day the weather is the master of the lands.

Now it is late spring, and a weather front has just cleared the state, and behind it, cumulus clouds dance across the desert, their shadows drifting across the desert floor. The May sunlight is intensified by reflection from the alkali soils and by reradiation from the fleecy clouds. The air is fresh, sharp, and invigorating, and the distant ranges, still partly dressed in their winter mantle, glisten in the sparkling air. Warmth, a comfortable pleasant warmth, comes from the rising convection currents and from the direct solar radiation absorbed by the body. The recent moisture and the mild spring temperatures have combined to bring a vivid green to the desert shrubs and a variety of colorful wildflowers. The desert experience on this day is an exhilarating one.

Such is the temperament of the climates of Southeastern Oregon. At times, the climate is almost repellent; at times it is benign. Landscapes reflect in part the geology, in part the season, in part the character of the day and even the time of day. Sun or shade, clouds or clear skies, wind or calm, each contributes to the atmospheric conditions of this region, which experiences heat and cold, drought and deluges, all within a given year.

The desert climate also brings on occasion a unique atmospheric optic phenomenon, a superior mirage. When there is a temperature inversion (warmer air aloft; colder air near the surface), light refracted from distant objects is distorted, even at times to the extent that objects beyond the horizon are seemingly raised into the sky. I have seen desert buttes rise above the horizon, expand, contract, and then when the temperature inversion breaks up, sink beyond the horizon again. This is not a new occurrence by any means. In 1862, the First Oregon Cavalry was returning from the Alvord Valley, where they had selected a summer camp. According to Frances Fuller Victor, on the return to Camp Henderson the troop amused itself for an hour with the mirage on the dry lake, which performed an amusing pantomime, figures of men and horses moving over its surface, some high in the air, while others were sliding to right or left like weavers' shuttles. Some horses appeared stretched out to an enormous length, while others spindled up, the moving tableau "representing everything contortions and capricious reflections could do."[6]

An early twentieth-century description of Harney County includes reference to the superior mirage: "Nature frequently vouchsafes to manifest one of her strangest and least understood phenomena. The hour of sunrise, always possessed of a sweet, inexplicable charm, is usually attended during the summer months by a delightful mirage. Towns, houses, mountain peaks, herds of peacefully grazing cattle or sheep rise up from the ground by magic and are pictured on the atmosphere with great distinctness of outline. It is said that distant objects are so vividly mirrored that persons several miles from home have identified without difficulty the different members of their families as they went about their work."[7]

Typically, winters in the region are cold with periods of snow. While the moderating effect of the Pacific Ocean gives coastal stations December and January maximums close to 50 degrees F. (10.0 degrees C.) and cities in the Willamette Valley readings around 45 degrees F. (7.2 degrees C.), the more continental location and higher altitude of cities such as Burns, Lakeview, and Ontario means that, in midwinter, daily high temperatures normally stay in the 35-39 degrees F. (1.7 - 3.9 degrees C.) range. Interestingly enough, given calm winds, clear skies and exposure to sun, the lower humidity of Southeastern Oregon often results in quite pleasant winter daytime outdoor experiences. However, once the sun has started to set, radiational cooling is rapid, and the mercury has usually plummeted below freezing by dusk and skidded below 20 degrees F. (-6.7 degrees C.) by early morning. At night, stars twinkle their messages in a sky so full of heavenly bodies that one is awed by the sight.

When high pressure positions itself east of the Cascades in winter, stagnant air, low level moisture and, in places an up-slope drift of air on the east sides of ridges combine to produce a damp, bone chilling, gloomy fog that is often persistent in the basins. At the same time, nearby mountains may be basking in brilliant sunshine.

The low-pressure system, which normally develops in the Gulf of Alaska by late fall, usually dominates the climatic pattern for the Pacific Northwest during the low-sun period. A succession of storm systems that sweep in from the Pacific beginning in November bring rains to the west side of the Cascades and snow to the eastern sections of both Washington and Oregon. To a large extent, the Cascades block much of the moisture, and while western stations receive 40 to 80 inches (1,021-2,043 mm.) of precipitation per year, in general most places in Southeastern Oregon receive 10 to 15 inches (255-383 mm.) annually. The winter snows, while at times disrupting travel, create mountain snowpacks, which later provide summer irrigation and moisture for desert ranges that support livestock in the spring and summer. Said pioneer stockman Bill Hanley, "It looks like (several) feet of snow. Let it come... means there won't be any water shortage next year. This old country covered with

Storm clouds hover over the eastern face of the Steens. View is from the unpaved highway that parallels the Steens between Juniper Lake and Alvord Lake. Photo by Marcus Haines, Burns.

snow seems to be full of life...."

Periodically, Mother Nature forgets about climatological averages. Southeastern Oregon may experience bitterly cold winters or weather so mild that area residents get spoiled and plant growth gets confused. Extreme cold follows when incursions of Arctic air spread west of the Rockies. Given sufficient moisture from the Pacific, deep snows may result. The winter of 1889-1890 resulted in the loss of thousands of livestock in Eastern Oregon. From 1860 to 1889, livestock owners did not grow supplemental hay for winter feed, as there had generally been an abundance of natural feed for the livestock. The summer of 1889 was exceptionally dry, and grasses had withered before summer's end. Heavy snows fell in December 1889, and the storms continued into January 1890. At Westfall, Malheur County, snow was 2-1/2 feet (0.78 m.) on the level, temperatures dropped to -20 degrees F. (-28.9 degrees C.) and reports were that all hay was gone. The *Burns Times-Herald* in its issue of January 30, 1890, reported that hay was the "same as gold in Harney County." The severe winter continued through February. At times, the

weather moderated and melted the top of the snow. Then strong cold winds returned, froze the crust, and chilled the livestock to death. Livestock losses were staggering. One sheepherder, McIntosh, lost most of his 3,000 sheep. The Brown Brothers lost over 6,000 sheep out of a herd of 9,600. Livestock losses were put at 75 percent in many areas. One positive aspect of the winter of 1889-1890 was that ranchers commenced to cultivate hay and store it for winter feed.

During the winter of 1894, an unusual tragedy occurred on Summer Lake. Some 2,500 sheep belonging to Wm. Harvey, Sr., drifted on to the frozen lake. High winds forced the sheep east towards a thin coat of ice. Sheepdogs intending to round up the sheep only got them more excited and bunched. The weight of the sheep broke the ice and the sheep dropped into the frigid waters. Only the lead goat of the flock, who climbed out of the lake on the backs of the sinking sheep, was saved.

In December 1924, the mercury dropped to a frigid -45 degrees F. (-42.8 degrees C.) on Christmas Eve in Burns and to a colder-yet -53 degrees F. (-47.2 degrees C.) in Riverside. A shortage of hay at the Paisley ranch of the ZX Company made it necessary to take several thousand cattle to ranches in the Blitzen Valley for winter feeding. The severe cold hit as the cattle were being moved. The *Burns Times-Herald*, January 17, 1925, recounted the event: "The story of the hardships of the men who took the last band of cattle across the desert for the ZX Company reads like a chapter from a romance of the early days of the history of Oregon. Battling storms and enduring the icy blasts of barren sagebrush wastes, open, unprotected desert stretches, in cold which drove the mercury to almost unprecedented depths, these vaqueros took the cattle through without complaining or deserting their posts — all because it was a part of the day's work....

"In going across the desert it was necessary to guard the cattle at night and during these cold watches the men were forced to fight the biting frost for hours at a time.

"In the daytime those in the lead built fires at frequent intervals along the trails and the men who followed warmed themselves and kept the blazes replenished for their companions further back. Thus a continuous line of fires was left along the desert trail in the wake of the benumbed brutes that were being taken out of the way of almost certain starvation. This was the only way in which the biting frost could be kept out of the bodies of the men even during the daylight hours.

"Those who were permitted a few hours of sleep at night found no warmth in their beds. Breath froze on the blankets, leaving them stiff with ice around the necks and faces of the tired men.

"The nostrils of the horses became caked with ice until quite often they could scarcely breathe, and the vaporous exhalations of the men froze on their beards and faces. The eyes of both horses and men were frozen shut at times when they were forced to be away from the fires for any length of time. At Wagontire thermometers registered below zero — and the men still "singin' to 'em" on guard to keep the cattle from breaking the herd toward almost certain death. Ears, fingers, noses and toes often felt the bite of the frost which no clothing by day or bed at night could quite keep out. Fifty-one of the cattle were left, victims of the intense cold. That the others suffered is attested by the men, but no word of complaint came from man or beast. It was all in the day's

work, and the cattle were taken through."

Every now and then, mild winters raise almost as many comments as do the severe ones, and some remarkable temperatures (for Southeastern Oregon) have been recorded in the region. Vale has registered several spring-like temperatures during the winter months, including 72 degrees F. (22.2 degrees C.) on December 2, 1908, and 80 degrees F. (26.7 degrees C.) on January 7, 1909. The highest-ever January reading in Oregon was the 81 degrees F. (27.8 degrees C.) registered at Fremont (Fort Rock Valley) on January 31, 1934. Such warm temperatures in Southeastern Oregon are usually associated with Chinook winds, where already mild air from the mid Pacific is warmed by compression as it moves downslope. Over the years, the effects of mild winters have been in evidence. In January 1934, farmers were in the fields plowing, livestock grazed outdoors all winter and moved to the spring ranges in February. At both Paisley and New Pine Creek, trees were in bud in January and crocuses bloomed in Lakeview by early February. January 1, 1959, reports from Plush stated that buds on peach trees were ready to burst open. By mid-January 1959, daffodils were blooming at Summer Lake. In the period December 1953-February 1954, Burns recorded 54 days when the temperature reached 40 degrees F. (4.4 degrees C.) or higher. When in December 1917, volunteer lettuce was sprouting in Burns and the grass remained green, concerns were raised that there would be no ice for summer!

Springs in Southeastern Oregon are often tardy and at times hardly worthy of the name. Usually there is a series of "false springs" — mild, sunny days with readings in the 65-75 degrees F. (18.3-23.9 degrees C.) range in late March, often followed by biting northwest winds and snow flurries just when high school athletes are out for spring sports. Tender plants put in by green-thumb enthusiasts (usually newcomers) in late April are frosted out by May freezes. Generally, the Treasure Valley area is the most favored area of Southeastern Oregon for spring vegetative growth, with the least likelihood of frosts.

Average maximum temperatures climb from near 50 degrees F. (10.0 degrees C.) in mid-March to 70 degrees F. (21.1 degrees C.) by late May in Burns and Lakeview, while in Adrian, in the Treasure Valley, the range is from 60 degrees F. (15.5 degrees C.) to 80 degrees F. (26.7 degrees

C.) during that same period. The earliest date that the average minimum rises above freezing varies from late March in Adrian to mid-April in Burns and Lakeview. However, Mother Nature often tends to ignore statistical averages.

Representative of newspaper accounts of late spring frosts include the following:

Ontario, April 18, 1960. "Extensive frost damage to beets and fruit in local area. 7,000-8,000 acres (2,000-3,200 ha.) of sugar beet destroyed. It cost $50-$60/acre (0.41 ha.) to reseed. Yields are expected to be down because of shortened growing season."

Even in mid-June, high-altitude locations in Lake County can experience damaging frosts. In mid-June 1952, temperatures at New Idaho (near Lakeview) dipped to 12 degrees F. (-11 degrees C.). Snow fell in Lakeview in that cold spell.

Temperatures below zero have been recorded in the region during April with, for example, a -4 degrees F. (-20.0 degrees C.) at Hart Mountain Refuge on April 18, 1973. Zero degrees F. (-17.7 degrees C.) was reported from Juniper Lake, in the Alvord Basin east of the Steens, on May 2, 1968. Interestingly enough, that afternoon the mercury climbed to 80 degrees F. (26.9 degrees C.). Despite the periodic cold spells, spring is welcomed by residents of Southeastern Oregon. Bill Hanley philosophized, "Spring is morning, teaches us that all will live again." Spring is the most colorful season of the year, with new green grasses and desert wild flowers.

It is the late spring rains (May is the second wettest month of the year at Ontario) that are critically needed for the growth of unirrigated crops and for the growth of range grasses. Typically, the maximum temperature for mid-June averages 75 degrees F. (23.9 degrees C.); minimums are around 45 degrees F. (7.2 degrees C.). In Ontario, the typical daily range is 84-51 degrees F. (28.9-10.6 degrees C.). In July and August, maximums normally climb to the mid-80s degrees F. and low 90s degrees F. (25-30 degrees C.). The Pacific High normally dominates the weather pattern over the entire American West throughout the summer and into early fall, and summers are generally sunny, dry and quite warm throughout the region.

Then, of course, there is the exceptional weather. How about snow the Fourth of July? There are those stories, almost legendary boasts, that "Yea, I remember when...." The *Lake*

County Examiner, May 18, 1950, stated that six inches (153 mm.) of snow had to be swept off the platform before the 4th of July dance in 1896 could get started. There were reports of four inches (102 mm.) of snow in Lakeview on July 4, 1903. More recently, the *Burns Times-Herald* issue of July 10, 1969, showed a photo (taken June 27 of that year) of Mrs. Wayne Purdy of the nearby Silvies Valley "pushing a lawnmower" with five inches (128 mm.) snow on the lawn.

Summer heat waves are much more common than summer snowfalls. Extreme maximums in Southeastern Oregon for the summer months include 113 degrees F. (45.0 degrees C.) at Blitzen June 28, 1932, the highest-ever Oregon temperature in June; 113 degrees F. (45 degrees C.) at Ontario on July 12, 1967; and 110 degrees F. (43.3 degrees C.) at Vale on August 11, 1910. It is extended periods of 90 degrees F. (32.3 degrees C.) or higher temperatures that constitute heat waves; of all the weather stations in Southeastern Oregon, Ontario is usually the leader of the heat brigade and can normally expect 60 days with maximums over 90 degrees F. (32.3 degrees C.) in a calendar year. In 1985, Ontario experienced 23 days when the mercury topped the century (37.8 degrees C.) mark, including ten consecutive days in July.

Another characteristic of the regional climate is the quick change in weather conditions. In Burns, snow fell on the city on June 17, 1973. On the 18th, the mercury hit 80 degrees F. (26.7 degrees C.). On July 7, 1981, Burns' high reading was a cool 60 degrees F. (15.6 degrees C.). The morning of the 8th, the minimum was 28 degrees F. (-2.2 degrees C.). Then on the 9th, the temperature zoomed to 86 degrees F. (30.0 degrees C.).

Summer heat when combined with weeks without rainfall has resulted in some devastating droughts. When drought occurred in 1889, the *Burns Times-Herald*, October 17, 1889, stated that such a drought had "never been known before and may never occur again." The prolonged drought that contributed to the abandonment of the homesteads in the years 1917-1920 is discussed in a separate chapter. In reality, the entire period from 1917 to 1937 was arid. In 1934, the U. S. government took over abandoned farm lands and Civilian Conservation Corps programs were initiated. During 1934, the drought contributed to severe dust storms in Southeastern Oregon. The Silvies River dried up completely by April that year. Springs failed; sheepmen hauled water daily for their flocks. Nationally, one-half billion dollars was appropriated for drought relief. Since the 1930s, several severe dry spells have impacted Southeastern Oregon. One of the worst was between 1976 and 1977, when precipitation at several Southeastern Oregon stations was below 50 percent of the long-term average. By March 1977, flow on the Silvies River was only 11 percent of normal. In May 1977, Oregon and Washington received one-half million dollars of congressional appropriation for emergency drought-relief measures. Three hundred thousand (300,000) head of cattle (20 percent of the total Oregon inventory) were sold by July 1977. Some cattle drives stirred so much alkali dust that many cattle died of dust pneumonia due to inflammation of the lungs. Crops in non-irrigated areas failed. Groundwater dropped in many areas. The drought losses in Northeastern and Southeastern Oregon were estimated at $70 million. Harney County cattle losses were placed at $1.9 million, with 25-35 percent of the beef herd sold prematurely. At the time, it seemed inconceivable that within a few years, some lake beds of Southeastern Oregon would fill with water and that ranchers in the Harney Basin would be seeking flood relief.

In summer when spirals of moisture move north from Nevada or California, dark clouds gang up to form towering thunderheads. Lightning flashes over the escarpments of Southeastern Oregon, triggering fast-moving range fires. Perhaps, as firefighters hope, deluges of rain accompany the storms. Then short-lived instant streams course across the desert lands. Such storms are usually intense but brief and soon give way to the desert sunshine.

To many people, the almost-traditional Indian summer weather of early- to mid-fall is the best weather of the year in Southeastern Oregon. The fierce heat of the summer has been tamed. The inevitable bitter cold, piercing wind, and snow are weeks away. Indian summer, that time after the first fall frost, is characterized by crisp, invigorating mornings and comfortably warm afternoons. It is in late August and September that some remarkable daily temperature ranges occur in parts of Southeastern Oregon. For example, at Fremont, Lake County, the mercury zoomed from a chilly 25 degrees F. (-4.0 degrees C.) low to a scorching 87 degrees F. (30 degrees C.) high on

For young children living in parts of the High Desert country, the isolation is a reality that must be coped with. The young boy proudly demonstrates his homemade guitar outside of his ranch located north of the Fort Rock Valley. Photo by Ray Hatton.

the same day — September 4, 1980. The following day the temperature range was from 29 degrees F. (-2.0 degrees C.) to 89 degrees F. (32 degrees C.). Extreme maximums during the fall months include a sweltering 104 degrees F. (40.0 degrees C.) on September 1, 1976, and a 96 degrees F. (35.6 degrees C.) at Rome, October 7, 1964. Even in

Oregon's Big Country. View looking west across the Catlow Valley from the southern end of the Steens Mountain Loop. Photo by Charles A. Blakeslee, Bend.

November, a warm 81 degrees F. (27.2 degrees C.) was recorded at Riverside (November 2, 1918).

Fall is harvest time. It is hunting season. Aspens that are tucked away in small valleys on Hart Mountain, or which spread over the upper gentle western slopes of the Steens, turn shades of yellow, orange, and reds, much to the delight of sightseers and photographers.

But the balmy Indian summer days are all too brief. The lengthening of shadows, the shortening of daylight, colder mornings and a higher percentage of cloud cover aloft indicate that winter is on its way. Residents have checked and restocked their woodpiles, cold-weather clothing is dusted and antifreeze levels in radiators are measured. Cold northwest winds bring snows, first to the mountain tops, then to the lower slopes. While it seems that temperatures were near 70 degrees F. (21.1 degrees C.) but a few days ago, they now struggle to reach 40 degrees F. (4.4 degrees C.). Fall readings below zero have been recorded at Fremont, -9 degrees F. (-22.8 degrees C.), October 29, 1971, and Silver Lake, -32 degrees F. (-35.6 degrees C.), November 26, 1896, two of the coldest readings in Oregon during those two months. Yes, winter comes early and stays late in the High Desert country of Southeastern Oregon.

Plant Life of Southeast Oregon

by Dr. Stuart G. Garrett

Southeastern Oregon is an igneous land, a land of frozen lava and volcanic ash. Glaciers have scoured its mountain tops. Huge lakes have lapped at its ancient shorelines, and the beaches remain as silent reminders of past mysteries. The extension of the western part of the North American continent has shattered this part of the world into a myriad of faults. The crustal blocks formed from this faulting have tilted to make numerous lake and desert-filled basins and mountain ranges. All of these factors have combined to produce a diversity of topography, soils, and weather, which fosters a rich and varied plant life.

The changes over time in Southeastern Oregon have been dramatic. From the more gentle eruptions of basaltic volcanoes to violent cataclysms such as the eruption of Mt. Mazama, which formed Crater Lake, a wide range of volcanism has left its fiery legacy. The rise of the Cascade Range has dramatically lowered precipitation to the east and correspondingly altered the plant life.

In early Tertiary times (c. 60 million years ago), the western part of our continent was low and uncut by the mountain ranges of modern times. Even and mild climates prevailed west of the Utah-Nevada line. Tropical forests extended north to Washington and temperate forests north to Alaska. Subsequently the Cascade and Sierra mountain ranges arose. During the last million years, Western America has become colder and drier. Northern coniferous forests covered the land but they have since retreated, except west of the Cascades in Oregon. Grasslands have developed in the interior, and pines and firs have moved to higher altitudes.

Deserts in Western North America are of relatively recent development, evolving over the last two million years. There were no desert conditions or vegetation in North America prior to this time. New plants have evolved to match these unusual habitats. During the last million years, glaciers developed in the higher elevations in Oregon. The retreat and advance of the glaciers is matched by a retreat and advance of species adapted to arctic and alpine environments.

In present-day Southeastern Oregon we find a blend of these types of plants. An observer may speculate what conditions might be like a million years from now. What plants that are rare now might become more common? What plants that are now widespread might be forced by climatic or other environmental changes to radically restrict their range?

This restriction of range is referred to in botany as endemism. Plants which are endemic occupy only a particular geographic area. The two main types of endemic plants are called paleoendemic and neoendemic.

A paleoendemic plant is a very old plant that was once much more widespread. Due to changes in the environment, this plant tends to be disappearing. Its range has become much more restricted. Classic examples of this type of plant are the coastal redwood (*Sequoia sempervirens*) and the Sierra big tree (*Sequoia gigantea*). Both of these plants were once found over much of Southeastern Oregon but are now restricted to small geographic areas. The coastal redwood is found in a narrow strip of the northern California and southern Oregon coast, while the Sierra big tree is found only in a small area of the Sierra Nevada mountains in California.

The other type of endemic plant is a neoendemic, one which has recently evolved and may be expanding its range. An example of this type of plant is the Malheur wire lettuce (*Stephanomeria malheurensis*). This plant, which grows only in a small area of the sagebrush steppe in Harney County, was recognized as new to science by Dr. Leslie D. Gottleib, a University of California geneticist, within the last 20 years. Growing on land administered by the BLM, this plant is one of two plants in Oregon currently protected under the Federal Endangered Species Act.

Unfortunately, this plant is also an example of the rise and fall of a given species. In the early 1970s, the only known population of this plant numbered several hundred. However, in recent years a gradual decline was noted, and in 1984 the plant became extinct in the wild. In 1987, the BLM in cooperation with environmental groups planted seedlings of Malheur wire lettuce raised from seeds that had been preserved in a frozen seed bank. It is hoped that this plant can be reintroduced into its natural habitat. This is a striking example of the care we need to exercise in our jobs as stewards of the land.

Southeastern Oregon has three main geologic provinces: The Basin-Range, the Owyhee Uplands, and the High Lava Plains. Each of these provinces supports a variety of plant communities, ranging in elevation from the low salt desert shrublands to the alpine communities.

The close association of salt deserts and alpine plant communities is seen nowhere else in Oregon but the Basin-Range. We can stand on the summit scarp of Steens Mountain amid alpine wild flowers, which are relics of the age of glaciers. At the same time we can stare down on the Alvord Desert, which maintains populations of plants that have migrated northward from the Sonoran and Mojave Desert areas. A visitor has a feeling of primal forces at work: ice deeply gouging the mountain, wind and rain eroding the "bones" of Steens Mountain into the Alvord Basin and the Blitzen Valley. Looking down on the Alvord, we are led to think about what defines a desert. A geologist might think of a desert as a place with little vegetation and low precipitation where there are a number of alluvial fans. To a climatologist, a desert may simply be an area where evaporation exceeds rainfall over a given period of time. But to a botanist, a desert is defined by the plants that grow there. A desert characteristically has little or nothing in the way of grass communities; it supports a variety of shrub-like vegetation and a number of annual forbs (small, non-woody plants).

The Owyhee Uplands have been formed by violent eruptions of silicic volcanoes. In the area of Leslie Gulch, north of Jordan Valley, these rocks have been eroded into grotesque and fascinating land forms. The unusual volcanic soils produced in these areas are host to a variety of endemic plants. Dr. Pat Packard of the University of Idaho has spent many hours searching these areas and has studied several plants new to science. These include Grimey ivesia (*Ivesia rhypara*), Packard's Mentzelia (*Mentzelia packardia*), Packard's sagebrush (*Artemisia packardiae*), *Senecio ertterae,* and Mackenzie's phacelia *(Phacelia lutea),* variety *mackenziorum.*

In traveling the wide-open expanses of Southeastern Oregon, one is not immediately impressed with the mark of man. To the untrained eye the land appears unchanged and unblemished.

But since the advent of European man, the natural environment has been radically altered. The obvious effects are seen in our towns, roads, mines, and farms. Less obvious are the subtle but profound changes in the natural world, especially the vegetation.

In many areas of Southeastern Oregon, the first settlers described lush meadows of native bunch grasses. Early settlers in the Christmas Valley basin described seas of grass up to the "belly of a buckaroo's horse." The cattlemen were pleased with these prospects and moved rapidly to take advantage of them. As large numbers of sheep and cattle began to graze on the ranges east of the Cascades, the type of vegetation began to change. This area never knew large herds of native ungulates, such as the bison. With heavy grazing, grasses became less dominate and shrubs increased. A rapid expansion of the juniper tree population has been noted. Old photos document this well.

There is controversy over the reason for these changes. Are they man-made or are they the result of the natural environment? Suppression of fire allows juniper to increase. Juniper is not a fire-tolerant species, and lightning and man-made fires of previous centuries helped to control its numbers. In the presence of regular or intermittent fire, the native Oregon bunch grasses are able to dominate or at least co-dominate the shrub steppe. They are able to out-compete the juniper and the sage for vital nutrients and moisture. Without fire, the sage and the juniper tend to out-compete the grasses. Improper grazing also decreases the grasses and allows an increase in other species.

The introduction of exotic species such as Russian thistle (*Salsola kali*) and cheatgrass (*Bromus tectorum*) has changed the plant composition of Southeast Oregon. These ruderal species (defined as ones that re-establish themselves early after soil disturbance) have taken over as pioneers; no one is sure what native species may have occupied this botanic niche in the past. Russian thistle and cheatgrass are found everywhere they can thrive in Southeastern Oregon. Russian thistle is familiar to motorists as "tumbleweed"; it dries up in late summer and separates from its root system, tumbling across the landscape and scattering seeds.

First recorded in the Northwest in about 1890, cheatgrass had spread through much of the area

Coyote Lake is a playa lake (one that periodically dries up) located in the Whitehorse Desert about 20 miles (32 km.) northeast of the Whitehorse Ranch. Playa lakes are highly saline and support few, if any, plants other than greasewood. Photo by Bob Kindschy, Vale.

and had become a prominent part of the plant communities by 1920. Possibly introduced by cattle or hay from the arid Eurasian steppes, the plant readily found its niche and expanded its range, frequently along rail lines. Cheatgrass is well adapted to its role of invader. It is one of the first plants to set seed in the spring. Its seeds are able to germinate in the fall and take advantage of the winter rain. In fact, its seeds are capable of germinating over approximately an eight-month span. Starting in February, it will begin to send out new shoots and roots. This early start allows it to set fruit and go to seed before other plants have even started growing. This gives it a jump on other species in the competition for germination, moisture and sunlight. In its new habitat in North America, it is even more common than it is in the steppes of Russia. Its seeds adhere as readily to the coats of animals as they do to the clothes of man.

Of what importance is this alteration of our natural world? Economically it is difficult to gauge. How many more cattle would range support if it isn't overgrazed or invaded by alien weeds? What is the value of an intact watershed that sponges up water and releases it slowly, leaving stream beds filled even in the heat of summer? Of what value is the native trout fishery such a stream would provide? Answers to these questions are just now being sought. Federal management agencies have been particularly interested in learning how management of the range in riparian areas affects the natural world. Experiments are underway in Southeastern Oregon in which streams have been fenced to exclude grazing animals and to allow the native streamside vegetation to return. The initial results are encouraging. Intermittent creeks begin to run all year; trout return to formerly "dead" streams.

JUNIPER

Juniper is the most common tree over most of Southeastern Oregon. Western juniper (*Juniperus occidentalis*) is found in its most well-developed forms in Central Oregon. This plant also grows in Washington, California, and Nevada. Plants can be either predominately male of female or a combination. They can also change sex from one year to another, depending on growing conditions! Male cones begin development in the fall and release pollen in March or April. Female cones develop in April and attain full size the first summer, but they require a second year to mature. They therefore stay on the tree for two years. Birds like to eat juniper berries. The "scarification" that the berries undergo when passing through the avian digestive system helps seed germination and reproduction of the tree.

The juniper has two types of leaves. The mature type has tight scales, but the juvenile leaves are quite bristly and sharp. Deer will occasionally forage on juniper. They prefer certain trees, which seem to be "ice cream" trees. They will browse heavily on these trees and leave adjacent ones untouched. The wood of juniper is widely used for firewood and fence posts. Native Americans used the bark of the juniper for containers and cordage fiber. The berries were used for flavoring. Sometimes they were eaten raw or pounded into cakes.

Juniper trees are not fire resistant. Any tree less than four inches (10 cm.) in diameter is very susceptible to fire. Juniper is expanding its range in Southeastern Oregon; some observers use the word "invasion". Young trees are growing in areas that previously were sage or meadow steppe. Several theories have been advanced to explain this phenomenon. One is that changes in the climate have allowed this tree to extend its range to areas that it couldn't inhabit before. Another maintains that fire suppression and grazing encourage juniper and are responsible for its increase. Whatever the reason, areas that formerly could not support stands of juniper are now heavily forested with this tree.

SHRUB STEPPE

What is referred to as the "desert" or "high desert" is actually the meadow or sage steppe in a botanical sense. Professor R. Daubenmire, well-known Washington State University ecologist, has said, "The few months of intensive summer heat and drought combined with the occurrence of cacti, rattlesnakes, scorpions and tarantulas that perhaps suggest 'desert' to the layman, do not impress the plant geographer as strongly as does the moderate to heavy stand of perennial grass that grew nearly everywhere before the era of domestic livestock. The term steppe is more appropriate to the botanist."

The Russian word *steppe* refers to a plant community in which grasses are able to exist in significant numbers, often dominating or co-dominating the community. Vast areas of the High Lava Plains and the Basin-Range areas of Oregon consist of this plant community. Occasionally one can stand at the top of a rise in the road and look for dozens of miles without seeing a tree. The land appears stark and monotonous to the casual observer. But for one who is willing to take the time to investigate, it is not so. The main grasses found in this community are the blue-bunch wheat grass (*Agopyron spicata*) and the Idaho fescue (*Festuca idahoensis*). The Idaho fescue will usually be found in slightly higher and moister spots; the wheat grass is able to tolerate drier environments. These native bunch grasses provide excellent forage for both domestic and wild animals that inhabit these areas. The shrubs of these communities comprise mainly species of sagebrush (*Artemisia* species) and rabbitbrush (*Chrysothamnus* species).

Sagebrush (*Artemisia* species) can survive in a variety of habitats, from harsh alpine areas to rich riparian soils. It was a plant widely used by Native Americans in this area. A member of the sunflower family, it saves its energy until September, when it flowers in the warmth of late summer. Sagebrush is not fire-tolerant and does not resprout once it has been burned. It serves as forage for native mammals.

The rabbitbrush (*Chrysothamnus* species) seems to do best in recently disturbed soils. In areas that have been heavily impacted, this will likely be the predominant shrub. It is somewhat salt-tolerant. Certain subspecies of this plant have high levels of a rubber-like latex. This was used by Indians for chewing gum and is currently being investigated for rubber production.

ETHNOBOTANY

A small group of expectant people look out from their rock shelter in the early dawn. The landforms are at first indistinct in the still, cool air. Scattered junipers punctuate the distant hills. They smell the sage in the freshening scents of the spring rain. Around a small smoldering fire of sagebrush limbs, they make plans for the future. They know that the thin and precious soils which mantle the eroding lavas are beginning to awaken with the earliest plant growth of spring. This band of Wadadika (seed eaters), later known as the Burns Paiute Tribe, are getting ready to begin their "seasonal rounds."

These people, especially the women, were accomplished botanists. They were expert observers, knowing when and where certain usable plants grew and how to harvest them and use them as food, dyes, medicines, shelter, and clothing. Their seasonal rounds were not random travels, but carefully anticipated and planned through the year from knowledge which was generations old. Their religious ceremonies were timed to the cycle of nature.

In the spring they began a trek that would move them over a 50-to-80-mile (80-130 km.) range. They would travel from one traditional campsite to another to take advantage of the natural bounty. In the spring, biscuitroot (*Lomatium* species) and bitterroot (*Lewisia rediviva*) were gathered. These, along with camas (*Camassia quamash*), were eaten raw, or they were dried and ground into a flour to be made into biscuits or ashcakes. Cattail roots (*Typha latifolia*) were also collected later in the summer. The ripening of the summer berries and fruits provided another opportunity for use of native vegetation.

These people made their sandals with sage bark and tules (*Scirpus* species). Yarrow (*Achillea millefolium*) was used for cuts and birth control. Sagebrush (*Artemisia* species) was used for colds and congestion. Rabbitbrush (*Chrysothamnus* species) was burned inside huts to clean the air after death and keep away spirits. Evening primrose (*Oenothera* species) was used as "love medicine". The bark of bitterbrush (*Purshia tridentata*) was used for measles. Smoke from bitterbrush was said to be able to cure snow blindness. Bitterroot was frequently boiled with salmon. Chokecherries (*Prunus virginiana*) provided not only fruit, which would be made into dry cakes, but also wood for bows. The inner bark could be used for diarrhea.

The shelters of these people were made out of a framework of willow (*Salix* species) covered with tules. Mats of rye grass (*Elymus cinereus*) and cattail were used inside the huts. Sagebrush was used to make thread and cordage, and willow shoots were used to make baskets. These Native Americans were very aware of and dependent on native plants.

Not only were the Native Americans dependent on the land, but so were the first European settlers. Farming in Southeastern Oregon is difficult. Good years are followed by bad years. Many of the first dryland farmers in Central Oregon arrived at the beginning of a series of good crop years with higher-than-average moisture. This situation only lasted a few years; the long-term prognosis for dryland agriculture in Southeastern Oregon was not very bright. Perhaps it would have been less cruel for the farmers to have had the bad years first, and a chance to move on before community roots were established. The High Desert is studded with abandoned town sites.

The white immigrants used the local pines and junipers as raw material to construct their homes and ranches. The native bunch grasses provided forage for the livestock. Local fruits such as wild Oregon plums (*Prunus subchordata*) added a delightful variety to their diet. Elma Linebaugh Campbell, a member of one early family, remembers with excitement her family's annual August trip to Summer Lake to pick wild plums at her uncle's ranch. The children would pick the fruit and play. They gathered the harvest to provide preserves for the rest of the year. This tradition of harvesting native plums continues today with the Springer family of New Pine Creek, south of Lakeview, who make the only available commercial plum wine.

HIGH LAVA PLAINS

Millican Valley

"Blink and you'll miss Millican," cracks the wise guy. Millican has never been big; for half a century the population has ranged from one to five. At one time Millican was featured in Ripley's *Believe it or Not*, when the mayor, chief of police, postmaster, watermaster and president of the Millican Chamber of Commerce was W. A. "Billy" Rahn. Rahn moved in, or should we say bought the town in 1920 and lived there alone for over 20 years. Not only did Rahn buy the town, he moved it too. When the state of Oregon realigned the serpentine Bend-Burns road, Rahn moved the town a half-mile north to be on the new highway.

In 1946, Bill Mellin, a retired Navy diver, purchased the "town" for $5,000 and moved in with his wife and stepson. With the birth of two children, the town grew 500 percent from the Billy Rahn era. Mellin expanded the services of the gas station to include a mechanic's shop and lunch counter (which subsequently closed after deaths in the family). Today, Millican supplies gas, beer and groceries to the few locals (those within 15 miles) and to the motorists heading across the desert to either Bend or Burns.

The store stocks the usual staples, but it is the "decor" that gives it character. Wall decorations include a rattlesnake skin, bobcat skin, antelope horns, and pictures of Western America — Indians chasing a stagecoach.[8]

Millican was named after George Millican, a stockman who in 1868 settled in the Crooked River country and later relocated in the valley which subsequently bore his name. When homesteaders arrived to farm the sandy soil of the Millican Valley, the first post office was to have been Mount Pine, so named after nearby Pine Mountain. However, because of possible confu-

Millican, located along the Bend-Burns highway, was named after George Millican, who homesteaded in the valley of the same name. W. A. ("Billy") Rahn, (top) purchased Millican in 1920 and lived there alone for over 20 years. There is no longer a post office, nor any services at Millican. Lower photo by Ray Hatton.

sion with La Pine, the alternative name Millican was adopted. At one time, the Millican Valley was dotted with homesteads and supported two schools. Increasing aridity forced the homesteaders to vacate their claims. Millican's well and parts of the old windmill can still be seen just west of "downtown" Millican. Here and there are scattered boards and juniper fence posts, relics of the homestead era. However, the valley has largely reverted back to sagebrush and bunch

The Dry River Gorge located west of the Millican Valley. During more pluvial times (Pleistocene epoch), water from the Millican Valley (after being dammed by lavas from Newberry Volcano) cut a new channel through Horse Ridge. In time, the stream cut a canyon 300 feet (93 m.) deep. The ancient river bed is now dry most of the time. Photo by Ray Hatton.

grasses. Sand dunes, obscured in parts by vegetation, cover part of the valley. Evidence of wetter times is seen in sedimentary lake bed deposits exposed in roadcuts west of Millican, and in the ancient (now dry) river bed that meanders across the valley floor. Although most drainage in southeastern Oregon is into interior, land-locked basins, the drainage from Millican Valley is northwestward into the Crooked River and Deschutes River system, then down the Columbia to the sea. For a time, during the Pleistocene Epoch, drainage out of Millican Valley was dammed by the lavas of Newberry Volcano, closing the old waterway south of Horse Ridge. Ponded waters eventually rose during a time of increased precipitation in this arid region, flooding Millican Valley until a new spillway was cut where the waters overtopped Horse Ridge. This spillway was lowered by vigorous stream erosion, draining the waters of ancient Millican Lake. The steep-walled canyon (300 feet [93 m.] deep) thus formed may be seen today from a viewpoint along U. S. Highway 20 west of Millican. Water still occasionally flows along parts of this dry canyon and at very infrequent intervals floods the canyon to depths of tens of feet, as evidenced by old log jams still preserved within the canyon.

Pine Mountain

Pine Mountain, which consists of a series of gently-shouldered ridges and rocky spines, rises 2,000 feet (621 m.) above the flat Millican Valley. While desert-like vegetation climbs high on the sun-beaten southern and western slopes, the protected north side cradles winter snows, and the more effective moisture supports stands of mature, stately cimarron-bark ponderosa pine. In early summer, lupines carpet the forest floor, and when springs are wet, some of the higher meadows.

During the early-day settlement of the Millican Valley, Pine Mountain was more than a sentinel to the homesteaders. The breezy summit area and pine forests provided cool picnic spots. Today, in summer, hangliders patiently wait for updrafts that sweep up from the hot desert below to send them airborne. Visitors to Pine Mountain's 6,300-foot (1,953 m.) summit are rewarded by views of nine Cascade peaks, bulky Newberry Volcano, the forested Ochocos to the north, and a vast expanse of Oregon's High Desert country. Winter snows on Pine Mountain are often quite heavy, and Nordic skiers seeking a change of scenery are able to ski logging roads on the mountain.

Despite the subtle beauty and relative solitude in the various ridges of the mountain, Pine Mountain's fame has come from research and findings from the astronomical observatory located on the summit. It was in 1967 that University of Oregon Professor Ed Ebbighausen established a telescope and observatory on Pine Mountain. Today, the Pine Mountain Observatory, the only continuously operating one in the Pacific Northwest, has three telescopes, a 15-inch, a 24-inch, and a 32-inch. In 1984, the University of Oregon budget to maintain the residence quarters for the caretaker, a graduate student and, when doing research, Professor James C. Kemp, was $27,000. In the past, federal grants have funded specific research programs. Private donations through the Friends of Pine Mountain have raised extra funds to repair the 32-inch telescope and to help provide money for publications and visitor education programs.

Each year, some 4,000 visitors negotiate the eight-mile dirt road that links Millican with the summit area. Several years ago, accompanied by visitors — friends from Canada — I made the

35-mile drive from Bend. By prior phone call, I had notified Dr. Kemp of my intending visit. The sun had already set behind the Cascade skyline, and the dark desert skies of Central Oregon became the stage for a multitude of stars. Those accustomed to seeing night skies from an urban environment are stunned by the brilliance of the Milky Way and by the earth's planets. During the course of a year the gathering of scientific data is possible on two-thirds of the nights.

I knew nothing of astronomy and was unsure what the visit would provide. Dr. Kemp, a tall, angular, energetic man, welcomed us. The aluminum dome of the observatory rumbled open and the telescope was sighted on low-on-the-horizon Venus. With enthusiasm and excitement, Dr. Kemp explained his research on binary stars, pulsating stars and exploding stars, some 2,000 light years away. Over the years, researchers at Pine Mountain have published over 40 scientific papers on their discoveries.

The crisp desert air chilled us as we made our way by flashlight back to the car. To the west, the lights of Bend illuminated the night sky. Overhead, the maze of stars twinkled as they have done for eons. Somehow those stars took on new meaning. The evening visit to Pine Mountain was a humbling experience.

Brothers

Brothers, which lies on an open windswept plateau 50 miles (80 km.) east of Bend, is a focal point for area ranchers, a place for motorists, hunters, or rockhounds to secure gas, coffee, or a meal, or for travelers to just stretch their legs at the state roadside rest area. State of Oregon highway crews and their families reside in the neatly-kept homes clustered on the edge of "town." A one-room grade school, where the graduation class usually numbers anywhere from four on down, faces the main highway. The Brothers school teacher lives in the mobile home next to the school.

The commercial heart of Brothers is the stucco-like Brothers Stage Station opposite the school. In addition to selling gasoline and groceries, the store contains a post office, a lunch counter, and a small gift shop. Scattered around the town is a mixture of the old and the new —

buildings left from the homestead era on the adjacent High Desert, mobile homes, and a glistening metal barn.

North of Highway 20 at Brothers, a "Hatfield Ranch" sign identified the property owners of that particular rangeland. I was looking for Doc Hatfield, veterinarian and rancher. The pavement ended some ten miles (16 km.) or so out of Brothers. I continued north, the usual desert dust following my car tracks. Off to the east, the abandoned and now decaying Pringle Flat community hall stood lonely and neglected. Suddenly, still a distance away, there were signs of habitations. "It has to be the Hatfield ranch," I mused. Talk about living in the boondocks!

Doc Hatfield greeted me warmly. I'd arranged an interview to learn more about the Hatfield approach to cattle-grazing on the High Desert range near Brothers. Doc explained, "We only allow cattle to bite once on the same desert plants [native bunchgrasses, crested wheat grass, Idaho fescue, needlegrass, for example] during the growing season (mid-April to July)." "The growing schedule for plants in this area relates to daylight and sunlight hours. It is the fall and winter moisture (that deeply saturates the soils) that is critical for the growth of plants. We allow grazing in fenced pastures from three days to three weeks, then move the cattle to another pasture. This allows the vegetation to recover from the shock of the first bite. Where range livestock [on BLM land, for example] may be moved four times in a summer, we move our cattle 15-20 times."

Brothers is the largest community on Highway 20 between Bend and Burns. In addition to the combined store, cafe, and gas station, there are a one-room school, roadside rest area, and State of Oregon highway compound located at Brothers. Photo by Ray Hatton.

Apparently, little labor is needed, as light-weight motorcycles are used to help move the cattle. Also, added Doc, "Our cattle are trained to move by a whistle. A little more fencing is required, but the big change in range management is the change in thinking. Tom Bunch, at one time with the BLM in Prineville, first applied this method with the Hampton Butte Grazing Association in the 1970s. I'll show you what we're talking about."

The little pick-up bounded and lurched over, well, I'll call them desert jeep trails. Doc pointed out the role of fire in trying to control juniper trees. "Junipers transpire (and waste) a lot of valuable moisture." Doc explained how overgrazing around the turn of the century had badly hurt the desert range. Deep, V-shaped gullies had been the legacy of homesteaders trying to farm valley bottoms. Doc pointed out fenced pastures that had been grazed that spring — vegetation was coming back and would be ready for next spring. In places, the higher water table, a result of good range management practices, had caused the withering of unwanted sagebrush and rabbit-brush. "This is quite good stock country," added Doc, "Just don't make it what it isn't."

Hampton Valley

East of Brothers, the straight desert highway slices the prehistoric lake bed now known as the Hampton Valley. Cattle browse and seek sustenance amidst acres of sagebrush and bunchgrasses. Near Hampton at the old Harmon ranch, giant sprinklers bring moisture to thirsty alfalfa, and the patch of bright green markedly contrasts with the grays and tans of the adjacent desert. To the north, Hampton Butte — a cluster of ancient volcanoes — broodingly watches over the valley.

As it was with many other old lake beds in Southeastern Oregon, the Hampton Valley was settled during the homestead era. Homesteaders gambled $10 that they could wrest a living from 320 acres of desert. They lost. In a taped interview (1953), Paul Brookings, whose family journeyed five days from Bend to the Hampton Valley in two covered wagons, recounted how his father failed at farming. However, when the Bend-Burns road was improved (by pulling two logs behind a four-horse team) in 1911, the family built and operated a ten-room inn, Brookings' "Halfway

Brookings "Halfway House," midway between Bend and Burns, was operated by the Brookings family for several years during the homestead period. Meals were 50 cents, rooms $1 a night. In 1912 the auto stage took nine hours to travel between Bend and Burns with an hour lunch stop at Brookings. The one-way fare was $20.

Hampton Station — cafe, gift shop, and gas station — following remodeling in the 1980s. Hampton is midway between Bend and Burns and on the opposite side of Highway 20 to where Brookings Halfway House was located. Photo by Ray Hatton.

House." Said Brookings, "We catered to those traveling between Bend and Burns and those coming seeking homesteads. Meals were 50 cents; overnight rooms were $1. In our register books we had the names of people from all over the United States." The *Bend Bulletin*, November 15, 1911, reported that "from a settlement of two in August, 1910, to 24 houses at present has been the remarkable growth of Hampton."

Today there are few evidences of the homestead settlements in the Hampton Valley area. Gone are the abandoned communities of Rolyat and Stauffer, the latter of which at one time supported a school. Nothing is left other than scattered remains within the sea of sagebrush.

The lonely windmill visible south of U. S. Highway 20 midway between Brothers and Hampton is a solitary reminder of what was once the settlement of Imperial. Imperial was advertised to become one of the "Great Cities of the Northwest", along with Portland and Seattle. The promotional literature included mention of

Geology   by Bruce Nolf

The High Lava Plains Province, as outlined by Dicken, is the 30-to-40-mile-wide (50 to 65 km.) Brothers Fault Zone, separating the Basin-Range on the south from the Blue Mountain Province to the north. Exposed in the Blue Mountain Province, north of the Brothers Fault Zone, are many rocks far older than those cropping out in the Basin-Range. These older rocks include marine sedimentary rocks of Mesozoic and Paleozoic age (roughly 100 to as much as 400 million years old), metamorphic rocks, and numerous bodies of intrusive granitic rock, feeders for old volcanic systems. Such rocks are now exposed at the surface as the result of significant uplift and erosion during late Mesozoic and Cenozoic time. South of the Brothers Fault Zone in Oregon, similar rocks are exposed at only one principal locality, at the base of the Pueblo Mountains, but they no doubt underlie at depth many of the younger volcanic rocks of the Oregon Basin-Range.

Along the Brothers Fault Zone occur hundreds of relatively small normal faults, oblique to the overall trend of the fault zone, with vertical offset typically measured in tens of feet. Spacing between faults is typically a fraction of a mile or so. Some of these faults merge southward into faults bounding major individual blocks in the Basin-Range. As a result of the nature of this faulting, the topography of the Lava Plains is characterized by the presence of many small escarpments, a number of which can be seen easily from Highway 20. Large uplifted blocks are absent from this zone. Faulting is young, but we do not yet have good data concerning the most recent activity.

Considerable recent (within the last 20,000 to 30,000 years) basaltic volcanism has occurred along the Brothers Fault Zone. The wide distribution of young basalt flows and vents along this fault zone led to the use of the term High Lava Plains before the nature of the fault zone was recognized. The most notable field of young basalts is that centered at Diamond Craters. Others include Jordan (Cow Lake) Craters and the Saddle Cave field.

Northwestward along the Brothers Fault Zone, this volcanism appears to merge with the basaltic activity of Newberry Volcano. Even farther to the northwest, the Brothers Fault Zone is aligned with, and possibly related to, the largest field of young basaltic volcanism in the Oregon Cascades, in the Santiam-McKenzie Pass area. As of this writing, no pattern of systematic change in age of basalts along the Brothers Fault Zone has been documented.

Because of the predominance of fluid basalt flows that have solidified at very low gradients, and because of the absence of faulting with large-scale vertical displacement, the fault zone is a remarkably easy route of east-west travel, passing between the rugged Blue Mountains on the north and the high-relief desert mountains of the Basin-Range to the south. Deep canyons and gullies are also generally absent, due to the youth of the rocks and the very low precipitation in the area. This route was used by the Meek immigrant party in 1845 and would undoubtedly have been more popular if water were not so scarce. One might almost say that the modern Bend-Burns highway (U.S. 20) is paved by young basalts!

An extraordinary alignment of centers of silicic volcanism also marks the Brothers Fault Zone, with a well-documented decrease in age of the silicic volcanism northwestward along the fault zone. Silicic volcanism in this sequence began about 10 million years ago at the southeast end of the Brothers Fault Zone and has progressed northwestward along the zone, until we have today essentially modern activity at Newberry Volcano. Silicic activity occurred less than 1,500 years ago in the caldera of Newberry Volcano, depositing a thick blanket of pumice on the east flank of the volcano. Several other silicic centers on the east side of Newberry Volcano are also less than a million years old.

When they were active, these high-silica (dacite and rhyolite) volcanoes along the Brothers Fault Zone erupted large amounts of tephra and lesser volumes of very viscous lava. The lava typically formed domes or thick localized flows. At some sites the rapid and voluminous eruption of tephra was associated with collapse of the roof of the emptying magma chamber, forming a caldera. The most notable example of this type of collapse is the Burns Caldera, a volcanic depression forming the center of the Harney Basin.

During the Homestead Period there were many small schools throughout Southeastern Oregon. In the Fort Rock-Christmas Valley area there were no less than 18 schools. Photos show the school at Stauffer (located south of Hampton) during its use and following its abandonment. Photos from the Gladys Workman Collection.

Isolation and easy-to-hide areas made the High Desert a good place for illegal whiskey stills during the Prohibition era. Photo from the Gladys Workman Collection.

"the fertile volcanic soil, and a climate (320 days of sunshine and 12-18 inches of rainfall) suitable for dry farming as is the fertile Palouse Country of Eastern Washington." The "town" was the dream of promotor Sherman Montgomery of Imperial, California, who in his brochure showed photographs of the streets of Portland but described them as "downtown" Imperial. Lots were sold from coast to coast. However, in October 1914, the population of the Imperial precinct numbered only 223. Four years later Imperial was abandoned. The Bend-Burns highway was realigned to the north. The succession of

dry years did the rest.

Years later, owners of the lots in Imperial were inquiring as to "how large the high school was" and what developments had taken place. Even in the mid 1980s, seventy years since Imperial was vacated, the townsite, 80 acres of desert divided into 2,500-square-foot lots, was still on the Deschutes County tax rolls. Eventually, the townsite became part of the giant ZX ranch. An electric pump has now replaced the windmill, which still creaks and groans in the desert wind. Today, most of the human activity in the Hampton Valley revolves around Hampton Station, a cafe that beckons the motorists who zip along the long straight stretch of desert highway, oblivious to the historical geography of the Hampton Valley.

Wagontire

The humorist can easily poke fun at Wagontire. Start with the name. It sounds like someone had left a wagon tire (or was it a wagon wheel?) in the vicinity. They did. Legend has it that an emigrant wagon was attacked and burned by Indians, and a wagon tire was found lying near the adjacent mountain, subsequently called Wagontire Mountain. Visitors stopping at Wagontire may note the "town's" population — two, recorded near the entrance to the "Wagontire City Hall." The parking meter, showing Expired, stands guard

A light dusting of snow in the Wagontire Country. Typically, light snowfalls quickly melt under the High Desert sunshine. Photo by Charles A. Blakeslee, Bend.

outside the store — at least during the day. "We take it in at night," said Bill Warner, co-owner. Across the highway, a dirt landing strip has been carved out of the sagebrush plain. "Sure, we get planes," answers Bill. "If a pilot decides that he wants breakfast, he lands. If he wants gas, we open the gate and push the aircraft across the highway. Then if he wants, he can take off along the highway." Highway 395 is the main link between Lakeview and Burns. "In winter we may see a vehicle every half an hour," Bill notes.

Nonetheless, things have changed at Wagontire. According to the 1910 highway map of Oregon, Egli, as the settlement was then named, was the focal point for four roads (or were they trails?). A road to the east connected Egli with the short-lived settlement of Kennedy, located west of Harney Lake. The road south of Egli diverged near Alkali Lake, one branch cutting across the desert to Paisley, the other skirting the west side of Lake Abert. Two roads diverged north of Egli, one to Hampton the other to the homestead community of Fife. It was only in later years, the 1930s, that Highway 395, the Yellowstone Cutoff, was aligned in its existing route through Wagontire. In 1919, the name of the Post Office at Egli was changed to Wagontire, reflecting the name of the nearby 6,504-foot (2,016 m.) mountain.

The "Wagontire City Hall" actually resembles and functions as a store, cafe, and gift shop. A sign in the cafe section priced coffee at 35 cents an hour. The gossip is free. On the occasion of my visit, three patrons, the U. S. mailwoman en route from Burns to Alkali Lake and a couple from

Wagontire (population 2) City Hall. The cafe incorporates a small gift section and post office. A motel and a camping area are next to the cafe. Note the lone parking meter out front. Photo by Ray Hatton.

Wagontire Mountain, elevation 6,504 feet (2,016 m.), broods over the sage-studded plains near Highway 395. Oregon Department of Transportation Photo.

Boise, were at the cafe counter. The conversation flowed as easily as the coffee cups were refilled. "Oh, I guess I drive 200 miles [320 km.] a day," ventured the mailwoman when asked. That made it easy to figure — 1,000 miles (1,600 km.) a week, 52,000 miles (83,200 km.) a year. Once again the geography of space was apparent. The couple from Boise confided that they planned on moving back to Lakeview: "We miss that country." Pride was expressed in the fact that the woman's great-grandmother, Alice Jones (Laird) was "the first white child born in the Warner Valley."

The owners of the store, Bill and Olgie Warner, purchased the store, cafe, and adjacent six-unit motel and small trailer park — a total of 18 acres (7.41 ha.) — at the end of 1986. They inherited

the official weather station and a donkey ("Willy") along with the real estate. Bill, formerly an engineer at MGM Grand Hotel and Casino, Reno, stated, "We wanted to own our own town. We like the people we meet here." On Sundays in winter, Bill and Olgie close the entire town. "That's the day we explore the desert country and visit neighbors — 40-50 miles [64-80 km.] away. The only thing we miss is bowling. It is 100 miles [160 km.] round trip to Burns for bowling. We like the peace and quiet here," added Bill, then paused, "except for the time cowboys branded their cattle right behind the store!"

Riley

Darlene Casey of the Riley Store and Garage calls it a "little green oasis in the middle of the desert." Motorists journeying from Lakeview or Bend and low on gas call it a "godsend." Apart from two highways and the occasional hustle and bustle in downtown Riley, the Silver Creek Valley, with its green alfalfa fields and cattle grazing, is characterized by a quiet, pastoral landscape.

Settlers came to the Silver Creek Valley in the 1870s, lured by lush grasses and by year-round water from Silver Creek. Peace in the valley was disrupted in June 1878, when an Indian war party of Bannocks and Paiutes 2,000 strong, led by Chief Egan, was ambushed by cavalry troops. After a skirmish in the Silver Creek Valley, the Indians were forced to retreat. Almost 109 years later a Springfield rifle made in 1877, evidently a relic from the Bannock War, was found hidden behind a rock on the South Ranch near Riley. Over the years, the Silver Creek Valley became settled. The post office in the valley has at different times been named Evergreen, Suntex, and Riley. When in 1956 the Bend-Burns highway was realigned to its present position, the Riley store relocated. Historical photos of the area and Western antiques help add character to the Riley store and garage, which includes a cafe and gift section. Although large trucks rumble along Highways 20 and 395, it is the Western legacy that still impresses Darlene Casey. "We still get cattle drives in the spring and fall." On a table in the cafe section of the store a photo album, put together by Darlene, is left open for visitors to browse through. The character of the Riley area is reflected by the many photos.

Riley is located at the junction of Highways 395 and 20 in the Silver Creek Valley. Following the battle between Bannock and Paiute Indians and cavalry troops in 1878, the Silver Creek Valley was homesteaded. The Riley business, shown at right, includes a store, cafe, and garage. Photo by Ray Hatton.

Above:
Abandoned cabin in the Brothers area is a silent testimony to man's lost battle in attempting to survive on the High Desert. Photo by Ray Hatton.

Left:
George Millican homestead about 1915.

OREGON'S BASIN-RANGE PROVINCE

Geology

By Bruce Nolf

Much of Southeastern Oregon falls within the Basin-Range Province of western North America, a large area characterized by youthful fault-bounded mountain blocks, sediment-filled inter-montane valleys, and relatively recent (Cenozoic) volcanism. Boundary faults trend roughly north-south, and as a result, both ranges and basins tend to be elongated in a north-south direction. Faulting is recent and continues in many places,

The Squaw Butte Experiment Station is located on the High Desert about 40 miles (64 km.) west of Burns. The experiment station, which was established in 1935, replaced the Harney Branch Experiment Station that was located just east of Burns in 1912. The Squaw Butte Experiment Station is involved in range livestock production and conducts research on range management. Photo by Ray Hatton.

Volcanic Fort Rock as seen from the south. Waves from a Pleistocene lake, which at one time covered the entire Fort Rock-Christmas Lake Valleys, eroded the southern flanks of the tuff ring. Vegetation in the foreground includes giant wild rye, rabbitbrush (a pioneer species that invades after soil is disturbed) and the characteristically gray sagebrush. Photo by Stuart G. Garrett, M.D., Bend.

generating considerable numbers of earthquakes in the region. Large earthquakes have occurred in the twentieth century in Nevada, and swarms of smaller earthquakes have been recorded historically in the Basin-Range of Oregon.

Faults tend to be steeply inclined, and displacement along faults is primarily extensional in nature (normal faults). This faulting in brittle upper crustal rocks accommodates the east-west stretching that is occurring at depth beneath the Basin-Range. Cause of this widening is a matter of considerable discussion at this time.

Because faulting is recent and because precipitation is generally low, drainage systems have not had time to integrate on a large scale. Most stream drainage is interior, giving rise to the term Great Basin, sometimes used roughly synonymous for Basin-Range. Sediment derived by erosion of uplifted ranges is typically deposited in adjacent closed basins, rather than being swept on out to the oceans. These flat-floored basins, shaped by sedimentary fill of fault-bounded depressions, are quite different in origin from valleys cut primarily by stream erosion. However,

the term "valley" is commonly used in Southeastern Oregon for these basins, such as Warner Valley, Catlow Valley, and Pueblo Valley.

During the Pleistocene Epoch (the last 2.5 to 3 million years), repeated advances of glaciers at higher altitudes and latitudes were accompanied by increased precipitation in the Basin-Range. The resulting high levels of numerous Pleistocene lakes are well documented by shoreline features commonly found hundreds of feet above the floor of now-dry desert basins. At their greatest extent, the eight major Pleistocene lakes in Oregon had a combined area of 3,500 square miles (8,960 km²), almost three times the area of the state of Rhode Island. Only Harney Lake, centered on a large caldera complex in the High Lava Plains north of the Basin-Range, had exterior drainage, using two overflow channels into the Malheur River at various times. Spectacular rise of water levels during the mid-1980s caused considerable cultural disturbance, especially in Harney Basin, but levels are still far below those attained repeatedly in the recent geologic past.

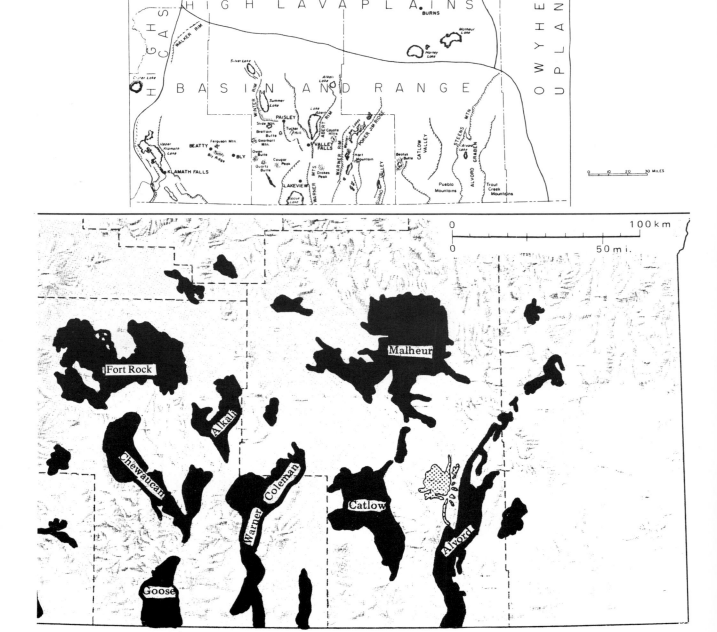

The extent of the Pleistocene lakes in Southeastern Oregon. Some idea of their sizes can be judged from the map scale. For example, the "Chewaucan" Lake extended 50 miles (80 km.) from one end to the other. The stippled area west of Lake "Alvord" represents Steens Mountain glaciation. Map from *Atlas of Oregon* (by permission).

SUMMARY OF THE STRUCTURE OF RANGES IN OREGON BASIN-RANGE

Most fault blocks in Oregon are notably tilted. The best-known block, the Steens, is broken by cross-faults into four roughly parallelogram-shaped pieces, each with different degrees of tilt. The northernmost piece is tilted very gently westward from the bounding fault on the east side of the range. The High Steens block, well known because it is traversed by the Steens Loop road, slopes more steeply westward and underlies at its western edge the sedimentary fill of the Blitzen Valley. The southern Steens block sags in its center in an open downfold (syncline), sloping gently westward from the east face, and eastward from its west edge (the northern Catlow Rim.)

Opposite:
The physical structure of the Basins and Ranges in Oregon.
Source: *Mineral and Water Resources of Oregon.* **1969.**

The portion of the Steens range south of the Long Hollow fracture zone is known as the Pueblo Mountains, and it is tilted far more steeply westward than other pieces of the Steens. This unusual degree of westward tilt has resulted in several thousand feet of greater uplift on the east side of the Pueblos, exposing the basement of pre-Cenozoic granitic and metamorphic rocks. These rocks are far older than other rocks exposed in the Oregon Basin-Range and are presumably representative of basement elsewhere in Southeastern Oregon. Greater uplift of the east side of the Pueblo block has also resulted in

greater erosion of the uplifted block and cutting back of the capping Steens basalt. The rim of the basalt is now about three to six miles (5 to 10 km.) west of the bounding fault and well behind conspicuous 8,625-foot-high (2,630 m.) Pueblo Mountain, a peak carved by erosion of the basement rocks which originally underlay the basalt. West of the crest, the layers of basalt curve upward again, forming a broad syncline across Rincon Valley and eventually forming the west-facing escarpment of the southern Catlow Rim.

Hart Mountain is a classic example of a horst, a block bounded on both sides by steep faults. The west side is so steep that in prehistoric times, it was the source of large high-velocity air-lubricated avalanches extending several miles westward across the flat floor of Warner Valley. Poker Jim Ridge, structurally a northward continuation of the Hart Mountain uplift, is quite different from Hart Mountain in cross-section. It is bounded on the west side by a very steep fault

Aerial view of Hole-in-the-Ground, a 300-feet-deep (93 m.), one- mile-diameter (1.6 km.) crater. Rising basaltic magma encountered abundant ground water, creating a steam explosion which, unlike nearby Fort Rock, deroofed the explosion chamber. Ponderosa pine grow in the more shaded north-facing inner slope (left), while the southern slope is devoid of trees. Photo by Ray Hatton.

Volcanic Fort Rock glows as the sun sets in the Fort Rock Valley. This view from the west presents a different perspective of the volcanic tuff ring from that seen from the south. Photo by Charles A. Blakeslee, Bend.

scarp, but on the east the layers bend down steeply and then flatten out toward the Catlow Valley, forming a monocline, a relatively rare form of fold in Southeastern Oregon.

The Warner Range is bounded on both sides by steep faults, with the bedrock layers tilted inward, away from the faults, on both east and west sides. The central "sag" of this uplifted block encloses a series of perched and poorly drained high valleys, including Big Valley, and localizes the cut-off road northward to Plush. The overall structure of this range is well viewed from Highway 140, which traverses the Warner block between Lakeview and Adel. Even better perspective may be gained from the lookout near Drake Peak, reached by good Forest Service roads north of Highway 140.

Winter Ridge is bounded on the east by a large fault, and the rock units slope westward from the rim. The block is largely comprised of relatively weak rocks and receives a little more precipitation than more eastern ranges. Hence the east face has been deeply incised by numerous large landslides, giving the rim a particularly scalloped appear-

ance. Many of the landslides reached the floor of the Summer Lake basin and are readily noted from Highway 31.

Fort Rock Basin

FORT ROCK VALLEY

The Fort Rock Valley is perhaps best viewed from the pumice-covered road that leads from Hole-in-the-Ground to Fremont. One minute, the traveler is among stands of mature pine; the next, as if a curtain were drawn, the desert landscape unfolds. From the hill overlooking Fremont, the Fort Rock Valley stretches far to the eastern horizon. Remnants of old volcanoes including circular, impressive Fort Rock rise conspicuously above the flat valley floor. In summer, where parts of the valley have been cultivated, swatches of bright green contrast with the beige of the untamed desert. Apart from the fields and pivot sprinklers, elements of the cultural landscape are few — just a scattering of isolated dwellings. Yet

TUFF RINGS:
A DIFFERENT KIND OF VOLCANO
by Bruce Nolf

Fort Rock Valley is bordered on the northwest by the gentle slopes of Newberry Volcano, a large shield-shaped volcano near the northwest end of the Brothers fault zone. The Newberry profile is dotted by hundreds of smaller volcanoes, mostly typical basaltic cinder cones. Basaltic volcanism in the Fort Rock Valley, however, produced vent structures of very different form, due to explosive formation of steam as a result of underground interaction between rising basaltic magma and abundant ground water.

Volcanoes produced by the explosive interaction of ground water and rising magma are commonly referred to as maars. Maars are relatively abundant along the Brothers Fault Zone, where youthful basaltic volcanism occurs in basins with considerable ground water. Where the explosive interaction was shallow, violent expansion of steam blasted away the overlying rock, producing spectacular craters rimmed by shattered pieces of bedrock. Hole-in-the-Ground, a crater approximately one mile (1.6 km.) in diameter and 400 feet (120 m.) deep, is a classic example of a basaltic volcano shaped in this manner. No lava flows were erupted at this site following the explosions. (photo page 37)

If mixing of water and magma occurs at greater depths beneath the earth's surface, the resulting mixture remains greatly compressed while confined by the overlying rock. When this mixture of steam, chilled magma, water, and broken rock finally finds a route to the surface, it erupts violently. However, because the steam in this mixture is highly compressed until it reaches the surface, the eruption cloud jets not only vertically upward, but also horizontally outward from the vent, flowing at high speed over the ground surface. Reasonable analogies are the flare of gases behind the bullet at the muzzle of a firearm as it is discharged, or the lateral surge of clouds at the base of a large nuclear explosion. Although initial speeds of such a base surge are high, the material being transported is relatively sticky, having essentially the character of a mudflow once steam is released. The flow slows down quickly, depositing a broad, low ring of ash around the vent. The radial distance of the ring from the vent depends on the vigor of the eruption. Repeated eruptions from the same vent may build the ring to significant height, as at Fort Rock.

Subsequent rise of lava, if access of magma to ground water is sealed off, may fill the ring of tuff with flat-lying flows of basalt. Flat Top, eight miles (13 km.) northwest of Fort Rock, is an example of a tuff ring filled in this manner.

Approximately 30 tuff rings are known in the area of Fort Rock Valley, ranging in diameter from less than a mile to more than five miles (8 km.). Some, such as Table Rock, are large and structurally complex. Many tuff rings in the Fort Rock Valley have been modified by the erosive effects of waves in ancient Fort Rock Lake, and some have been totally obliterated by wave erosion. The Fort Rock ring has been breached on the south side by wave erosion, and prominent shoreline terraces have been cut into the steepened sides of the eroded ring. Another notable field of particularly large tuff rings is the Harney Basin, between Wrights Point and Harney Lake. The most conspicuous is Dog Mountain, more than four miles (7 km.) in diameter, easily viewed from Wrights Point south of Burns.

man has occupied the Fort Rock Valley as long ago as 13,000 years. While the desert landscape predominates today, the valley was at one time inundated, and a vast lake extended to the east beyond Christmas Valley and to the south to include Silver Lake. In more recent history, cattlemen, sheepmen, and homesteaders have come and gone. Their story is part of the history of the Fort Rock Valley.

The early settlers in the Fort Rock Valley inadvertently came across evidences of Indian occupancy in the valley. In March 1915, the skulls and bones of four Indians, along with shell beads and remains of old grass mats, were discovered at the base of Table Mountain. Many homesteaders simply gathered artifacts from the lands they were clearing. One rancher, George Menkenmaier, collected an estimated 10,000 arrowheads.

In 1928, an Indian burial ground was discovered in the Fort Rock Valley. The bleached bones and the artifacts — spear points, knives, and arrowheads — were exposed by the wind blowing across the dry bed of the old lake. In 1929, the skeleton of an Indian woman was discovered in drifting sand near the Connley Hills, east of the town of Fort Rock. However, it was in 1938 when University of Oregon anthropologist, Dr. Luther Cressman and his crew methodically sifted through layers of volcanic ash and pumice in a small cave recessed into an ancient weathered tuff ring, less than a mile from Fort Rock. The artifacts that were unearthed indicated that the Indians (Northern Paiutes) had occupied the cave during at least four different times periods, the earliest dating back 13,000 years, the most recent being 3,000 years ago. Climatic changes accounted for fluctuations in the water level of the lake. A gap in the occupancy of the cave coincided with the eruptions of Mt. Mazama (Crater Lake) about 6,600 years ago. Strong southwesterly winds evidently brought several inches of ash and pumice to the Fort Rock Valley, choking springs and marshes and forcing abandonment of the area.

Anthropologists have subsequently learned much about the lifestyles of the first occupants of the Fort Rock Valley.[9] The sagebrush was an important resource of the Indians, and the bark peeled from the big sage (Artemisia tridentata) was used for floor coverings, padding, and for bedding. Strips of the bark fibers were rubbed and the softened material was used for making blankets, skirts, aprons, sandals, and mats. Professional and amateur archaeologists have discovered sandals fashioned from twisted sagebrush bark in both the Fort Rock cave and a cave at nearby Cougar Mountain. The sage was used for temporary shelters by piling the brush chest-high in a circle several feet in diameter. Indians of the Great Basin have long used sage for medicinal purposes. Sage poultices healed cuts, pains, and bruises. Sage tea helped clear lung congestion. Sage leaves were chewed to treat stomach disorders and indigestion.

Ironically, the sagebrush, such an important resource to the Indians thousands of years ago, was considered a problem for the twentieth century settler. The plant had to be grubbed before the land could be plowed. It provided refuge for the jackrabbit, a great pest. Overgrazing by sheep and cattle led to a change in the desert ecosystem, and the sagebrush spread at the expense of the bunchgrasses.

Stockmen were the first white people to settle in the Fort Rock Basin, in particular the Silver Lake country in the 1870s. Adverse climatic conditions, principally severe winter and drought, affected the livestock herds. The depression of 1907 led to an interest in new opportunities away from urban areas. Then the Revised Homestead Act (1909), whereby settlers were granted 320 acres (131 ha.) of land provided they paid a $10 filing fee, occupied the land within six months, and improved their claim within five years, brought hundreds of potential settlers to the Fort Rock Basin.

Homesteaders were attracted to the Fort Rock area, as they were to other parts of Oregon's High Desert country, by newspaper claims. The *Silver Lake Leader* in May 1909 reported that the "entire Fort Rock Basin is covered with a luxuriant growth of sagebrush" (thereby indicating fertility of the soil). Water in abundance is found everywhere from 60 feet [18.6 m.] to 40 feet [12.4 m.] and the name previously applied to this section — "desert" — is a misnomer. This vast territory is capable of supporting a couple of thousand families. It now has 300 settlers and every day brings more in. Soils have been tested by the State Agricultural College and pronounced to be of the richest and highest productive qualities. This entire section, we fully believe, will in a few years be one vast grain field." There were claims as to the climate being suitable for fruit such as pears, apples, plums and cherries. Irrigation, it was claimed, was not necessary, with the annual precipitation being 16 inches (406 mm.). "All grains such as wheat, rye, oats, and barley will be grown under the dry-farming system."

When J. J. Rhoton located in the Fort Rock Valley in April, 1907, there was no cabin in the valley. By May 1910, there were three schools and six post offices and an estimated 250 families. A Fourth of July celebration held in the "crater" of Fort Rock that year attracted 300 who watched or participated in horse races, baseball, and dancing. In December 1910, membership of the Fort Rock Literary and Debating Society had reached 100. As the valley was settled, community gatherings became an important aspect of the homesteaders lives. Dances attracted people from many miles around. Dancing, which generally included qua-drilles, heel-and-toe polkas and other now-forgotten steps, started early in the evening and ended at dawn the following morning. Sleepy children went to bed on benches around the wood stove or in the coatroom. An orchestra may have consisted of two men, one playing an mandolin, the other an accordion.

Following the summer of 1912, nearly 20,000 bushels of grain were threshed in the Fort Rock Basin. During the period 1910 to 1916, the Bend, Silver Lake, and Lakeview newspapers included weekly reports, largely optimistic, from the various communities in the Fort Rock Basin. For example, the *Silver Lake Leader*, July 14, 1916, stated that the Fremont Creamery turned out 4,000 pounds (1,800 kg.) of butter during the month of June. The creamery paid 24-1/2 cents a pound (0.45 kg.) for butterfat, and its payroll was $900 for the month. The newspaper added, "This country will produce more than sagebrush and jackrabbits." Christmas Valley people even re-commended a name change to Pleasant Valley on the basis that Christmas suggested cold weather and retarded development.

In January 1915, the *Fort Rock Times* boasted that "Three years ago there was not an acre of cultivated land in the valley. Now hardly an acre is not taken. Houses are seen in all directions on every 320-acre claim." At the height of the homestead period, 1916, the population of the Fort Rock Valley was estimated at 1,200. As more people moved in, improved homesteads became valuable, at least temporarily. In the spring of 1915 the W. L. Powers homestead (160 acres, 66 ha.) near Loma Vista sold for $2,500. Roy Nash, Fort Rock, traded his 320 acres (131 ha.) and his wife's 160 acres (65.6 ha.) of land, valued at $20,000, for 500 acres (205 ha.) valued at $30,000 in the Willamette Valley near Salem, the differ-ence being paid in cash. Adding further zeal to the homesteaders' optimism was the surveying of the Strahorn rail line, intended to run from Bend to Lakeview via the Fort Rock Valley.

The dependence of the Fort Rock Valley people on the "outside world" was well stated by the following *Fort Rock Times* news item included in the June 3, 1915, *Lake County Examiner*:

"Some of us Fort Rock Valley people get up at the alarm of a Connecticut clock, button our Chicago suspenders to our Philadelphia pants, wash our faces with Cincinnati soap in a Pennsyl-vania basin, sit down to a Grand Rapids table, eat Nebraska bacon, eat our biscuits made of Wis-consin flour and Kansas lard, walk out of a house plastered with a Scotch mortgage, do business with money borrowed from the East, advertise with printed matter produced in Portland. At bedtime we read a verse from a Boston Bible, say a prayer composed in Jerusalem, crawl under a New Jersey blanket, and are kept awake by the yowling of a Fort Rock Valley cat, the only home product of the entire outfit."

Cautionary notes soon crept into the news items. From Christmas Lake Valley, there were reports of the difficulty of finding drinking water that was not impregnated with salts. Jackrabbits were multiplying and consuming vast amounts of grain. The *Lake County Examiner*, October 28, 1915, reprinting from an earlier *Silver Lake Leader*, featured a story entitled "Has Farming Proved a Success at Fort Rock?" Failures were attributed in part to the homesteaders' lack of capital (costs of farming were greater than anticipated), to inexperience, to using wrong seed for the area, and to pests, especially a small yellow worm working underground on plants. Yet successes had been achieved with the harvest of grain, which had increased from 200 bushels in 1912 to 25,000 bushels in 1915. The February 11, 1916, issue of the *Silver Lake Leader* reported, "L. O. Girton has raised only one good crop in four years." However, it added, Mr. Girton was staying, awaiting irrigation waters. "With the government back of the irrigation," he stated, "the project looks good to me. However, the land without irrigation is just about worthless." Gir-ton supported his family, a wife and four children, by freighting for the Fort Rock merch-ants.

The large-scale abandonment by homesteaders of the Fort Rock Basin started about 1917. Precipitation at Silver Lake dropped to a meager 7.20 inches (183 mm.) for the years 1914-18. By a coincidence, the first homesteaders had settled in the Fort Rock area when yearly precipitation, although still modest, was above what has proven to be the long-term average. For example, the Silver Lake weather station recorded an average of 11.61 inches per year (295 mm.) of precipita-tion for the five-year period 1909-13. The long-term mean annual precipitation for Silver Lake is less than 10 inches (254 mm.). Crops failed, hordes of jackrabbits attacked any leftover

Abandoned homestead in the Fort Rock Valley. By the late 1980s there were few such cabins left standing. Photo by Ray Hatton.

St. Bridget's Church in the Cougar Valley, an extension of the Fort Rock Valley. The church was built in 1918 and named after Bridget Godon who, with her family, homesteaded nearby in 1911. Photo by Ray Hatton.

stunted grains, and vegetables were hit by late-spring and midsummer frosts. (Later observations [1947 to 1953] taken at The Poplars ranch six miles [10 km.] southeast of Fort Rock showed the average frost-free period to be 20 days.) As the aridity intensified, winds picked up the parched soils and swept them across the valley. Isolation from any railhead added to the cost of shipping goods to the region. Furthermore, freight lines from Bend were handicapped in winter by deep snows and in the spring by muddy roads. Irrigation schemes that had been promised to homesteaders failed to materialize.

By 1917 the exodus from the valley had begun. The *Silver Lake Leader* gloomily reported first a trickle, then a flood of homesteaders leaving. Typical of the reports was, "F. E. Cook and family left Monday with teams and wagons for Idaho where they expect to make their home." Crops were a total failure in the summer of 1918. Water in wells had dropped considerably, and adding to the problems, the labor supply in the valley as elsewhere was greatly reduced by the drafting of young men for World War I. Many older men readily found work in Portland shipyards or in one of Bend's two lumber mills.

There were, however, those with hope and confidence. *The Bulletin* (Bend), July 12, 1919, stated that F. C. Eichemeyer, a large landowner in the Fort Rock Valley, urged homesteaders not to lose hope and pleaded for funds to study the water possibilities in the valley. Meetings to discuss the prospects of investigating the water situation in the valley were attended by most of the remaining homesteaders. A poem written by M. R. Holtman, printed in the *Silver Lake Leader*, June 10, 1920, optimistically predicted better times:

There is a little valley, In the heart of Oregon,
Where sagebrush and junipers Are the only things that's grown
Winds and drouth and jackrabbits Have ruined all the crops;

Cheer up my friends, there'll come a time;
When all this bad luck stops,
For we'll soon have irrigation;
No doubt artesian water too,
Then we'll show the knockers A few things that we can do.
Next we'll get the railroads, We will need them it is true
To link us with civilization, And to put our produce through.
Then will come the cities, They will spring up thick and fast
Fort Rock will be a metropolis,
And Silver Lake will forget its past.

However, by 1920 the exodus had taken place. Throughout the Fort Rock Basin most post offices and schools closed. Examples of post office closures included Arrow (February 1918), Cliff (June 1920), Fleetwood (July 1920), Fremont (May 1921), Loma Vista (May 1918), and Sink (August 1920). When school bells should have rung in the fall of 1918, eleven schools in the Fort Rock Valley did not open. The 1920 census taker, expecting to list 300 names, told the *Lake County Examiner* (February 5, 1920), "The country is almost depopulated. Only one-eighth of the expected number is left."

In the early 1920s a temporary wet spell revived

hopes for those who had stubbornly resisted moving. Springs that had been dry for a few years were flowing again. Water in wells, which had dropped two feet (0.6 m.) or more, crept back upwards. The state legislature appropriated $10,000 to test for possible artesian water in the basin. In the spring of 1921, prospects of a good crop for summer looked excellent. Then on July 1 and 2, severe frost ruined grains throughout much of the Fort Rock area.

The *Silver Lake Leader*, October 6, 1921, reported that crop failures due to the drought in the past five years had bled people white. "With the irrigation questions solved [referring to the construction of Thompson Reservoir] it is reasonable to expect that many settlers who have left will return and others looking for cheap land will avail themselves of the opportunities." In October 1921 a demonstration well drilled at the Ernst ranch southeast of Fort Rock produced up to 1,000 gallons of water a minute. A crowd of 150 gathered to witness the pumping demonstration. H. M. Parks, Director of the Oregon Bureau of Mines and Geology, was of the opinion that beneath the desert of the Fort Rock Basin lay a yet-to-be-tapped body of water. Electricity for pumping the water, it was believed at that time, would come from a hydroelectric plant to be built on the Deschutes River at Pringle Falls. In reality, it would be 34 years before electricity arrived in the Fort Rock Basin. This, as will be shown, was the key to changing the economy and landscape of the region.

The drought returned with even more of a vengeance. In July 1924, it was so severe that Bridge Creek at Silver Lake went dry for the first time in memory. Dust storms followed the drought. The *Silver Lake Leader*, March 19, 1925, reporting from Fort Rock, stated, "Well, we have had one more real dust storm and talk about a real estate transfer! We think we got most of what Fremont lost. Have been shoveling it for two days but can't even make a showing."

Descriptions of the desert landscapes as seen shortly after most of the homesteaders had left was provided by Isaiah Bowman and by Isabel McKinney. After his visit through Southeastern Oregon in August 1930, Bowman wrote:

"Between Fort Rock and the eastern border of the Deschutes National Forest in a distance of ten miles there are 15 uninhabited and two inhabited houses on or quite near the road that runs through the driest and worst part of the valley. There are perhaps twice that number of houses on the hilly border of the plain, but they were too far away from me to see whether they were occupied or empty. In the midst of the plain lies Fremont, once an occupied hamlet and now wholly abandoned. Fort Rock has but two or three occupied houses besides the combined post office and general store. In all of the ranch yards there are windmills if the house is occupied, and half of those unoccupied have this lingering sign of the hopeless homesteader.

"Settlement ventured far in the High Desert between Bend and Burns but still farther in the Low Desert that includes Fort Rock Valley and Christmas Lake Valley. There are about twenty-five houses between Silver Lake and Fort Rock. Not a single one is inhabited. If the house is not boarded up the windows have all been broken or the place is in ruins. The sheds have not been in use for a long time. The yards are unkempt. Sagebrush is all about. A third of the houses in the town of Silver Lake are unoccupied and the windows broken. There are no sidewalks. Heavy dust lies everywhere. Sage grows right up to the back yards. The town boasts a good high school and grade school with five teachers and about eighty pupils. Some of the parents move into the village when winter sets in and stay until spring."[10]

Years later, Isabel McKinney, writing for the *Oregon Journal*, recollected her family's move in May 1920 to a foreclosed ranch located at the edge of the Fort Rock Valley:

"What a strange country we drove down into. The past seemed to be unrolling before us. Silent houses, mere one-room shacks, stared at us vacantly through gaps that once were windows. They stood there like monuments to an abandoned hope. This land seemed to have absorbed everything and given nothing in return. It just lies there silently waiting — waiting for water — water for irrigation which has never come."

"We stopped at one shack out of curiosity to read a sign hung over the door. 'Abandon all hope, Ye, who enter here.'

"I noticed an old tin trunk and walked over to it and lifted the lid. Down in the bottom were some old faded portraits and books. I picked up a book. It was a complete volume of Shakespeare's works. There were many notes written on the edges of the pages. Its owner must have been a lover of the classics. I couldn't make out the owner's name. The writing was too dim, but the date was still clear enough for me to see that it had been written May 17th, 1893. I couldn't leave that book; 1893 was before I was born. I took it and several others. Why not? The name wasn't legible and I would take good care of them. Where was the owner anyway? The wind answered with a hollow moan, 'Gone, gone, gone,' and sucked more dirt out from under the house.''[11]

Bud Parks of The Poplars ranch, long-time resident of the Fort Rock Valley, recollected the landscape of the valley. He noted, "In 1929 as one stood on the top of Hayes Butte [8 miles (13 km.) southeast of Fort Rock] the country, as far as the eye could see, was dotted with abandoned homestead cabins.''

Later, many of these cabins were burned by government employees. Others were moved to remaining farms and used for storage sheds. Few of the cabins remain today.

The drought which started in 1917 continued intermittently for nearly 20 years. Indeed, the *Lake County Examiner*, May 23, 1935, reported, "crops planted this year have been blown out of the ground or cut off by the wind-blown sands. Rye that was showing green above the parched sandy soil was mown down as if by a close-cropping lawnmower by the sand, driven by a high wind.... What few cattle [are left] will have to be sold or mortgaged to provide food for human consumption, and unless something is done before fall, all but a comparatively few who have irrigated ranches will be forced off the land with nothing to show for years of heart-breaking, self-sacrificing work and industry.''

Stated the *Lake County Examiner*, October 13, 1938, "Fort Rock has now become a ghost town. Those who have weathered the years of drought, improving their homes loath to sacrifice what they have built up. Now [with increased precipitation] they are making a living, crop conditions are improving, and they love the desert country. The strange fascination of its ruggedness and even the barrenness and loneliness holds them like a spell of enchantment.''

Although hundreds of homesteaders had left the Fort Rock Valley, special occasions such as the July 4, 1939, picnic and rodeo were held at The Poplars, described as a veritable oasis with its grove of poplars and elms and adjacent lush green alfalfa fields. As many as 500 people came from all parts of the county to participate in or watch bucking contests, calf roping, and steer riding and enjoy the picnic organized by Mr. and Mrs. H. M. Parks. The Lakeview newspaper described the event: "... a demonstration that Western people can still furnish and enjoy their entertainment just as the pioneers did a few decades ago. It was a day steeped in the flavor of old-time hospitality and neighborliness.''

On March 31, 1949, some 110,000 acres (45,100 ha.) was transferred to the Bureau of Land Management. This ended the chapter on the homesteading of the Fort Rock Valley. The tragedy of the homesteading period has been one of the main historical episodes in the Fort Rock Basin. Each September, members of the Fort Rock Pioneers, some of whom remember the homestead days, gather at Fort Rock to participate in the Saturday evening dance and Sunday potluck or to reminisce about the "good old days.'' They remember them as a time when the elements and economic conditions hit them with the worst possible combination. One would think that the homesteaders would hate the place, yet they revel in these annual gatherings on the desert. Their attitude seems to be, "We were hit with the most tragic circumstances imaginable and we survived! Our own resourcefulness and that of caring neighbors carried us through. Nothing which happens in later life can erase our confidence in our ability to carry on in the face of appalling adversity.'' Fittingly enough, the activities are in the Fort Rock Grange, a large structure that was once one of three schools (Fleetwood, Connley, Loma Vista) of the homestead era.

In her Ph.D. dissertation in the late 1970s, Barbara Allen interviewed old-timers still living in the Fort Rock Basin. Allen found that of all the topics of "talk about the past", the one that informants most frequently mentioned was home-steading.

Referring to the time of exodus by the homesteaders, old timers' comments included "...A lot of them walked away and left their furniture and everything." Recalled Mrs. Ward, ''I remember as a kid we used to go and explore the shacks left around here... at that time many of these places had trunks full of things, cupboards full of dishes, clothes hanging in a closet or behind a curtain... people had gone away, maybe to go to work [in Bend or Portland], and never came back....''[12]

The key to unlock the desert lands was water.

A SENSE OF PLACE

I was in one of my desert-exploring moods. On this occasion I poked around the periphery of the Fort Rock Valley, visiting and photographing abandoned homesteads. One isolated cabin in particular caught my attention. While the ravages of 60 winter snows and 60 summers of fierce sun had left their mark, the homestead had been soundly constructed. Dust and debris littered the interior and partly covered a crudely-made chest of drawers.

My curiosity got the better of me. I heaved open the chest. Buried under years of blown soil were a number of left-behind personal papers, including a report card for daughter Gladys (mostly As, including one in Geography!) and a letter postmarked Kansas (postage 2 cents) addressed to J. W. Hatter. In addition, there was a teacher's bulletin for February 1917, a blackboard eraser, and a collection of vacation songs.

I wandered outside. A roll of barbed wire, still serviceable, lay coiled next to the barn. Various machinery parts lay rusting around the old cabin. Once again the tragedy of the homestead period became so apparent. I tried to picture the last days of the Hatter family in their Fort Rock Valley home. The school where J. W. Hatter taught, the Valley View School, was losing students as families left the valley. The decision to stay or leave was clearly made... or was it? What were the thoughts of the family members? After moving from Kansas and investing so much time, energy, and capital into building the homestead cabin and barn, digging (perhaps by hand) a well, what a heart-breaking situation it must have been to leave. What to pack? What to leave? As the family left the home, took one last look back at the receding cabin, what were their thoughts. What memories of the Fort Rock Valley followed them back to Kansas?

I thought of the Hatter family. Are there grandchildren of Mr. and Mrs. J. W. Hatter who live in Kansas or elsewhere, who have heard stories passed down from their grandpa about the Fort Rock Valley in Oregon? I slowly wandered back to my car. To my mind a verse from Ada Hastings Hedges' *The Desert Wife*. I looked back at the homestead. A sense of sadness engulfed me.

XIII

Only a wall is left... the fallen frame
Lies like a bleached and scattered skeleton,
And they who thought to build and to reclaim
Are gone, as wilder tribes have come and gone.
With sun and wind across the burning sand,
The desert ruthlessly has taken all
That marked their brief intrusion save a strand
Of sagging fence, a reach of silvered wall.
Indifferent and timeless as the stars,
Few are the records it will not erase—
The futile footprints and the surface scars
Of men too puny for its light and space.
From age to age the waste shall brood and dream,
Mysterious and silent and supreme. [13]

As early as 1937 H. M. Parks was still of the opinion that with power, Bonneville power for example, 40,000 acres (16,400 ha.) of Fort Rock Valley land could be brought into production. However, it was not until the mid 1950s that electricity reached large areas of northern Lake County. On October 28, 1955, the arrival of Rural Electrification Association power attracted 500 to Silver Lake for a celebration. People came from Bend, Klamath Falls, Lakeview, and Burns; many were homesteaders who had left their desert claims over 30 years previously. A pessimistic Oregon State University Experiment Station report on the Fort Rock Valley, pointing out the short growing season and great distances to market, temporarily deterred development of the valley. Within two years, however, the landscape of the Fort Rock Valley was undergoing change. Where sage had covered the desert in 1955, there were fields of waving grain and green alfalfa. Electric pumps and sprinklers, and bales of hay in late summer, became part of the desert scene.

The years have come and gone, and in summer, parts of the Fort Rock Valley are as green and lush as the Willamette Valley of western Oregon. But looks can be deceiving, and those who know the desert understand its subtleties. Writes Bud Parks:

"To me, the Fort Rock Valley appears as an enigma. Viewed on a typical fall day it seems delightful. Calm, with the temperature just right; imagination and dreams project one's mind into what it can become, far beyond what meets the eye.

"The typical spring day," on the other hand, is likely to find a bitter wind howling, dust blowing, and the season's soil moisture dissipating so rapidly it's as if it were immaterial whether there ever had been winter rain and snow. At these times the mind focuses on what it is. The dream of what it can become grows dim.

"On balance, most years seem weighted with bitter winds and dust. Their impact on the senses is all but overwhelming. Yet, with the return of the calm, pleasant days the dream is there again. The great valley holds a hypnotic attraction, but its promises seem just out of reach — next season —in the future." [14]

By far the chief crop of the Fort Rock Valley is alfalfa. Loma Vista Farms, located midway in the triangle between Fort Rock, Silver Lake, and Christmas Valley, grows alfalfa on 3,000 acres (1,230 ha.), producing 250,000-300,000 tons a year. Alfalfa is one of the richest crops grown for livestock, especially dairy cows, having large amounts of proteins, minerals, and vitamins. The plant is a perennial. During the growing season the plants send up bright green shoots up to three feet (1 m.) high. The crop is cut after five or six weeks and the shoots grow once again. In the Fort Rock Valley, farmers can expect to get two, sometimes three cuttings per summer.

One unique feature of Loma Vista Farms is the making of cubes of alfalfa, which are shipped to Japan. Despite the cost of shipping, Japan has been eager to buy the high-protein alfalfa.

Water is the key to much of the development in the High Desert, as it is in other semi-arid lands. Despite the long, cold winters interspersed with periodic blitzes of snow, summers are likely to be hot and mostly dry. Evaporation rates are high. Today, one of the keys to the continued economic viability of the Fort Rock Basin is its underground water resources. Where water is pumped from the ground, the desert blooms. Each acre of irrigated land may yield three tons of top quality alfalfa per growing season. By 1984, the 200 or so farmers in the Fort Rock Basin were irrigating nearly 50,000 acres (20,500 ha.) of land, only about three percent of the basin's 2,500 square miles (6,500 km²).

Alfalfa is a thirsty crop. Each acre requires about one-third of a million gallons of water. In places, quarter-mile pivot sprinklers spray 1,000 gallons of water a minute over the growing crops. From the air, the revolving sprinklers create huge green circles on the tan desert.

The cost of establishing large-scale operations in the desert is not cheap. For starters, undeveloped lands in the mid-1980s went for $300-$350 an acre (0.41 ha.), or close to $50,000 for a 160-acre (65.6 ha.) tract. The pivot sprinklers sold for $32,000-$37,500 each. Well drilling, assuming a well permit were granted, cost $24.40 per foot (0.31 m.): from $2,205 for a 90-foot well to as much as $27,440 for a well 1,120 feet (347 m.) deep.

In 1985, a decline in ground water levels was attributed to increased pumping and a moratorium was placed on drilling new wells. Land prices plummeted to $100 an acre (0.41 ha.). In 1960, 12,000 acre-feet of water was pumped out of the valley each year. Hydrologists at that time estimated that each year an average of

125,000 acre-feet of water was entering the ground water table. This figure was later disputed and a revised figure of 60,000 acre-feet was given. Water withdrawal increased from 20,000 acre-feet in 1970 to 90,000 acre-feet by 1980. The number of wells in the basin in 1980 climbed to 400, up considerably from the hundred documented in 1970. Donn Miller, of the Oregon Water Resources Department, noted a 3-foot (1 m.) decline in ground water levels in the early 1980s. By mid-decade, following a period of much-above-normal precipitation, a reverse trend in the water level had begun. In addition to less-than-certain water supplies, a decline in alfalfa prices, high interest rates on equipment purchases and on loans for seeds and fertilizers, and soaring electricity rates created some economic hardships for many farmers in the Fort Rock Basin. By the 1980s the population of the basin, which was put at 300 in 1960, more than tripled to over 1,000, coincidentally about equal to the population of the peak of homesteading in 1916.

CHRISTMAS LAKE VALLEY

The Christmas Lake Valley, the eastern arm of the Fort Rock Basin, is a region of contrasts. Sagebrush and open sandy stretches are interspersed with the deep green of alfalfa fields. Here and there, weathered cabins, relics from the homestead days, stand next to shining mobile homes. While Silver Lake and Fort Rock are older pioneer communities, Christmas Valley, the largest settlement in Lake County after Lakeview, is of relative recent origin.

The valley extends unbroken for mile after mile in an east-west direction. To the south, tilted fault-block mountains, associated with the Basin and Range geology, form the southern limit to the valley. Youthful symmetrical cinder cones and black lava flows delimit the northern edge.

During the homestead period, settlements such as Cliff, Viewpoint, Buffalo, Sink, and Lake sprouted amidst the sagebrush, flourished for a few years, then withered. At most, each community consisted of a combined store and post office and a school.

Christmas Valley dates back only to 1961. That year the Penn Phillips Company purchased from a cattle company 70,000 acres (28,700 ha.) of sagebrush-studded desert land, most of it for $10 an acre (0.41 ha.). Previously, the cattle company had acquired most of that acreage from Lake County for 25 cents an acre (0.41 ha.). In turn, Lake County had assumed possession of the land through tax delinquency. The Penn Phillips Company, with the help of engineers and architects, put together the plan to develop Christmas Valley into a rural retirement area with part-time farming to possibly supplement retirement income.

A test plot for agricultural experimentation was established. However, the major developmental part of the plan was the creation of a 30-acre (12 ha.) lake, a nine-hole golf course, lodge, dude ranch, airfield, motel, and water system. The town of Christmas Valley was platted into small city lots while the adjacent desert land was divided into various-sized acreages. A total of 2,700 parcels was spread over a five-square-mile (13.0 km²) area.

An intensive advertising campaign touting Christmas Valley as the "rich heartland of America" was carried over radio, television and newspapers throughout urban areas of California. Glossy color brochures included an "artist's conception of the plan." The promotion blitz succeeded. Land-hungry Californians, seeking property at "giveaway prices," purchased many of the lots site unseen. By 1966, some 99 percent of the development had been sold, some "city lots" going for as high as $1,100 an acre (0.41 ha.). However, most of the parcels of land that were sold ranged from 20 to 40 acres in a region that takes 60 acres (24.6 ha.) to support one cow.

As might be expected, there were those who were disappointed, to say the least, with the land they had purchased. Some 25 percent asked for and received their money back after viewing the property. Others in time defaulted on their payment contracts. Some, buying for speculation, resold their property. In all, the Penn Phillips investment at Christmas Valley was pegged at $3 million. Estimates of the corporate profits varied from $8 million to over $20 million. [15]

Today, land consolidation has occurred in the vicinity of Christmas Valley, and some of the original Penn Phillips holdings are successfully growing alfalfa. Furthermore, many of those who have settled in the valley are enthusiastic about their decision and contend that despite drawbacks—isolation from urban areas for shopping, medical facilities and distances to schools—the wide-open spaces, clear skies, fresh desert air, and nearby recreational opportunities are more important.

Christmas Valley is a community that has seemingly sprouted from the sagebrush plains. The only industry in the vicinity is the Oil-Dri Production Company plant, which mines and processes (into kitty litter) diatomaceous earth — fossilized material formed from diatoms, microscopic aquatic life that settled at the bottom of the lake that once covered the entire Fort Rock Basin. The rural fringes of Christmas Valley consist of scattered farms. In town, mobile homes and conventional houses circle the commercial heart of Christmas Valley.

First-time visitors, after driving through miles of open desert and farmlands, may be surprised by the variety of businesses in the town. The Christmas Valley Lodge, an imposing A-frame structure anchored by ranch-style sections, has been a focal point for both visitors and local residents who gather to dine or patronize the adjacent cocktail bar.

Recreationists come to Christmas Valley to explore some of the nearby unique natural features, including Crack-in-the-Ground, the Lost Forest, and the Sahara-like sand dunes in the Fossil Lake area. Seen from a distance at night, the lights from homes and ranches illuminate the sky and tend to greatly magnify the apparent size of the community.

NORTHERN LAKE COUNTY'S "SARAHA", "BONEYARD" AND LOST FOREST

Although the unirrigated lands within the Fort Rock Basin appear arid, they do not generally create the Hollywood stereotype of a desert — waves of shifting sand dunes. However, about 20 miles (32 km.) northeast of Christmas Valley are 12,000 acres (4,920 ha.) of rolling, sahara-like dunes. This desert landscape is part of the Fossil Lake country.

It was in the 1870s that cattlemen, searching for their stock, wandered into the Fossil Lake area and discovered what proved to be a veritable boneyard of paleontological finds. In 1876, Professor Thomas Condon, a geologist at the University of Oregon, visited Fossil Lake and discovered fossilized shells and bones of elephants, camels, and birds. Three years later, paleontologist E. D. Cope of Philadelphia investigated the old lake bed.

Cope discovered the fossilized remains of two species of extinct horse, a huge sloth, a large

Crack-in-the-Ground, located 10 miles (16 km.) north of Christmas Valley, is two miles (3.2 km.) long and, in places, is 70 feet (21 m.) deep. The "crack", according to Dennis Simontacchi, geologist with the BLM at Lakeview, is one of three tension cracks in the area. Lava may have collapsed into lava tunnels that were associated with the recent (last 1,000 years) volcanism at the nearby Four Craters lava flow. Ice often lingers into the summer in deep sections of the crack. Photo by Ray Hatton.

grizzly bear, a mammoth, and several small mammals — some extinct, some not. In addition, Cope noted that among his finds were the bones of different birds and fishes. Scattered everywhere on the lake bed were chips of obsidian flints, evidences of Indian occupancy in the vicinity.

Since the 1870s, other scientific finds have been made at Fossil Lake. One of the most interesting was the remains of an anadromous salmon, indicating that the waters of the Fort Rock Basin, in more pluvial times, had a water link to the ocean. That being the case, scientists have analyzed the geology of the basin and have concluded that, given the geology and topography of the region, the link to the Deschutes River and hence to the Pacific Ocean was through an outlet from the Fort Rock Basin.[16] Here, it was

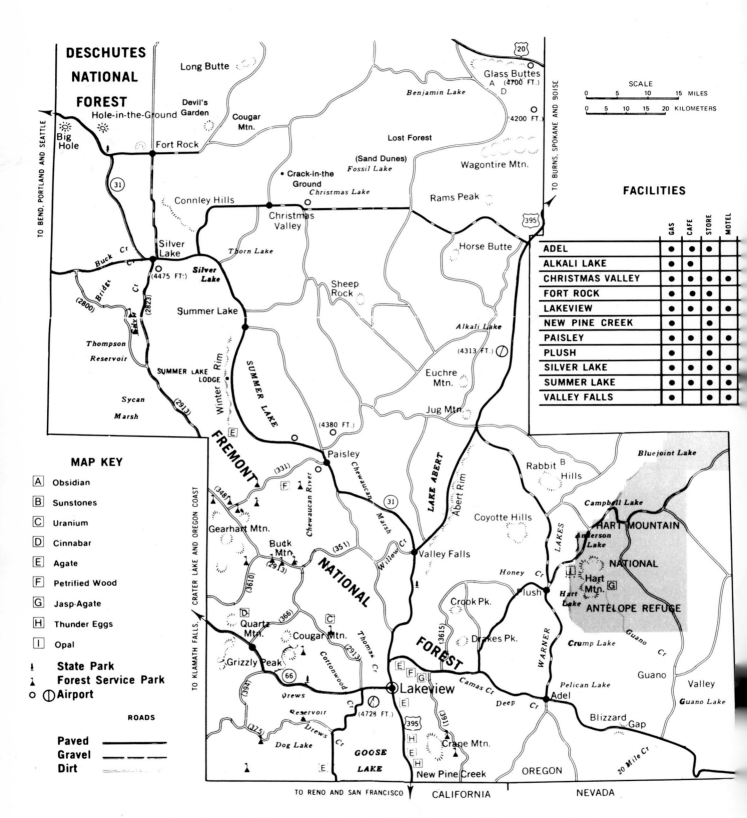

MAP KEY

A	Obsidian		
B	Sunstones		
C	Uranium		
D	Cinnabar		
E	Agate		
F	Petrified Wood		
G	Jasp-Agate		
H	Thunder Eggs		
I	Opal		

⚑ **State Park**

⚑ **Forest Service Park**

○ ◔ **Airport**

ROADS

Paved	———————
Gravel	— — — —
Dirt	‒ ‒ ‒ ‒ ‒

FACILITIES

	GAS	CAFE	STORE	MOTEL
ADEL	●	●	●	
ALKALI LAKE	●	●		
CHRISTMAS VALLEY	●	●	●	●
FORT ROCK	●	●	●	
LAKEVIEW	●	●	●	●
NEW PINE CREEK	●		●	
PAISLEY	●	●	●	●
PLUSH	●	●	●	
SILVER LAKE	●	●	●	●
SUMMER LAKE	●	●	●	●
VALLEY FALLS	●		●	●

Lake County, which was created October 24, 1874, covers 8,340 square miles (21,684 km²). It has a population of less than 8,000. The map shows the major physical and cultural places mentioned in the text. Map courtesy of Lake County Chamber of Commerce.

Rolling dunes cover 12,000 acres (4,920 ha.) of Lake County, northeast of Christmas Valley. The dunes are of interest to recreationists who come to photograph, hike, or ride over the dunes. Photo by Ray Hatton.

View across the western section of the Lost Forest to the sand dunes near Fossil Lake (background). The Lost Forest encompasses 9,000 acres (3,690 ha.) of ponderosa pine and juniper in an area that receives less than 10 inches (25 mm.) of annual precipitation. Photo by Ray Hatton.

suggested, water flowed out of the Fort Rock Basin northward in pre Newberry times to the Deschutes River. Relatively recent volcanic activity associated with the Newberry Volcano had subsequently dammed that outlet. Changes in the climate shrank the lake, and today Fossil Lake is a mere puddle left over from when the Fort Rock Basin was covered by a vast lake.

Fossil Lake is now closed to vehicular use, but the sand dunes to the east attract many recreationists and visitors — off-road vehicle enthusiasts, photographers, students on field trips, naturalists, and those who see the fascinating beauty of the dunes.

From the top of Sand Rock (a volcanic tuff ring), except for a string of power lines and distant irrigated farms, the landscape of the eastern part of the Fort Rock Basin today is similar to that described by Cope in 1879: "The scene was impressive from its wild desolation. As far as the eye could see was the same sagebrush desert, the same waterless region of death. Many a man has entered this region never to escape from its fatal drought, especially during the first days of the overland emigration to Oregon."[17] It is hard to believe that an emigrant road skirted the north side of the Fossil Lake dunes. A couple of springs, Mounds Springs and Sand Springs, supplied water for the migrants. In general, the landscape must surely have been a bleak one for those early travelers of Oregon's High Desert country.

At first the Lost Forest looks like a mirage, especially when seen from the bumpy "road" that

approaches from the north. It is literally a "lost" forest, a 9,000-acre (3,690 ha.) stand of ponderosa pine and juniper, located in an area which receives less than 10 inches (25.4 mm.) of annual precipitation, half of what is normally required for ponderosa pine. Furthermore, the mature pines seem very much out of place so far from any other stands of ponderosa and adjacent to the Fossil Lake sand dunes. Some of the junipers in the forest are among the largest known and measure five feet (1.55 m.) in diameter.

Students of the Lost Forest have concluded that the bed of an ancient lake provides an impervious layer to sustain whatever moisture falls. A contract surveyor for the General Land Office who surveyed the Lost Forest in 1877 described the area as being heavily timbered with an abundance of bunch grass adjacent to the forest. Logging in the 1950s has thinned the pine, and young trees in the stand seem few. In places, sands from the Fossil Lake dunes have encroached into the Lost Forest.

SILVER LAKE

Silver Lake Valley was first settled by the white man in the early 1870s when stockmen, making use of the thick bunch grasses watered by Buck Creek and Silver Creek, brought sheep and later horses and cattle to the area. However, Silver Lake was extremely isolated. At first, mail service, delivered only every six weeks, came from Willow Ranch, California. The first post office was established in the winter of 1874-75 near the body of water known as Silver Lake, nine miles

(15 km.) east of the present site of the town. In 1884, the present Silver Lake was settled and within a few years had a hotel, feed barn, two stores, school, saloon and blacksmith's shop. Mail services subsequently came from Lakeview, then from Prineville, at that time the largest town in Central Oregon.

By 1894, Silver Lake had a population of 150. However, tragedy struck the small town. On Christmas Eve, some 170 men, women, and children, many traveling some distance to Silver Lake, crowded into the Chrisman Building, a 24x50-foot (7.4x15.5 m.) room, for a Christmas Eve celebration. Towards the close of the festivities, one of the audience, wishing either to get a better view of what was going on or to leave the hall, accidentally struck a hanging Rochester oil lamp with his head. The spilled flammable oil ignited and within seconds spread across the hall. Panic ensued. The fire spread rapidly. People jammed the one exit door or broke windows on the south end of the building and climbed onto a small porch to escape. The porch collapsed, plunging people to the ground. Within two minutes the whole building was aflame. Nineteen women, sixteen men and eight children were killed by the fire, and just about every household in Silver Lake and vicinity was affected by the tragedy. Today in the Silver Lake Cemetery a large marble gravestone, erected in 1898, bears the names of the 43 who had died.

For a few years Silver Lake continued as a small cattle town and trading center, being on the stage and freight lines that ran from Prineville to Lakeview. In 1904, in addition to the usual businesses, Silver Lake had two hotels and two newspapers. When the homestead rush in the Fort Rock Basin got underway after 1909, Silver Lake benefitted from the influx of settlers and the promise of a railroad through the town. The *Silver Lake Leader*, March 24, 1916, carried the headline "Strahorn Engineers Making Survey Through Silver Lake" and added, "The prayers of the people for the past twenty years are now being answered. The Railroad our financial salvation." The paper portrayed a photo of Robert E. Strahorn (promoter of railroads in Central Oregon) with the caption, "The Man of the Hour." In the April 28, 1916, issue of the *Silver Lake Leader* the newspaper proclaimed,

"Silver Lake, The Coming Railroad Center." During this period Silver Lake was a bustling town of 500 with a variety of services including a drug store, two sawmills, barber shop, lawyer, dentist, and a physician, Dr. Thom. Dr. Thom, who started his practice in Silver Lake in 1905, faithfully served the community until 1924.

In 1915, when the country was growing, the *Silver Lake Leader* urged the state to drain Silver Lake. It was calculated that the lake bed would yield oats at 60 bushels per acre (21 hl. per 0.41 ha.); with 114,000 acres (46,740 ha.) to be sowed, the harvest would be valued at $437,760, which would have greatly benefitted the Silver Lake school funds. Nature intervened and in 1917, following a number of winters with light snowfalls, the lake dried up completely.

Local ranchers claimed the "new" land, and considerable acreage of the lake bed was seeded with grain. Newcomers to northern Lake County proceeded to occupy the land by building small cabins and assuming "squatter's rights" on their claims. Conflicts broke out and lawsuits over land ownership were filed. Nature, however, ended the hostilities. A generous snowfall in the adjacent mountains in the 1917-18 winter was followed by a large runoff and the lake bed filled once again, floating squatters' cabins off their claims.

Silver Lake had been reported dry in the 1850s and in 1896; it became dry again in the early 1920s. The construction of dams and reservoirs along the creeks to the south of Silver Lake prevented waters from reaching the lake bed. In recent years, only in times of much-above-normal precipitation has even part of the Silver Lake bed been covered with water.

The railway never came to Silver Lake, nor to any part of the Fort Rock Basin. With the exodus of the homesteaders from the region, Silver Lake declined in population. Only after rural electrification reached the Fort Rock-Silver Lake country in 1955 did the population increase. For a number of years a small lumber mill added diversity to the town's economy. Today, other than the establishment of a district ranger station of the Fremont National Forest, Silver Lake is much as it was 100 years ago — a community whose economy is based on agriculture, principally cattle, and a trading center servicing the valley and those traveling Highway 31.

Chewaucan Basin

SUMMER LAKE

On December 16, 1843, explorer Captain John C. Fremont entered into his diary:

"We traveled this morning through snow about three feet deep, which, being crusted, very much cut the feet of our animals. The mountain still gradually rose; we crossed several spring heads covered with quaking aspen; otherwise it was all pine forest. The air was dark with falling snow, which everywhere weighed down the trees. The depths of the forest were profoundly still; and below, we scarce felt a breath of the wind which whirled the snow through their branches.... Toward noon the forest looked clear ahead, appearing suddenly to terminate; and beyond a certain point we could see no trees. Riding rapidly ahead to this spot, we found ourselves on the verge of a vertical and rocky wall of the mountain. At our feet — more than a thousand feet below — we looked into a green prairie country, in which a beautiful lake, some twenty miles in length, was spread out along the foot of the mountains, its shores bordered with green grass. Just then the sun broke out among the clouds, and illuminated the country below, while around us the storm raged fiercely. Not a particle of ice was to be seen on the lake, or snow on its borders, and all was like summer or spring. The glow of the sun in the valley below brightened up our hearts with sudden pleasure, and we made the woods ring with joyful shouts to those behind; and gradually as each came up, he stopped to enjoy the unexpected scene. Shivering on snow three feet deep, and stiffening in a cold north wind, we exclaimed at once that the names of Summer Lake and Winter Ridge should be applied to these two proximate places of such sudden and violent contrast."[18]

When they set up camp along the western shore of the lake, Fremont again noted how they enjoyed the summer-like temperatures, justifying "the name we had given it." Distrusting the appearance of the eastern shore (today it still looks barren, and inhospitable), Fremont followed a "plainly beaten Indian trail along the narrow strip of land between the lake and the high rocky wall from which we had looked down." Today, Highway 31 follows that same strip of land. Fremont commented on the little springs or streams of pure cold water, the fresh green grass, and the white efflorescence (alkali) along the shore of the lake.

Today, on most December days, the contrast between the forested, snow-covered Winter Ridge and the "beautiful lake" stretched along the foot of the mountains — Summer Lake — would be just as great as that described by Fremont. However, the cultural scene in the valley has changed. Ranches that were established nearly 30 years after Fremont's explorations, a paved highway that skirts the lake, scattered homestead cabins (some tucked away under tall poplars), glistening mobile homes, and irrigated fields, all reflect the historical geography of the valley. The small community of Summer Lake occupies the relatively confined area of flat land between the high-water mark of the lake and the precipitous rim that towers 3,000 feet (930 m.) above. In summer, cattle graze the strip of green meadowlands between Highway 31 and the green waters of Summer Lake. While in earlier years Summer Lake was just as much noted for its fruit trees and its cattle raising, the valley is now exclusively hay and cattle country.

Summer Lake Valley was settled in the 1870s. James Foster, who had heard of Summer Lake from Gilbert Quincy, a member of the 1843 Fremont Expedition, left Benton County in the Willamette Valley in 1871 along with four other men and 125 head of cattle. The party found the valley covered with bunch grass up to three feet (1 m.) high. Foster returned to the Willamette Valley to bring over his wife and eight children. From modest beginnings in a log cabin, James Foster built a twelve-room home in 1884 to shelter the family, to put up travelers, and to stage gatherings for other Summer Lake settlers.

Foster forecasted that Summer Lake Valley, which was favored by "an absence of insect pests, blight, scale, decay, or mildew," would be known as the "Second Hood River" with the growth of peaches, English walnuts, apricots, plums, and small fruits such as strawberries. All of the fruit was grown without irrigation, reflecting the greater precipitation of that period. For years, Summer Lake fruit, which also included pears, cherries, and apples, attracted buyers from a wide region. In 1908, Foster sold over $450 worth of peaches, all obtained from 22 Elberta trees. One remarkable aspect of the Summer Lake fruit-growing was the short time that it took for young trees to produce fruit — apples only three to five years after setting.

Another remarkable climatic aspect of the valley was the general absence of spring frosts in those early years. Perhaps the larger volume of water in Summer Lake helped ameliorate night-time temperatures. Also a success in Summer Lake Valley was the growing of watermelons and corn which was, according to the *Lake County Examiner*, October 22, 1908, "eight feet [2.48 m.] tall, and yielding ears of a most excellent quality." At one time, Summer Lake Valley had four schools, the Ana River, the Foster, the Withers, and the Harris School. The picturesque Harris School was still standing in 1988, a silent reminder of the homestead era in the valley.

Summer Lake is fed by the Ana River, which in turn originates in a series of springs. The river, which has been dammed near its headquarters, then flows only five miles (8 km.) south into Summer Lake. Along its short course are signs of the homestead period — vacant substantial houses, relics of once prosperous fruit orchards, and workings of old irrigation systems. Summer Lake itself, as seen from the overlook south of Picture Rock Pass, is often a shimmering body of water, sometimes greenish, sometimes blue. The lush meadows along the western shore contrast with the dark green forests on Winter Ridge (or Winter Rim, as it is now commonly known) and with the beige sand dunes and parched barren hills east of the lake.

Summer Lake itself is shallow and its waters quickly recede and expand, depending on the climate. During the extended dry period in the 1920s, winds frequently picked up the alkali dust left by the evaporating lake and almost suffocated both people and livestock in the Summer Lake area. During the summer of 1931, the waters in Summer Lake, lowered in part by the use of Ana River for irrigation, dried up for the first time in the memory of the oldest inhabitants. Roots of tree stumps, which are found in other lake beds of Lake County lakes, indicating vegetation growth in extended periods of arid climates, were not found in the lake bed of Summer Lake. The waters of Summer Lake often reflect the direction and velocity of winds in the valley. A strong southerly wind will push the surface waters a considerable distance northward along the valley, leaving exposed mud flats along the south shore.

To the south of the lake, a small metal bathhouse enclosing a 15-x-30-foot (4.65x9.3 m.) tank cooled to 100°F. (38°C.) has long served local residents and travelers using Highway 31. In 1901, the hot springs were called "mud springs" and were touted for their great healing qualities. The *Lake County Rustler* stated, "Many who have bathed in them for rheumatism claim they are very beneficial." The bathhouse itself dates back to the 1920s. Hot water is not only used for the bathhouse but is piped to heat the owner's adjacent home.

The tiny community of Summer Lake, located north of the lake, consists of a store (which also functions as the post office), a cafe and motel, a church, an Oregon Highway Department maintenance yard, and a rest area with a historical marker that recounts Fremont's discovery of Summer Lake.

PAISLEY

To Lake County residents, Paisley means the ZX Cattle Company, the Chewaucan Valley, the Paisley High School Broncos, and the Mosquito Festival held annually to salute the town's most prolific and most obnoxious species of wildlife. To a newcomer from Glasgow, Scotland, the name Paisley must surely invoke memories of home. Paisley, Scotland, is a large industrial city on the western outskirts of Glasgow, whose metropolitan population approaches 2 million. Paisley, Oregon, which is home to some 275 people, was named in the 1870s after the Scottish city by an early-day immigrant from that part of Scotland.

For the most part, Paisley (the Lake County one!) has changed little in several decades. Early in the twentieth century, Paisley supported three general stores, a drug store, a blacksmith's shop, livery stable, saloon, barber shop, brickyard, carpenter shop, and a "first-class hotel" — the Chewaucan. Power from the Chewaucan River, which flows through the northern edge of town, was used for a flour mill. The community's newspaper was the weekly edition of the *Chewaucan Ripple*. The *Oregon Almanac*, a 1915 State of Oregon publication aimed at attracting new settlers to Oregon, stated that "Paisley, population 300, is in the 'heart of the Chewaucan Valley,' and that the area is adapted to dairying, general farming and fruit raising."

Paisley is quite a compact community. The

MINERAL SALTS OF SUMMER LAKE
AND ALKALI LAKE

As the levels of Lake Abert and Summer Lake sink lower, wide expanses of white salts are left along the shoreline. These salts were for many years the object of prospective large-scale mining ventures that were going to greatly influence the economic geography of the lake areas. The State of Oregon had been declared legal owners of the lakes, as they were navigable bodies of water at the time of surveying. In December 1914, the state was offered $1,500,000 for mining rights to both Lake Abert and Summer Lake. A Portland syndicate countered with an offer of $2 million. Then, according to *The Oregonian*, May 10, 1914, a New York capitalist offered to buy the lakes outright for $9 million, payment to be part cash and part common and preferred stock. The State Land Board declined all of the offers, largely because U.S. government surveys of the area and "leading chemists" throughout the United States valued the potash and soda and common table salt at a minimum of $75 million and a maximum of $200 million.

Beginning in 1915 a Chicago businessman, Jason Moore, investigated plans to mine salts from the two lakes. Moore had several plans, some that seem "far out" now, if not then. Moore felt that the waters from Lake Abert and Summer Lake could be piped to the Columbia River, where a hydroelectric plant would be constructed and electricity used to extract nitrate, carbonate, caustic soda, baking soda, and bleaching powder from the alkali lake waters. The State of Oregon was to get royalties from the sales.

Rumors of the mining development at Summer Lake sent real estate developers scurrying for land. A general store opened at Summer Lake, a sawmill was being planned, and local ranchers turned down offers of $200 an acre (0.41 ha.) for their land.[19]

In 1916, Moore's plan changed. He proposed to run a pipeline to Lakeview, which was then a railhead. Laboratory tests on the salts from Lake Abert and Summer Lake were conducted at the University of Nevada at Reno. The lab estimated that the waters of the two lakes contained 40 million tons of salts and concluded that, with World War I in progress, there would be a demand for soda and potash. Instead of building a pipeline, Moore set up an evaporating plant on the south shore of Summer Lake. However, by 1918 the lake level was so low that the plant was left high and dry. For years Moore anticipated a railroad running through the Summer Lake-Lake Abert basin. It was never built, and his equipment stood useless. Before Moore finally abandoned plans to extract salts from Lake Abert and Summer Lake, he had invested over $100,000.

Interestingly enough, during the same time period that Jason Moore was conducting plans to mine salts at Summer Lake, soda deposits were mined at Alkali Lake, 20 miles (32 km.) north of Lake Abert. Alkali Lake, which had been secured from Indians in an 1864 treaty, had been surveyed in the 1870s, declared navigable and thus state property. The navigability of the lake was later disputed, thus opening up Alkali Lake to mining claims. Soda, which had been discovered at Alkali Lake in 1901, was mined in April 1916. A furnace was shipped from San Francisco. In August 1916, John D. Spreckles inspected the lake with a view to shipping the soda to San Francisco. The *Lake County Examiner*, April 26, 1929, stated that the Alkali Lake soda deposits belonging to the Spreckles interests totaled 700,000 tons, and that at $40 per ton equaled in value all the timber in Lake County.

Chewaucan River, which clearly marks the northern and western limits of town, tumbles out of the nearby forested mountains. In times of heavy rains or rapid snow melt, the Chewaucan has overflowed the levees that line its banks and has inundated sections of Paisley. Timber from the adjacent mountains is a resource for the local lumber mill. Both east and south of Paisley, cattle ranches occupy much of the upper Chewaucan marsh, whose grasses provide winter and summer feed for thousands of cattle. Beyond the marsh, the barren, even forbidding Coglan Buttes dominate the natural landscape and help direct the Chewaucan River southeastward towards Lake Abert.

A century of more of growth of cottonwoods

and poplars mark much of Paisley's residential and commercial areas. "Downtown," where Highway 31 abruptly jogs to the east for a short distance, consists of two general stores, a library, a cafe, tavern, garage, and two churches. The neat, imposing two-story Paisley High School and the rustic brown Fremont National Forest ranger station are located alongside Highway 31. The Paisley High School, one of only two high schools in all of Lake County, provides education to students from as far away as Christmas Valley. Paisley is an important trading place, servicing motorists traveling between Lakeview and La Pine as well as ranchers who live in the Chewaucan Valley.

THE ZX IN THE CHEWAUCAN VALLEY

From Highway 31, the ZX doesn't look any bigger than other ranches in Southeastern Oregon. In fact, except for the large sign ZX painted on a large shed roof, the ranch looks quite modest. Mention the ZX in Paisley or Silver Lake or Lakeview and people nod, "Yes, the ZX." The ZX is a giant among big cattle ranches. From its headquarters, located a couple of miles south of Paisley, the ZX territory extends intermittently northward to and beyond the Bend-Burns highway, over 100 miles (160 km.) distant. The ranch territory includes part of the Silver Lake country, where a subsidiary ranch (primarily used for haying operations) is located. The Viewpoint Ranch east of Christmas Valley is headquarters for the desert operations. ZX cattle also graze the Sycan Marsh in Klamath County. In all, the ZX encompasses 1,300,000 acres (533,000 ha.), an area one-and-one-half times that of Rhode Island. Over 30,000 head of cattle, mostly Herefords, graze on ZX and leased lands.

The cattle are moved in the spring from their winter feeding pastures near Paisley. In early March some cattle are moved to the desert range, as they have been for decades. *The Bulletin* (Bend), April 7, 1935, reported the spring ritual:

"Cattle on Way to Rangelands"

Headed for spring range in the Benjamin Lake region southeast of Bend, 5,560 ZX cattle were moved from the Chewaucan Land & Cattle Co. ranches in the Paisley area yesterday, with 15 cowpunchers directing the great herd into the high country.

"When the cattle came through the Dry Fields gate yesterday and headed for the open ranges they strung out five miles.

"Cows and December and January calves comprise the 5,560-head herd. This herd is just a portion of the 20,000 or more cattle owned by the ZX people."

Around the first of May, some are driven in what is typically a three-day drive to the Sycan Marsh. Then in early June, once deep snows have gone, other cattle are taken to forest grazing areas. The cattle are normally driven back or taken by truck to the winter grounds before Thanksgiving, and some of the yearlings are sold. However, early snows in the higher elevations have at times created problems for the cattle and their buckaroos. In November 1983, for example, 18 inches (45.72 cm.) of snow buried the Klamath Marsh country, temporarily stranding 87 truckloads of cattle.

The ZX employs some 24 to 26 professional buckaroos, each with a string of eight horses, mostly quarter horses. During the winter, the ZX employs a crew of 70. However, in the summer months, hired hands needed for haying boost the payroll to over 100. The ZX normally puts up 65,000 tons (13,000,000 kg.) of hay a year, winter feed needed for the hungry cattle.

The ZX is virtually a self-contained operation; in addition to buckaroos, there are hay crews, cooks, well drillers, and mechanics to keep dozens of pieces of high-priced equipment in running order. The ZX typically operates 80-90 haying machines. To help feed the buckaroos in either the forest or the desert, the chuck wagons are fully stocked with provisions and equipped with LP gas refrigerators. The ZX has its own commissary that supplies the chuck wagons and cook houses. The ZX provides housing for most of its employees. Single men live in bunkhouses, married men in ZX housing in Paisley or in Silver Lake. Despite the mechanization of the farm operations and the computerization of the office, many aspects of the cattle-ranching operations are similar to what they were near the turn of the century.

LAKE ABERT

It was on October 16, 1832, that explorer John Work came across an Indian encampment by a small spring next to what Work called "Salt Lake." Two days later, Work wrote, "We journeyed 19 miles [30 km.] along the west side of the lake to its south end where we encamped on a small river [Chewaucan]."[20]

Eleven years later, on December 20, 1843, Captain John C. Fremont visited "Salt Lake" and named it and the adjoining rim for his chief, Colonel J. J. Abert of the U.S. Topographical Engineers. Fremont ascended Abert Rim at what is now called Fort Creek. In 1932, the remains of Fremont's stone fort were still to be seen on the south side of the creek.

Most of the inflow into Lake Abert is from the Chewaucan River, which enters the extreme southern end of the lake. There is no surface outlet, and the water balance of the lake surface depends largely on winter snowpack in the watershed of the Chewaucan and annual evaporation of the lake. As a consequence, a succession of wet or dry years drastically changes the surface area of Lake Abert.

In 1883, when the level of Lake Abert had dropped, cowboys reported seeing an emigrant wagon in the water on the east side of the lake near Poison Creek. In the 1920s, the level of the lake was dropping, and once again the wagon was spotted. By 1924, Lake Abert was entirely dry except for a few wet spots. The receding waters aroused the curiosity of relic hunters, especially when the emigrant wagon became visible. In the fall of 1927, the wagon was pulled from the lake bed. Near it was found a child's skull. Legend had it (told by an old Indian in 1929) that in the 1840s when Lake Abert was dry, a wagon train was attacked by Indians and the occupants killed. The Indians ransacked the wagon and took sacks of flour, which they dumped for the empty sacks.[21] Indian artifacts have been found near the mouth of the Chewaucan, and Indian petroglyphs are etched on large boulders along the east shore of the lake at the foot of Abert Rim.

In the early 1930s, a new highway, dubbed the Yellowstone Cut-off, was constructed along the east side of Lake Abert. (The old highway from Lakeview to Burns was via Paisley, then across the desert north of Lake Abert to the Alkali Lake area.) Two rock forts, believed to have been built by General Crook's men from Fort Warner, were discovered during the construction. Indian artifacts and paintings were found along the old lake shoreline, 50 feet (15.5 m.) above the shoreline at that time (1931).

Despite the interesting historical events that have occurred near Lake Abert, the landscape today, except for a solitary ranch near the mouth of the Chewaucan, is similar to that described early in the twentieth century:

"The strange, wild beauty of the landscape here can hardly be described in words. Viewed from the south the deep, blue-green water is seen stretching away in the distance; on the left a rugged slope of rock scantily overgrown with sage brush, rises from the shore; on the right huge boulders, fallen from the cliffs above, lie in confused masses on the water's edge; above these tower the mighty cliffs, rising fully one thousand feet above the lake, black, silent and majestic. Far into the distance stretch these awful heights, their colors mellowing and contours softening until they are lost in an indistinct mountain mass on the far horizon. We look in vain for a sign of life; a single sail upon the broad expanse of water; the smoke of a settler's cabin on the shore; all is silent and desolate; nature is alone in her grandeur."[22]

VALLEY FALLS

Three miles (5 km.) south of Lake Abert, at the junction of Highways 31 and 395, is located the small community of Valley Falls. The community was established in 1909, when homesteader C.W.F. Jennings operated a store, saloon, and a hotel, which also housed the post office. At that time, Valley Falls, named after the small fall in the nearby Chewaucan River where it empties into Lake Abert, was located under Abert Rim, a mile (1.6 km.) east of its present site.

During the homestead period, Valley Falls was planned to become a station on the proposed Oregon-Eastern Railroad. At that time, Lake County advertising touted Valley Falls for its potential for excellent fruits, vegetables, and grains. "On new dry land, potatoes produced 6,000 pounds per acre; wheat 20 bushels; field corn and garden vegetables grow in profusion." The railroad never came to Valley Falls. However, when the "Yellowstone Cut-off" (Highway 395) was built along the east side of Lake Abert, Jennings relocated the store and post office fixtures to the new highway. Later, the old hotel was also skidded by mule team and added to the store.

The Valley Falls post office closed in 1944. In excavating for the basement of a new addition to the store, human bones, believed to have been those of an Indian, were uncovered. In 1948 Jennings sold the store and moved to Pacific City, Oregon.

Some two dozen families live in this south end of the Chewaucan Valley. The combined store and gas station is the focal point for locals and service center for motorists passing through this section of Oregon's Big Country. The owners, Jeff and Carol Sullivan, also rent trailer spaces and a couple of small cabins. To the east, Abert Rim dominates the landscape just as it did when Valley Falls was first settled.

Goose Lake Valley

LAKEVIEW
Visitors arriving at Lakeview from the north are confronted by a geyser that spouts to over 100 feet (31 m.) every 80 seconds and greeted by a 30-foot (9.3 m.) tall wooden man erected in the mid-1950s: "Howdy Pardner! Welcome to the Tallest Town in Oregon." At 4,800 feet (1,488 m.), Lakeview is indeed the highest incorporated settlement in Oregon and, as I can testify, a town of friendly folks. Although a ridge of mountains up to 7,000 feet (2,170 m.) in elevation tower over Lakeview to the east of the town, for the most part Lakeview's outlook, history, and economy have traditionally been associated with the pancake-flat Goose Lake Valley, which stretches to the west and south of the city.

The Goose Lake Valley is the most economically developed and most populated region by far in Lake County. In the mid-1980s, over half of the 7,500 people of Lake County lived in the valley. The Goose Lake Valley was a focal point for travelers as early as the mid-nineteenth century. Settlement by non-Indians near the California border dates back to the 1860s, a time when Indian raiders were being subdued by the military. After the threat of Indians was diminished, settlers — farmers, sheepmen, cattlemen, and miners — flocked to the fertile, well-watered Goose Lake Valley, then a part of Jackson County. In the early 1870s, a mail route was established connecting Ashland and Linkville (now Klamath Falls) with two Goose Lake Valley

post offices. Due to the distance and relative difficulty of travel to Jacksonville (at that time the county seat of Jackson County), and due to the population increases in the Klamath Basin and Goose Lake Valley, a separate county, Lake County, was created in 1875. The temporary county seat of the new county was the small town of Linkville. A year later, 1876, after a county-wide vote, Lakeview was declared the county seat due to voting support from the then more populous Chewaucan and Goose Lake Valleys.

The site of Lakeview was on Bullards Creek, which tumbled down the mountains east of town. The site had perhaps been the scene of Indian battles. While excavations for a new flume were being carried out in August, 1914, at the mouth of Bullards Creek, the skeletal remains of Indians were discovered. It was believed that the location was either that of an old Indian burial ground or the scene of some savage battle. In the early 1870s, the waters of Goose Lake washed the shores of Eagle Point, one mile (1.6 km.) south of town, and the cries of waterfowl were heard in Lakeview day and night. Freight teams passing through Lakeview quenched their thirst without unhitching. In the 1880s, when the lake covered an area 40 miles (64 km.) by 18 miles (28.8 km.), a boat was used to haul wood and wheat from Lakeview to New Pine Creek. By 1890 over 2,500 people were living in Lake County, including 1,000 in Goose Lake Valley. In 1885, Lake County added Warner Valley, which previously had been a part of Grant County.

By 1900, the Lake County economy had expanded with increased activities in the cattle and sheep industry. The county population climbed to over 2,800 with Lakeview, despite its remoteness

Opposite top:
  The steep eastern scarp of Winter Rim (Ridge) provides the background for the now abandoned Harris School at Summer Lake. The Harris family, after which the school was named, settled in the Summer Lake area in the late 1880s. Oregon Economic Development Photo, Salem.

Opposite bottom:
  Abert Rim is the scarp of a normal fault separating the horst to the east (right) from the graben now occupied by Lake Abert. Lake Abert, the sink of the Chewaucan River, is a closed basin lake which loses its water by evaporation. It is too alkaline to support fish today. During the cooler and wetter climatic periods of the Pleistocene, this valley held pluvial lakes up to 300 feet deep, containing fresh water which supported a variety of fish and other wildlife. Photo by Pat McDowell, Ph.D., University of Oregon.

from any railroad, a bustling town of 760. A devastating fire on May 22, 1900, destroyed all of the business section, but within a few years, advertising of fertile Goose Lake Valley lands attracted hundreds of prospective settlers. Lakeview quickly rebuilt. Early in 1908, grant lands, the old Oregon Central Military Wagon Road Company lands, were purchased by the Oregon Valley Land Company (OVL), a land promotion and development firm based in Kansas City, Missouri. Throughout 1908 and much of 1909, the *Lake County Examiner* boasted of the area's climate and agricultural potential, including pending irrigation. The climate was classed as "mild and healthful without extremes of heat or cold. Goose Lake Valley has maximum sunshine, pure fresh air and hot mineral springs valuable for the treatment of various diseases and ailments."

In September, 1909, a giant land auction by the OVL Company attracted hundreds of people to Lakeview. The city was, in part, a tent city with over 1,000 people arriving from every section of the United States. Tents lined streets temporarily named after distant places — Missouri, Kansas, Chicago, Iowa. Adding to the excitement were the 200 gamblers who joined the throng. Beginning September 10, 1909, the auction proceeded with three auctioneers selling two or three tracts a minute to eager bidders, both local and out-of-state people, who crowded into a huge tent. In seven days, 24,000 tracts of land were sold! However, the promised irrigation program did not come about until the completion of the Drews Creek system (1917). Later, 1922, the Cottonwood Dam was constructed. Many of the OVL

lands never did receive irrigation waters. Today thousands of deeds, lands purchased in 1909, are scattered around the U.S. The deed holders, descendants of original purchasers, are perhaps dreaming of their Goose Lake Valley paradise they have heard about, but never seen.

The boosterism of the Goose Lake Valley continued after the OVL auction. In 1910, the *Lake County Examiner* was printing 2,300 copies a week, many of which were mailed to prospective migrants. Each week, the newspaper ran success stories of local farmers. To be fair, many of the reports were true. However, in those early years, climatic conditions were exceptionally favorable. Lakeview's precipitation between the years 1887-1907 (data for six of the years is missing) was 17.3 inches (43.2 cm.), compared to 10.2 inches (25.9 cm.) for the period 1913-32. In addition, spring frosts occurred less frequently than in later years.

On December 10, 1911, a narrow gauge railroad, the Nevada-California-Oregon Railroad, connecting Lakeview with Alturas, California, was completed and the first train was greeted by 500 citizens and a brass band. By 1913, the Goose Lake Valley farmers were raising 53,000 bushels of grain, half of which were wheat. A 65-foot (20 m.) launch was used to transport farm machinery and building materials across Goose Lake to settlers on the Westside area and to ferry people across the lake to and from the resort town of Fairport, California. Some indication of the population of Goose Lake Valley was seen when, in 1916, 2,000 people attended the Fourth of July celebrations at Fairport.

As settlement in the valley took place, sage-

(Left) Lakeview prior to the May 22, 1900 fire. (Right) The fire destroyed 64 out of 66 businesses and several adjacent residences. The loss in 1900 was $250,000. Two entire blocks and parts of six other blocks were consumed in the blaze, which was observed in the night sky at Klamath Falls, 100 miles (160 km.) distant. After the fire, the citizens of Lakeview rebuilt and by October 1, 1900, 15 brick buildings had been constructed. Oregon Historical Society Photos.

brush, which at one time had covered all but the low-lying area around the lake, was cleared and the land converted to agricultural use. By 1914, the climate of the Goose Lake Valley, as elsewhere in Southeastern Oregon, was turning drier. The Drews Dam Reservoir and Cottonwood Reservoirs were constructed to bring irrigation waters to the western lands of Goose Lake; a system of canals and laterals was built, and today the Westside district, as it is known, is a prosperous-looking agricultural area with scattered well-established ranches sitting amid fields of golden grain, green alfalfa, and meadows. Livestock graze the meadows. A small school, the Union School, and a general store at Westside are the focal points for community activities.

The widespread drought adversely impacted all agricultural activities. In northern Lake County, after droves of homesteaders had abandoned their claims, the population of the county dropped from 4,658 in 1910 to 3,991 by 1920. In the same period, Lakeview's population shrank from 1,253 to 1,139. However, the lumber industry became established at Lakeview in the 1920s, and by 1930 the census listed Lake County's population as 4,833, an increase of 842 in a decade. In that same time period the population of Lakeview climbed to 1,799 from 1,139. However, in northern Lake County, the Fort Rock and Silver Lake precincts respectively declined from 300 to 145 and from 405 to 258.

The lumber industry in Lakeview, as well as the town's function as a government and retail center, has helped sustain a modest population growth. By 1984, the Lake County population had increased to 7,600, with 2,755 living in Lakeview. In the mid-1980s, four lumber mills in Lakeview employed over 500 people. When a recession in the lumber industry forced widespread layoffs or cutbacks in employment throughout most of Oregon in the early 1980s, mills in Lakeview (and the Paisley mill) continued to operate. This was due in part to the use of the "restricted working circle system" in the Fremont National Forest, a system created in 1944 by the U.S. Forest Service: preference in the cutting of nearby timber was given to local mills to promote economic stability in isolated areas. When the Southern Pacific Railroad announced in 1983 that it was closing its branch line connecting Lakeview and Alturas, California, Lakeview postmaster, Orval R. Layton, concerned about the potential

Downtown Lakeview is a mixture of the new (for example, the courthouse and the library) and the old. The downtown area is quite compact, hemmed in by steep hills to the east and by residential areas to the west. The sturdy building shown here, built in 1913, reflects the optimism placed in the future of Lakeview. Photo by Ray Hatton.

loss of lumber sales and jobs that brought the $1.5 million in annual wages to the community, set about saving the railroad. Through the use of Oregon lottery funds ($475,000) and contributions from the four mills ($85,000), the county purchased the railroad. Great Western Railway Co. of Loveland, Colorado, provided the rolling stock and was awarded the contract to operate the railroad, named Goose Lake 55 (55 miles—88 km.—to Alturas) by Lakeview High School senior Molly Peterson. Because of Lakeview's isolation from trucking lines, the processed lumber and wood chips from the Lakeview mills, which fill over 1,000 lumber cars a year, are cheaper to ship by rail.

Lakeview is more than a "mill town." It is headquarters for the Bureau of Land Management, the Fremont National Forest, and the Hart Mountain Antelope Refuge, and county seat of sprawling Lake County. It is also a service town and, modest as its downtown shopping is, it serves people from a wide trade area. The geothermal energy in Lakeview is awaiting commercial development.

Today, Lakeview stretches for some two miles (3 km.), largely along Highway 395. When seen from Black Cap, a prominent mountain that broods over Lakeview to the northeast, the landscape reflects the key geographical assets — the flat, productive Goose Lake Valley, shining Goose Lake, and the forested mountains to the west — that have helped shape the "tallest town in Oregon."

Lakeview's answer to Old Faithful, Old Perpetual, which first erupted in 1923, "performs" every one minute and 20 seconds. The geyser is located next to Hunter's Hot Spring resort. Photo by Ray Hatton.

NEW PINE CREEK

Fifteen miles (24 km.) south of Lakeview, straddling the Oregon-California border, is the small settlement of New Pine Creek. Most of New Pine Creek's businesses, including a grocery store, cafe, gas station and post office, are in Oregon. So are most of the town's residences and the church, a key historical landmark in the community. New Pine Creek, founded in 1876, has long been noted for its vegetable gardens and orchards of cherries, peaches, pears, and apricots.

Prior to its founding in 1871, A. Z. Hammersly built a grist mill at the foot of the elongated mountain range that towers 2,500 feet (775 m.) or higher over the east side of Goose Lake. A flume from the mountains channeled water to run the mill, which was next to the old Lakeview-New Pine Creek road, half a mile (800 m.) east of Highway 395. The mill was operational until the late 1940s. In the mid-1980s, the sturdy beams supporting the structure (owned by Roy and Margaret Simpson) still reflected the quality of cedar and craftsmanship used in its construction.

Evidence of more humid times in the Goose Lake Valley are seen in this photo of a boat that once sailed the waters of Goose Lake. Oregon Historic Society Photo No. 54246.

Even the original equipment used to run the grist mill seemed capable of once again grinding grain. Years ago, grains (especially wheat) were grown quite extensively in the New Pine Creek area.

In October 1911, fire destroyed all of the New Pine Creek business section except for a brick store (which was still standing vacant in 1986), a dress shop, and the imposing three-story Lake Hotel. A mining boom early in the twentieth

HUNTER'S HOT SPRINGS

It was in 1919 that Harry A. Hunter, owner of large tracts of land in the West, had the idea of developing a sanatorium (a place for therapy treatment) at the hot springs just north of Lakeview. A corporation involving Hunter, the Favell-Utley Realty Co., and Dr. H. E. Kelty, local physician, was formed. Long before this time, Indians had used the steaming waters as cookstoves. (Maoris at Rotorua, New Zealand, still do this today.) In later years, early settlers at Lakeview used the hot springs for scalding hogs. Hunter recognized both the healthful nature of the hot springs and the geothermal potential for heating the town of Lakeview.

In September 1923, well drillers seeking hot water for the resort struck hot water at 55 feet (17 m.), creating the first geyser. News of the erupting geyser brought hundreds of Lake County residents to the hot springs area to see the phenomenon. At 160 feet (50 m.), the drill tapped boiling mud. Entrepreneurs thought that the fine mud could be sold as a skin beautifier. By late October 1923, there were three geysers spouting 50-75 feet (15-23 m.): by then, they were tourists attractions. Further drilling towards the adjacent hills struck hot water at 450 feet (140 m.). This was used for heating and furnishing hot water for the sanatorium, which opened in 1926, and was planned to be used for heating homes in Lakeview. The *Lake County Examiner*, January 27, 1927, reported: "With its two long wings and sweeping facade and the courtyard between the wings, the structure presents a pleasing appearance. The investment now is about $100,000 and more is to be spent later. H. A. Hunter is president of the corporation known as the Hunter Chlorine Hot Springs Club. The chlorine water has been found to have excellent curative effects upon many diseases. Mud baths and other treatments are given."

In May 1930, new management took over the Hunter's Hot Springs Hotel. In 1931, the hotel was listed as a "Charming Asset to the City" with its swimming pool, rooms for tourists, and individual bathhouses, each equipped with hot mineral waters.

During the next few decades, ownership of Hunter's Hot Springs Hotel changed on several occasions. The resort was not maintained and by the mid 1980s had deteriorated markedly. In 1985, Jim Schmit purchased the run-down Hunter's Hot Springs and proceeded to remodel the buildings and landscape the entrance. Walkways and platforms for viewing the geyser Old Perpetual (which erupts every 1 minute and 20 seconds) were constructed. The restaurant, which features Chinese and American food, was renovated. The motel units were refurbished. A museum, including memorabilia from the Seattle World's Fair, was added. In 1988, in partnership with basketball Hall of Famer, Rick Barry, Jim established a membership sports club which included racquetball, exercise classes, pool and jacuzzi facilities. By the late 1980s Hunter's Hot Springs was once again an asset to the City of Lakeview.

century in what was called the High Grade District, southwest of New Pine Creek, contributed to the prosperity of New Pine Creek. Gold mining brought the inevitable rush of miners and others to the town. The gold mining towns of High Grade and Bradly (both just across the state line in California) had a combined population that was estimated to have reached 5,000.

In 1928, New Pine Creek was called the "Garden Spot of Lake County" and at that time boasted two restaurants, two stores, a bakery, garage, and blacksmith's shop. However, the end of the mining boom and quicker access to Lakeview contributed to a decline in New Pine Creek's population. The small community remained relatively obscure until early 1985, when California questioned the position of the state border, legally the 42nd parallel north. This latitude is actually one-half mile (800 m.) north of State Line Road, the designated and accepted border for over a century; if the border were moved, the whole of New Pine Creek would find itself transferred from Oregon to California. The dilemma brought nationwide media attention to the small community, something that the normally peaceful New Pine Creek residents did not want. At stake were Oregon's pride, a question of sales tax, vehicle registration, insurance, and educating of high school students in Lakeview or in Modoc County, California. As of 1988 no action on the boundary change had taken place.

THE GOOSE LAKE DUST BOWL

The shallow lakes of Southeastern Oregon, modest reminders of what they were during pluvial times, rapidly respond to fluctuations in precipitation. During the extended arid period in the 1920s and 1930s, all of the lakes in the Warner Valley except Crump Lake dried up. Silver Lake in northern Lake County has been dry most of the years since early in the twentieth century. Lake Abert and Summer Lake just about shriveled up during the 1930s.

In late June 1918, the waters of Goose Lake evaporated, exposing large areas of alkali. Winds picked up the alkali and filled the skies to the extent that the *Lake County Examiner*, June 29, 1918, reported, "It was impossible to see fences only a few yards away." In August 1926, the dust storms in the Goose Lake Valley so darkened the sky that chickens went to roost, as they do during the eclipse of the sun. Stock were hard to find, except for their coughing and wheezing. Reduced visibility impaired driving. The dust settled so thickly on house floors that they looked more like the floors of flour mills. The blowing alkali dust was blamed for taking the paint off anything that was exposed to it. The once verdant Goose Lake Valley, the dream of early pioneers, took on a look of desolation. All the people of the valley could do was to pray for moisture to refill the lake again.

The dry lake bed during the 1920s revived tales and accounts of earlier years when Goose Lake went dry. A story told about 1920 by an old Indian was that in the days before the white man there was no Goose Lake. In the center of the valley was a small swamp in which tules grew around a small creek which entered from the north. The valley was then covered with sagebrush. In the early 1860s a severe winter followed by a rainy summer filled the valley and formed Goose Lake. The dry lake episode in the 1920s was similar to what occurred in the 1840s. In 1845 the Applegate immigrant trail (the "Old South Road") crossed the dried lake bed of Goose Lake. A description by Peter Burnett of the immigrant party stated, "One evening we camped at what was then called Goose Lake. The water in the lake was very low and putrid." In 1926, the old wagon trail was visible for miles across the lake bed, taking a southwesterly direction from the flourishing resort of Fairport. A large spring in the lake bed near what was the Everly Ranch (in California) appeared to have been a source of water and a camping spot. Two roads branched off from the spring, one going southward, the other heading northward.

The *Lake County Tribune*, editorializing on the old wagon trail, commented that although it was of "historical value, just the same, a whole lot of dampness on top of it would give us a lot more cheer." Heavy rains fell in the fall of 1926, and by late November the waters of Goose Lake stretched 15 miles (24 km.). Three years later the waters had evaporated entirely and alkali dust, "tasting like soap," fell on Lakeview. Driven by a south wind, the fine alkali sifted through doors and windows. In September 1931, the dust smothered crowds attending the Lake County Fair. Reported the *Examiner*, "This dust storm created the dreariest day of 12 years of the annual fair." Late in November 1932, dust storms blasted Lakeview for three days and "made life miserable for all who ventured outside."

Mrs. Ruby E. Hammersly of New Pine Creek recollected that the dust storms ruined many farmers. The alkali dust covered forage crops, and with no feed for livestock, hay had to be brought in at extra expense from Tulelake. In 1937, Goose Lake started to fill again. However, by 1943 a number of valley cattlemen favored draining much of the lake so as to add 200,000 acres (82,000 ha.) of grazing land. Actually, as early as 1905, U. S. government officials considered draining waters from the lake to create "valuable meadow and agricultural land." In 1956, a move by California to channel waters into the Pit River drainage and thus help irrigate Sacramento Valley fields was strongly opposed by Lakeview residents who remembered or had heard of the dust storms of earlier years.

Although the connection has not been substantiated by instrumental evidence, there were those who remembered that when Goose Lake was filled, there were fewer summer frosts and several kinds of fruit were grown in the valley. When the lake started receding in 1915, frosts occurred each summer and by the 1920s it was much more difficult to raise crops.

Warner Valley

"The principal portion of the valley is sterile, barren greasewood desert with only an occasional marsh or salt lake varying the monotony. It would be difficult to imagine a more desolate and God-forsaken region outside of Assyria, Arabia, or the Great Sahara." Such was a description of the Warner Valley in *West Shore*, January 1880. The Warner Valley extends 50 miles (80 km.) north-south, much of it bordered on the east by the steep scarps of Poker Jim Ridge and Hart Mountain. Within the valley, actually a basin, is a series of lakes, many of which are interconnected.

The gradient from Crump Lake in the south to Blue Joint Lake in the north is a scant twelve feet (3.7 m.). Principal tributaries into the basin are seasonal creeks such as Honey Creek and Deep Creek, which bring in substantial waters in the spring runoff but are mere trickles in late summer. All of the lakes in the basin are extremely shallow and their sizes vary according to seasonable snowpacks in surrounding highlands, underground seepage, and evaporation. While the basin may be almost a vast body of water in humid periods, in extreme dry spells, such as between 1918 and 1934, all but Crump Lake may completely evaporate.

The naming of the Warner Valley reflects the early explorations and history of the region. In October 1832, John Work of the Hudson's Bay Company may have visited the valley. Work's journal for Friday, October 12, 1832 noted, "[We] proceeded...along a valley, reached a small lake or rather the end of a chain of lakes." Next day Work noted again the "continuation of lakes close to each other as far as the eye can reach," then proceeded to the south through the "valley of lakes." Early maps of what is now called Warner Valley, including one prepared under the direction of Colonel J. J. Abert, U. S. Engineer, show a string of lakes connected by the "Plants River" (Charles Plant, also known as Plante, had accompanied John Work in 1832). In December 1843, Captain John C. Fremont explored the valley, naming one of the lakes (possibly what is now Hart Lake) Christmas Lake. On December 25, 1843, Fremont wrote:

"Dec. 25. — We were aroused on Christmas morning by a discharge from the small arms and howitzer, with which our people saluted the day, and the name of which we bestowed upon the lake. It was the first time, perhaps, in this remote and desolate region in which it had been so commemorated. The day was sunny and warm, and, resuming our journey, we crossed some slight dividing grounds into a similar basin, walled in on the right by a lofty mountain ridge. The plainly beaten trail still continued, and occasionally we passed camping grounds of the Indians, which indicated to me that we were on one of the great thoroughfares of the country. In the afternoon I attempted to travel in a more easterly direction, but after a few more laborious miles was beaten back into the basin by an impassible country."

Later, due to unexplained circumstances, a small body of water in the Fort Rock Basin of northern Lake County was named Christmas Lake. In 1849 Captain William H. Warner explored Lake Abert and Warner Valley. In September 1849 Warner was ambushed and killed by Indians in Surprise Valley, California, just south of Warner Valley. In 1864 Lieutenant Colonel C.S. Drew, First Oregon Cavalry, believing that Captain Warner had been killed in Oregon, named the valley "Warner" in his honor.

During the period 1859-1886, various maps of Southeastern Oregon showed the Warner Valley with a single lake identified first as Christmas Lake, then as Warner-Christmas Lake or Lakes. However, by 1921 the separate lakes in the Warner Valley had been named as now known. Ironically, not one of them is called Warner Lake.

Following the massacre of Warner, bands of hostile Indians pursued and sometimes killed migrants crossing Southeastern Oregon. When gold was discovered in Eastern Oregon and Idaho in the early 1860s, military camps or forts such as Fort Bidwell (California), Fort Klamath, Camp Alvord, Camp C.F. Smith, and Old Camp Warner (discussed in section on Hart Mountain) were established to protect the miners and travelers. In the summer of 1867, New Camp Warner, a carefully selected site having one approach, a large spring of pure water, and large pines was constructed. [23] It was in the move from Old Camp Warner (on Hart Mountain) to the new camp site that Major General (then Lieutenant Colonel) George Crook and his soldiers, in order to negotiate a narrow stretch of the south end of Hart Lake, used lava rocks to construct a causeway to reach the west side of the Warner Valley. The causeway, later called the "Stone Bridge", subsequently sank into the silt of Hart Lake, but in dry periods the "bridge" is still visible among the reeds and grasses of the lake bed. On November 5, 1912, the Stone Bridge was proclaimed a National Monument by President Taft, setting aside parcels of public domain at both ends of the causeway. Nothing was ever done to mark or preserve the site, however, and National Monument status was revoked on January 20, 1948, after more than 35 years. Finally in 1971, nearly 104 years after the Stone Bridge was built, something was done to preserve and mark the site. Boy Scouts of Troop 95, sponsored by the Lakeview Elks Lodge, undertook the task. Brush was cleared from the causeway and a redwood sign was erected to mark the Stone Bridge's eastern portal.

Camp Warner was abandoned in the fall of 1873. An early twentieth-century description of the abandoned site stated: "The site of Camp Warner is now an isolated ranch, many miles from any other habitation. The ranch house occupies the old parade grounds, and a beautiful meadow spreads out in front, and from this the stockman cuts enough hay annually to feed his band."

"At first sight one would not recognize the evidences of the former days, but with a little information and a further investigation, one finds enough to convince one that it was really a military post; and there are many things to remind one of this. An old rock chimney stands alone on the hillside near the ranch house. It shows awkward, but substantial, construction. In front of the fire place, cut in this old chimney, the foundation logs of the former building still remain. On the opposite side of the parade grounds from the officers' quarters were the stables of the command. Here may be found mule shoes, harness buckles, parts of harness and traces, bridle bits and many other things required to handle the mounts. And about the grounds may be found old cooking utensils, broken sabers, officers' epaulets and other remnants of the equipments of the fort which were abandoned by the soldiers upon leaving it.

"But up on the hill, nearby, surrounded by a grove of towering pines, are sadder evidences of the former days. Wooden headboards here and there, lying about the ground, tell in very dim

letters of the death of this one or another who was a member of a certain company.[24]

The early-day settlement of Warner Valley, then part of Grant County, was not without controversy, with farmers of small acreages competing with individual stock raisers and large cattle corporations. Dispute over thousands of acres of "swamp land" was contested at various levels of law courts for years. The crucial point whether the lands between Crump Lake and Coleman Lake were indeed swamp lands on March 12, 1860, was difficult to prove, because no settlers lived in the area at that time. During the late 1870s and 1880s various parcels of land were settled, claims were filed, and land cultivated.

Litigation continued through the 1890s. One level of court awarded large tracts of land to the Warner Valley Stock Company. Another court upheld the rights of individual farmers. A decision reached in Lakeview, February 3, 1900, favored the small settlers, a decision based on the belief that the lands in question were, on March 12, 1860, "the bed of a lake and were open to settlement." From 1864 to 1881 the lands were covered with water but by 1889 had become dry. The February 3 decision was appealed by the Warner Valley Stock Company and was reversed by the General Land Office on November 6, 1900. Even this verdict was reversed, and titles reverted to the settlers. Then on March 16, 1903, Secretary of the Interior Hitchcock overrode the previous verdict, stating that "the lands were swamp land, subject to overflow and unfit for cultivation." In 1909 the lands were opened for homesteading. Today, most of these lands are in private ownership.

In the northern Warner Valley is the Stone Corral. Built of lava rock by Chinese laborers, the corral is a perfect circle with walls five feet (1.6 m.) high and four feet (1.2 m.) thick at the base. One story is that ranchers employed Chinamen to build the corral. Another story is that a group of Chinamen, en route from California to the John Day gold fields, became stranded in the northern Warner Valley and built the corral for their own protection. The corral, located at the western base of Poker Jim Ridge, is difficult to reach at times of high water in the valley.

Settlement in the Warner Valley in the late 19th and early 20th century was largely agricultural, including stock raising. However, in 1908 a gold rush took place in the Warner Valley. The discovery of old mine workings in the Coyote Hills, a few miles north of Plush, brought prospectors to the region. Three of the original miners were killed by Indians; the fourth, away securing supplies at the time of the Indian raid, never returned to the mine shaft. By July 1908, a townsite named Goldrun was laid out, and for a time mining activity was "fever high." The gold mining venture soon ended, and the Warner Valley went back to what it does best — raising hay, sheep and cattle.

About 25 miles (40 km.) north of Plush, in the northern part of the Rabbit Basin section of the Warner Valley, is a small area (2,500 acres — 1,025 ha.) of Bureau of Land Management land set aside for sunstone collection. To the geologist, sunstones are a type of aventurine feldspar. To local rockhounds and gem collectors, they are known as "Plush diamonds." Indians may well have collected sunstones in the Rabbit Basin years ago. Indian artifacts found at Table Rock (near Medford) and displayed in the Jacksonville Museum include a group of small stones which show characteristics identical to the Warner Valley specimens, hinting of possible trade with Rogue Valley tribes.

The sunstones, which occur in yellow, pink, red, green or even blue, were formed by crystallization in a magma chamber at temperatures greater than 1,100°C. The "Plush diamonds" have volcanic origins dating back two to five million years. The smaller gems are used as key chains, bracelets, pendants, and necklaces, while the larger ones are displayed in rock and mineral shows. In June 1987, the Oregon State Legislature designated the sunstone as Oregon's state gemstone.

Plush (which supposedly got its name when a Paiute Indian who was participating in a card game had difficulty in pronouncing the word "flush,") benefitted from the gold mining in the Coyote Hills. At one time Plush had two large hotels and three saloons. The *Oregon Journal*, January 25, 1953, reported that one of the hotels, the Sullivan, was standing vacant "with sagebrush around the doors, wind-blown tumbleweeds piled high against the grey, weatherworn walls with its windows missing...tired and worn out...." In March 1939, Plush staged a Frontier Days with a parade, a dance, and a basketball game between the Hart Mountain CCC Camp and the Plush Buckaroos. In March 1941, the Irish Celebration at Plush, attended by 300, saw participants in foot races, boxing, and horse racing. Today, Plush is a quiet village during the long winter, but it bustles with activity in the summer months. As it is the gateway to the Hart Mountain Antelope Refuge and the upper Warner Valley, recreationists, bird watchers, photographers, members of the Order of the Antelope, rockhounds, sightseers, and various kinds of hunters — duck, archery, black powder, antelope, bighorn sheep, deer — all converge on Plush.

The Hart Mountain store at Plush sells gas, houses the Plush post office, and is the local watering hole and "community center." There is a certain unique character to small town stores. The one at Plush is no exception. A cozy alcove provides space for a table and chairs. In the corner is a small television set and the "Plush library." "People bring in their paperbacks and exchange them with what's on the shelves," said Virginia Abbe, store owner. During the winter, the store sponsors a Big Fish Contest and contests in cribbage and pinochle for local residents. An antelope head mounted on the wall surveys the activities in the alcove. In the center of the store are a pool table and a potbellied stove. The store has a line of groceries, including a good selection of essentials such as beer. A customer walks in, grabs a mug, helps himself to the coffee from a pot on a hot plate, and takes a counter stool. A deck of cards and a pair of dice lie on the counter top. Tacked on the wall behind the counter are signs such as "Hot Sandwiches", "Crime doesn't pay, Neither does farming", "Where the hell is Plush?" Historically, Plush derived much of its business from the sheep industry. Stated Virginia, "Irishmen took bands of sheep from the OO country [in Harney County] to Ft. Bidwell [California]. With open winters in the Warner Valley, many sheepmen settled in the valley. About 40 people live in Plush now. There are maybe 70 in the northern Warner Valley."

In town there are a church and a grade school. Added Virginia, "We have six students commute to Lakeview. There is no bus service. My boys drive, leaving at 7 a.m. and returning at 4:30 p.m. or 7 p.m. if there is a high school game. The biggest problems in winter are ground blizzards. You just can't see the road." The phone rings. "It's for you," said Virginia, handing the phone to the customer. While the store is busy serving travelers during the summer, it is the locals that keep the owners in business year round.

From the top of the grade west of Plush, the view extends up and down the Warner Valley and up to Hart Mountain, which rises like the formidable obstacle it was to early explorers and migrant wagons. Lake terraces indicate more pluvial times in the valley. The levels of the lakes in the Warner Valley change seasonally and yearly depending on climatic variations. The higher lake terraces are 215 feet (66.7 m.) above the valley floor. A well drilled in the south end of Warner Valley was sunk 585 feet (181 m.) without reaching the bottom of the lake sediment. The drill passed through well-preserved juniper logs. In the 1920s all of the lakes except Crump Lake dried completely, revealing many Indian artifacts including weapons, mortars, and pestles. Further evidence of Indian occupancy of Warner Valley was confirmed in 1933 by the discovery of rock writings — petroglyphs on the meander line of the ancient lake.

When the lakes were dry, sands from the lake bed were deposited in ridges as high as 50 feet (15 m.) or more at the north end of the lake basin. Several of the lakes such as Flagstaff, Upper Campbell, and Campbell have smooth, rounded lake basins. The dry lake beds have been used for crop growing. In 1931, when Hart Lake had but a small pond in the center, 2,000 acres (820 ha.) of the lake bed were planted with hay and grain. However, the use of the lake bed in the 1920s and 1930s led to disputes over ownership of the newly-created lands. Dixie Dixon Basta, who by 1969 had lived in the Warner Valley 54 years, recollected, "In 1931 everyone was fighting for feed. Hart Lake was like a battlefield. In fact, they named it "Big Smoke" as many haystacks were [deliberately] burned. One house went up in smoke and fences were cut.... After the pasture was gone, people began to move out with their stock and never did move back to South Warner...."[25] As quickly as the lakes dried up, given a season or two of heavy precipitation, especially snows in the adjacent mountains to the south and west, the lakes filled up again ending the contest of disputed lands.

On account of the gradual gradient in the Warner Valley, water flows from Crump Lake to Hart Lake, then to Anderson Lake and so on until it reaches Bluejoint Lake. In times of high water the lakes of Warner Valley join almost as one. In January 1908, during a "wet cycle," some residents of Warner Valley thought of dredging the channels between the series of lakes so that a small steamer could ply between them. The navigable water would have stretched 70 miles (112 km.).

When seen from the rim of Hart Mountain, the Warner Valley is a place of strange beauty. Parts of the valley have been tamed, and the green irrigated meadows adjacent to Hart and Anderson Lakes contrast with the stark sand ridges around Flagstaff Lake and the two Campbell Lakes and the desolate-looking desert to the west. Powerful forces of nature created the Warner Valley. Climatic cycles have left their marks with the former shorelines of the lakes visible in many places. Beginning with the Indians, humans have occupied the valley for centuries, but taken as a whole, it is the work of nature that predominates.

Hart Mountain

The pavement may end at Plush, but the Hart Mountain adventure is only just beginning. From Plush, the gravel road skirts the north side of Hart Lake and makes a beeline for the base of the seemingly impenetrable buttress of Hart Mountain, which towers 3,000 feet (930 m.) over the Warner Valley. The Hart Mountain road then parallels the base of the escarpment past a couple of working ranches and the site of a CCC camp, then starts its ascent of Hart Mountain.

From the vicinity of Campbell Lake, elevation 4,462 feet (1,383 m.), the narrow road switchbacks up the face of the mountain, clings to cliff edges, and in three miles (5 km.) ascends 1,500 feet (465 m.). For the faint-of-heart motorist the journey may be a little unnerving. If it is at all comforting, imagine driving it in winter! Nonetheless, the views of the Warner Valley lakes and surrounding desert lands are spectacular. To the north, Poker Jim Ridge stares down at Bluejoint Lake and Stone Corral Lake. Once at the top, the gravel road descends slightly (4 miles — 6.4 km.) to the Hart Mountain National Antelope Refuge Headquarters.

The refuge, which encompasses 275,000 acres (112,750 ha.), is host to some 750 antelope, 450 bighorn sheep and over 1,000 mule deer. In addition, grazing permits allow 1,500 cattle on the refuge. The headquarters' buildings consist of stone structures built by CCC workers in the 1930s and various equipment buildings. An official weather station at the headquarters has been in existence since 1939. There are facilities for two government biologists and their families at the remote refuge. During the summers, additional workers help with various repairs and maintenance tasks. Each year, some 17,000 visitors travel to the Hart Mountain Refuge, all but a handful of them between Memorial Day and Labor Day.

The first recorded visit of white men to the Hart Mountain area was the Fremont Expedition of 1843. For a time, trails leading to Idaho gold fields cut across the desert lands north of Hart Mountain. A stage line was established, only to be abandoned because agents and passengers were plundered by hostile Indians. By the 1860s settlers came with livestock to graze grasslands in the Hart Mountain region, only to find danger from Indians. After numerous massacres in which families were murdered, homes burned, and livestock scattered, the U. S. Army, led by General Crook, established a military post, Camp Warner, in 1866 amid the ponderosa pines (at 6,500 feet — 2,000 m.) on the eastern slope of Hart Mountain. The winter of 1866-67 was, according to historical accounts, a severe one — at least at that altitude — and soldiers suffered greatly because of deep snows and frigid temperatures. General Crook ordered the camp relocated, and on July 29, 1867, the company moved to a site at a lower elevation to the west of the Warner Valley. Within a few years General Crook succeeded in suppressing the Indian raids, allowing stockmen to settle the area.

The actual name Hart is a corruption of the word "heart", a brand used by the Wilson Ranch in the 1880s. By the early 1900s the land on and around Hart Mountain had been seriously over-grazed, and dense sagebrush replaced native grasses.

In 1931, a severe drought impacted the antelope

The fleet-footed, graceful antelope ranges widely throughout the High Desert country. Antelope, which browse shrubby plants like sagebrush, bitterbrush, and saltbush, have keen eyesight and good speed — to 50 mph (80 km./hr.). Oregon Economic Development Photo, Salem.

on Hart Mountain. The plight of the antelope was reported in the August 6, 1931, edition of the *Oregon Journal*:

"America's last big herd of antelope will soon be extinct unless the Oregon State Game Commission takes immediate steps to aid these dainty animals, which are dying of thirst in Lake County after being driven from the few remaining water holes with high-powered rifles by hunters placed there by the commission."

"... it was estimated that 10,000 head of antelope had gathered near Hart Mountain because their water sources across the wide desert had dried up in the drouth and the only water available was on some of the Hart Mountain ranches. But there the antelope ate and destroyed the hay and drank the water needed for livestock. Ranchers had sued the game commission and two Lakeview high school boys, with a dog and rifles, had been placed on one of the ranches to drive the antelope away from the water."

This well-publicized incident was the spark which resulted in the formation of the Order of the Antelope in 1932. In a move largely initiated by Forrest Cooper, Lakeview attorney, invitations were sent by the Lake County Chamber of Commerce to a select group throughout the state. Twenty-two attended that first meeting on Hart Mountain, in the grove which has since become known as the "Blue Sky Hotel". The group, growing in numbers, met at the Blue Sky each year, and on December 21, 1936, President Roosevelt, despite initial opposition by some Lake County business leaders, signed a proclamation establishing the 275,000-acre (110,000 ha.) Hart Mountain National Antelope Refuge. The government then purchased most of the ranches on Hart Mountain and added them to pre-existing public lands to form the refuge.

Since 1932, the Order of the Antelope has made its annual trek to Hart Mountain. In the late 1970s, criticism of the group's actions — noise, drinking, gambling — led to a review of the permit for exclusive use of the Blue Sky Hotel site near old Camp Warner. With some restrictions, the order, whose original mission was one of conservation, has maintained its annual meeting.

In October 1937, as part of the Civilian Conservation Corps program, a camp was established on what had been the Stein Ranch in the western foothills of Hart Mountain. This camp was one of the most isolated CCC camps in

Oregon. Poor roads contributed to the difficulty in transporting materials. When on November 10, 1937, a severe wind blew down tents and partially constructed buildings, one CCC enrollee from the South remarked that it was "awful wild country." Other enrollees had more profane descriptions of the country and of the weather conditions. Within two years CCC workers had constructed the refuge headquarters (using native lava rock), a road up the mountain, installed telegraph lines from Plush to the headquarters, and miles of truck trails, and had developed water resources on the refuge.

Hart Mountain, because of its altitude and height above the Warner Valley, has different vegetation zones. In the Warner Valley, elevation 4,400 feet (1,364 m.), vegetation includes the saltbush, greasewood, sagebrush, and various species of grasses. Between 5,000 feet and 7,000 feet (1,550 m. and 2,170 m.), depending on slope exposure, are small stands of ponderosa pine. One of the best examples is near Old Camp Warner on the east side of Hart Mountain. On colder, higher ridges where snow may remain into the summer clusters of quaking aspen cling to the mountain. Above the timberline, grasses cover much of the mountain. In late spring, especially if rains have come to Southeastern Oregon, Hart Mountain is a carpet of green bedecked in places by wild flowers, such as monkey-flowers, phlox, starflowers, different-colored paintbrush, and white, yellow or purple violets.

Hart Mountain has different meanings to different groups. Hunters, hikers, geologists,

Opposite Top:
This view from the steep fault scarp that forms the west side of Hart Mountain shows the shallow modern lakes of the graben known as the Warner Valley. The photo was taken during the early 1980s when a series of wetter-than-normal winters resulted in high water levels in lakes from Oregon to Utah. Water stands above the normal shoreline of these lakes, and a field of sand dunes within the valley is also "drowned". The dunes were created during dry periods of the last 5,000 years. During the last pluvial period, 25,000 to 10,000 years ago, Warner Valley held a lake about 300 feet (93m.) deep that covered the entire basin floor. Photo by Ray Hatton.

Opposite Bottom:
Hart Mountain, a large fault block mountain, rises 3,600 feet (1,116 m.) above the Warner Valley (foreground). Several deep gorges, Hart, De Garmo, and Potter Canyons for example, cut deeply into the steep western flanks of the mountain. Photo by Ray Hatton.

wildlife conservationists, photographers, and general sightseers all view Hart Mountain in their own way. Except for hunting season, the only campground open on the refuge is at the Hot Springs Camp, where the bathhouse with its warm thermal springs attracts campers and day visitors. Hikers to the summit of Hart Mountain, Warner Peak, elevation 8,017 feet (2,483 m.), are rewarded by panoramic views over Warner Valley, the Catlow Valley, and large areas of Oregon's arid southeast quarter.

To the resident wildlife biologists and families, Hart Mountain means a different lifestyle. Their main task is to closely monitor the animal population of Hart Mountain. The bighorns were native to Hart Mountain. Indians hunted them; petroglyphs found in the vicinity show the hunting of the sheep. Early land survey crews hunted the sheep on Hart Mountain for camp meat. In the early years of the twentieth century hunters shot the last bighorn sheep. In September 1939, Rocky Mountain bighorns were brought to Hart Mountain from the National Bison Range, Montana, but they did not survive. Then in 1954, California bighorns were brought from British Columbia to Hart Mountain. By the 1980s the bighorn sheep, which numbered 450, ranged along the steep western slopes below Hart Canyon to Poker Jim Ridge, a distance of 15 miles (24 km.). The California bighorns adapt to severe winter weather, blizzard conditions and below-zero temperatures, by eating plants in spots that the winds clear off snow and sometimes by digging through snow to reach edible plants.

It is the antelope, not the bighorn sheep, that visitors to Hart Mountain are more likely to see. By spring, the antelope have moved northward from their winter quarters on the Sheldon Refuge located in Nevada. The pronghorn antelope stands about three feet (1 m.) high at the shoulders. The does produce their young, usually twins, which weigh four to five pounds (2 kg.) in mid- to late May. By the third day after birth the kid antelopes are hard for humans to catch. From the fourth day on they can easily outrace any humans, reaching sustained speeds of 30 to 40 miles (48-64 km.) per hour with bursts to 50 mph (80 km.). The pronghorn is the only hoofed animal that sheds its horn annually from a bony core. The horn has a prong which projects forward from the main stem, unlike the horns of true antelope, bison, and mountain sheep. The pronghorn has a complex stomach and is a cud chewer, feeding on a variety of plants including grasses, forbs, and sagebrush.

Harsh winter weather that deters visitors from trekking up Hart Mountain tests the stamina of refuge personnel. In February 1970, a resident biologist reported, "For another week we received no visitors...." The December 14, 1972, bulletin from Hart Mountain (in the *Lake County Examiner*) reported that the refuge was "hit by extremely frigid conditions with temperatures to 26 degrees below zero [-32°C.]. The fuel line to the residents' generators froze on two nights, so we were without electricity.... After much work and some occasional swearing, the fuel line was sufficiently insulated. At this writing, the Witte generator No. 2 is not running, but we're working on it!"

In an interview in October 1983, a resident biologist commented on the isolation. For the sake of his wife and children they would try to go to town (Lakeview) once a week for food, fever (cabin), and friends. The biologist's wife grew up in Eureka, California, home of the redwoods. Her view from any room of the headquarters house was one of open desert, treeless ridges, and barren mountains. She said that after four years, it was a challenge to survive emotionally and mentally. When in Lakeview she stocked up on food and books.

The wildlife biologist and his family may have been lonely, but he was certainly not idle. On foot or horseback, by helicopter or plane, he monitored the antelope and bighorn sheep and counted animal populations. During the course of a year, he repaired equipment, maintained the generators, fixed cattle guards and fences, picked up litter, and provided information for hunters and visiting tour groups, as well as assisting in law enforcement with game violations!

Harney Basin and the Blitzen Valley

HARNEY BASIN INCLUDING BURNS-HINES

The Hollywood stereotype of the American West — Indians, cavalry, migrant wagons, cattlemen, sheepmen, gunfighters, homesteaders — is part of the history of the big Harney Country. In

GEOLOGY
By Bruce Nolf

Harney Basin lies astride the Brothers Fault Zone, bounded on the north by the relatively gentle southward slope of the Blue Mountains (Strawberry and Aldrich Ranges), and on the south by blocks of the Basin-Range. The center of the basin is a large caldera, formed by collapse accompanying very large and explosive volcanic eruptions in the late Cenozoic time (65.9 million years ago).

Considerable precipitation occurs in the drainage of the basin at higher elevation, much of it as winter snow in the headwaters of the Silvies River and on Steens Mountain. Since the time of formation of the central part of the basin, many hundreds of feet of non-marine sediment have been deposited in the basin, carried there by runoff from surrounding mountains. Volcanism has also occurred intermittently since caldera collapse. Excess runoff from the mountains has overtopped the basin sill to the east and cut several stream channels to the Malheur River, flushing sediments once accumulated within the Harney Basin farther downstream into the Snake River Drainage. Current lake level is approximately 10 feet (c. 3 m.) below the elevation of these spillways. On several occasions in more pluvial times, the lake level has been at least 100 feet (c. 30 m.) higher than at present.

addition, as if that drama were not enough, this frontier part of Oregon has experienced mining ventures, a struggle against drought, disasters from flooding, and the fluctuating fortunes associated with the cyclic nature of the lumber industry. Most of all, Harney County is cattle country. Annual revenue from the 100,000 cattle in the county is over $20 million. Hay and other forage crops generate about $3.3 million in revenue. Grain adds another $1.1 million.

The Harney Basin, although appearing flat and low-lying when viewed from the Blue Mountains to the north or from the towering Steens to the south, is actually at an elevation of 4,100 feet (1,271 m.). Three lakes, Malheur and Harney Lakes and tiny Mud Lake, occupy the heart of the Harney Basin. The two main streams that feed the lakes of the Harney Basin are the Silvies River and the Donner and Blitzen River. The Silvies has its source in small streams that rise in the mountains to the north of the Harney Basin. Throughout most of its course, the Silvies is a small sluggish stream, alternately flooding in the spring and shrinking by late summer or early fall to a mere trickle. Given heavy winter precipitation in the Strawberry Mountains and a rapid runoff, the Silvies inundates hundreds of acres of meadow lands near Burns each spring. These flood waters, however, cause little harm. Indeed, they provide moisture needed for the cultivation of wild hay. Historically, the lack of control of the Silvies waters, coupled with a low winter snowpack and a dry spring, have caused economic hardships to ranchers in the northern section of the Harney Basin.

The Blitzen, as it is more commonly named, provides over half of the inflow to Malheur Lake. This stream, along with its tributaries, Fish Creek, Indian Creek, and Ankle Creek, rises high up on the western slopes of Steens Mountain. The Blitzen enters the valley of the same name near the P Ranch, a mile east of Frenchglen. From that point on, the stream bed has been partly dredged. In its lower reaches it sluggishly meanders northward to its discharge into Malheur Lake.

Within the Harney basin are a number of smaller basins or valleys, each of which has provided opportunities for settlements. Virginia Valley, located southeast of Malheur Lake, was where water flowed through the Malheur Gap into the south fork of the Malheur River in an earlier geological time period. The small community of Princeton is the only settlement in the Virginia Valley. The Sunset Valley lies between prominent Wrights Point and the Narrows, where water may flow from Malheur Lake into Mud Lake. North of Malheur Lake, the Harney Valley occupies the flat-as-a-pancake real estate located between Burns and Crane. South of Malheur Lake, merging with the elongated Blitzen Valley, the lush green Diamond Valley receives waters from Kiger Creek, Cucamonga Creek, and McCoy Creek, all of which tumble out of the northwest flanks of the Steens.

Before the coming of the white man to the Harney Basin, Paiute Indians roamed the region, establishing seasonal camps around Malheur and Harney Lakes, in the Steens area, on the High Desert, and in the fall, in the Blue Mountains north of what is now the city of Burns. Beginning in the 1870s, however, the Paiutes found that their hunting grounds were being taken over by the newcomers.

The creation of the Malheur Indian Reservation in September 1872 was not by any means a satisfactory solution to the tribe's loss of land. Furthermore, plundering of Indian villages by soldiers resulted in an Indian revolt. Bannocks from the east and Paiutes, led by two of their chiefs, Otis and Egan, combined against the whites in the Bannock Wars of 1878.

Following the defeat of the Indians, the Paiutes were evicted from their homeland to a reservation in the Yakima, Washington area. In November 1929 the Paiutes received payments of $661,448 as compensation for lands set aside as a reservation back in 1872. Not until 1973 did the Paiutes acquire a reservation of their own, although tribal members had previously returned to the Burns area.

Today the Paiute Indian Reservation is a minuscule 1,200-acre tract of desert land. Some of the 250 or so tribal members live in typically suburban ranch-style houses that line the curving paved streets of the reservation on a plateau a mile north of Burns; others live on individually owned lands elsewhere in the vicinity of Burns.

The Paiute Tribe has its own administration office, law enforcement officers, and court system. Some of the members work for the tribe; other are employed in various jobs in the Burns area. Some Paiutes continue their heritage by making and selling baskets, jewelry, and beadwork, some of which are sold at Buchanan, a tiny hamlet located on Highway 20, about 20 miles (32 km.) east of Burns. Other attempts to preserve the

Paiute Indians participate in the Harney County Fair parade, an annual event in Burns each September. Photo by Marcus Haines, Burns.

Opposite top:
A summer thunderstorm rumbles over the desert near the headquarters of the Hart Mountain National Antelope Refuge. Flowering rabbitbrush add color to the desert landscape. Photo by Ray Hatton.

Opposite bottom:
Meadowlands grace the "front entrance" to the "Big Sky Hotel" on Hart Mountain, the site of the annual meeting of the Order of the Antelope. The site, set amidst ponderosa pine, was the location of General Crook's military post during the winter of 1866-67. Hart Mountain still retains winter snows in this June photo. Photo by Ray Hatton.

Paiute culture include the gathering and preparing of traditional foods (especially roots and plants) and the incorporation of Paiute crafts and culture within the Harney County 4-C and Headstart programs.

It was in this Harney Basin setting that white people first settled in the 1870s. This was the country vividly described by cattleman Bill Hanley: "And at last, I saw the great Harney Valley that I had heard of for so long, the big valley of the Oregon plains country that Indians had fought for. I didn't wonder. It seems a resting place for space and that which flies or roams seemed to have found it.... I was afire with feelings for its bigness, its grass, its water."[26] An even earlier account of the landscape of the Harney Basin was provided by Schuyler (Skip) Whiting:

"My story begins in the fall of 1874 when Harney County was yet unsettled. The Harney Valley was truly a beautiful country with the wild grass waving seven or eight feet high all over the prairie and only the winding, willow-bordered Silvies, and the hills and mountains rising in the distance to break the lonely monotony.

"The county was over-running with bands of antelope, deer, prairie wolves, coyotes and hundreds of jack rabbits.

"During all seasons of the year but especially in the spring, the sky was alive with birds. Sometimes they were so thick in the sky the sun couldn't be seen. White geese would alight on twenty or thirty acres and it would look like solid snow.

"There were no traveled roads then and when a wagon passed through the grass it left a deep, flattened lane in its wake. In the winter the eight-foot bunch grass would stick out two or three feet above the snow. Also, during that time the whole hill behind Burns was covered with juniper trees. Only it wasn't called Burns then, it was known as Rocky Point.

"Harney County was a great stock country in those days. There was so much feed, even in the winter, that the stock wintered out and were fat and sleek all year long. There was no machinery then for harvesting hay so there were no haystacks

dotting the landscape as there are now."[27]

Despite the seemingly peaceful setting, miners traveling to Idaho, settlers, and migrant wagons traveling through the Harney Basin found their safety threatened by Indians. Indians had resented the settlement of what had been their lands. To protect the Harney Basin settlers, several military camps were established in Harney County. Camp Harney was located on Rattlesnake Creek at the northern edge of the basin and on a traveled route to and from the mining town of Canyon City. It was in June 1878 that the Bannocks and Paiutes started on their warpath. A warning was sent around the country by a man on horseback, and settlers quickly moved their families to Fort Harney (as it was locally named). In Happy Valley, Indians killed John Smyth and his father before setting fire to the ranch buildings. The Indian raiders then swept through the Diamond and Blitzen Valleys. The cavalry caught up with the Indians on Silver Creek, where Chief Egan was wounded. The Indians were finally subdued in the John Day country, and brought back to Camp Harney.

Camp Harney, named after Major General W. J. Harney, had previously been named "Camp on Rattlesnake Creek," "Camp Steele," and "Camp Crook." Prominent Harney County stockman Bill Hanley recollected his visit to the camp: "Then I visited Camp Harney where the white settlers had taken refuge from the Paiutes. It was the only thing in the whole country that looked like civilization. There was a long row of officers' quarters, soldiers' barracks and the guardhouse, painted white, shining in the sun. And there was the settlers stove and big commissary building."[28]

The first post office in Harney County was established at Camp Harney, August 10, 1874. The camp was officially abandoned in 1880 and lumber from the buildings was used for the construction of housing for settlers who stayed in the vicinity. A new settlement, Harney City, had been established in 1879 near the camp. The post office was moved from Camp Harney in 1885, and later became the county seat. A photo of Harney City taken in 1885 showed about 50

Opposite: **Harney County's area, 10,185 square miles (16,904 km²) is the largest county in Oregon. The county has less than 10,000 people. This facsimile of a Chamber of Commerce map shows places discussed in the text.** Map by permission of Harney County Chamber of Commerce.

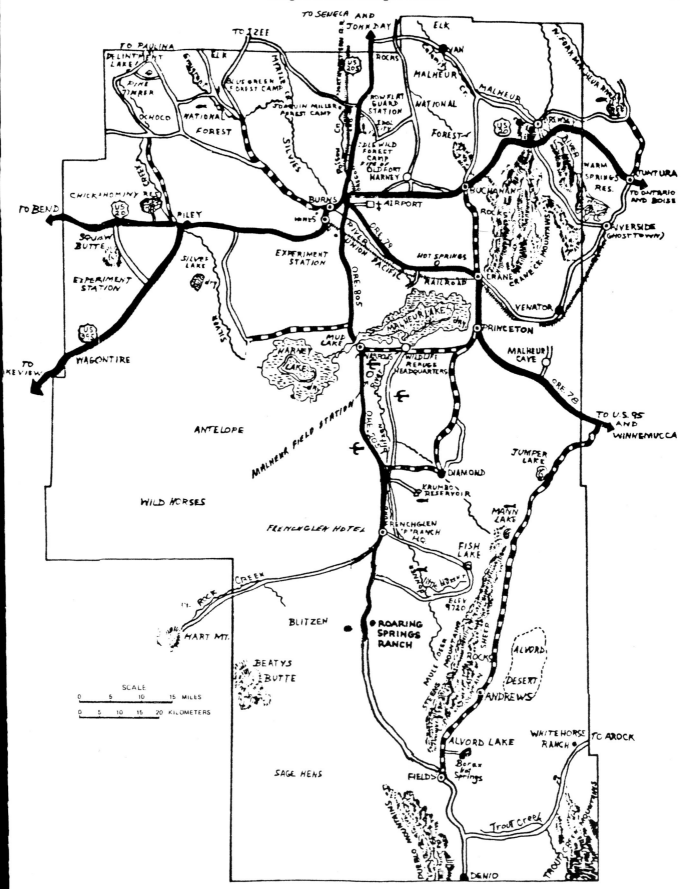

HARNEY COUNTY SAGEBRUSH SYMPHONY ORCHESTRA

The Oregonian, September 28, 1916, published a concert review of Oregon's youngest symphony: "Harney Youngsters Absorb Harmony From Desert — Concert is Wonderful — Techniques of Sagebrush Orchestra Surprise Artists of City. Every Number is Encored."

It was in 1910 that Mrs. Mary V. Dodge arrived in Harney County with her husband Mott V. Dodge, a civil engineer who was employed for a survey of the Silvies Creek and Silver Creek Reclamation Project. Mrs. Dodge, a college graduate from Boston, had taught for several years at the Shattuck School in Portland. In 1911 Mrs. Dodge started private violin classes in Burns, and the following year she organized what became known as the Sagebrush Symphony Orchestra with children ages five to fifteen, sons and daughters of Burns area citizens and ranchers. The stringed instrument section of the orchestra numbered 24; there were two cornets, two trombones, two clarinets, a French horn and a flute. The organ, drums and piano rounded out the orchestra.

Recalled Frank Loggan of Bend, a former member of the orchestra, "We gave recitals throughout Central Oregon — Canyon City, John Day, and Bend." A highlight for the orchestra was the trip to the Willamette Valley, where performances were given at the State Fair at Salem and at a Portland Theater. The orchestra, accompanied by some of the parents, was driven to Bend in Model T Fords. A special Pullman car was put on the Oregon Trunk Railroad for the journey to Portland. For most of the orchestra members, it was their first train ride and their first experience in a city with high-rise buildings and elevators. The Imperial Hotel, where the children stayed, was decorated with branches of sagebrush. The orchestra's performance was filmed by Pathe' Film Exchange and shown internationally in the Pathe' Weekly News. Every available seat at the concert was filled; according to *The Oregonian*, September 28, 1916, "Hundreds were turned away for lack of room.... The young musicians played from memory and their bowing and general violin techniques are excellent.... Several of the children are conductors and they do admirable work...." The world famous operatic contralto Mme. Schumann-Heink, visiting Portland at that time, invited the orchestra to her hotel room.

After Mr. Dodge was transferred back to Portland, about two years later, the Harney County Sagebrush Symphony Orchestra folded. In Portland, Mrs. Dodge's enthusiasm for the encouragement of young musicians prompted her to establish the Junior Symphony of Portland. Today, the Portland Youth Philharmonic, as it is now known, has been recognized as one of the leading youth orchestras in the nation. Mrs. Mary V. Dodge died in Portland, December 31, 1954.

structures. After Burns was narrowly voted the county seat in 1889, Harney City quickly lost its importance. Hope for Harney City's revival was placed in the gold mining at Idol City, 15 miles (25 km.) to the north. Here, optimistic miners thought that the real Blue Bucket gold was located. Following a short-lived gold rush, the Idol City post office, established in March, 1892, closed in August the following year. The *Oregonian*, August 24, 1900, reported, "For years, Harney [City] has been at a standstill. The houses have gradually gone to rack, the paint has washed off, the sun and dry winds have cracked the walls until Harney looks everything but an Eastern Oregon town."

Burns, the county seat and by far the largest community in Harney County, was named by one of the city's founders, George McGowan,[29] a native of Aberdeen, Scotland, after the famous Scottish poet Robert Burns. Today, athletic teams at Burns High School are aptly named the Hilanders. When Burns was established in 1883, it already had a rival in Egan, located two miles (3.2 km.) away. The *East Oregon Herald*, December 21, 1887, noted that in 1881, P. M. Curry of Egan was dispensing whiskey for 25 cents per drink at the only business house in Harney County. Mail came weekly by horseback from Canyon City; at that time, 1881, the Harney Basin was part of Grant County. By 1882, a general mercantile store and post office and hotel had been established at Egan. Egan and Burns consolidated in May 1883 and the post office was moved to Burns. More settlers moved into the Harney

The Harney County Sagebrush Symphony Orchestra poses on a float on the High Desert outside of Burns. The orchestra was founded in 1912 by Mrs. Mary V. Dodge, and gave performances throughout Central Oregon. The highlights of the orchestra were performances in Salem and Portland in 1916.

Basin, and with the Grant County seat at Canyon City being several days' journey, a new county was deemed necessary. Harney County was created February 25, 1889, with a temporary county seat at Harney City. Later that year Burns was voted the permanent county seat of Harney County.

The Burns population grew from 250 in 1884 to nearly 1,000 by 1900. Yet despite the growth, Burns was still an isolated frontier town with no railroad and no local markets for the thousands of cattle in the county. The big cattle companies didn't use or need the services offered in Burns. John Devine obtained his saddles from San Francisco; Bill Hanley ordered his hats from Chicago. Mail came into Burns twice a week. The town was isolated in winter by deep snows and in the spring by mud. Nonetheless, Burns did and still does service Harney Basin residents. In its early years, Burns had three blacksmith's shops, four livery stables, five saloons, a drugstore, several merchandise stores, and 11 lawyers. At one time Burns boasted three newspapers, *Harney*

Items, *The Times*, and the *East Oregon Herald*. In the early 1900s, wooden (vulnerable-to-fire) structures were replaced by ones built of brick and of local stone.

When the railroad was extended from Crane, the first train into Burns on September 27, 1924, was greeted by 4,000 people including Indians in full ceremonial regalia. The railroad to Burns was the impetus needed for the Burns area to grow once more. The Edward Hines Lumber Company's vast sawmill was constructed at the planned city of Hines in the late 1920s. Hines was designed with curving streets and parks by the wife of company founder Edward Hines because she was tired of seeing straight streets and identical houses at the company's other mill towns. Contractors Stafford-Derbes & Roy, who had built in other lumber towns — Klamath Falls, Marshfield (near Coos Bay), and Bend — constructed Hines. A variety of two-bedroom houses (86 different plans) were built around a large city park. Electricity for the houses came from the Hines mill. Timber for the mill itself largely came from the Malheur and the Ochoco National Forests, both located in the Blue Mountains north of Hines. A company-owned railroad, the Oregon & Northwestern Railroad, transported logs from Seneca, 50 miles (80 km.) north of the mill. There were expansions to the mill with the addition of a remanufacturing plant (1955) and a plywood plant (1965). At full capacity, the total mill operations had a payroll of over 1,000.

In 1980, as mortgage interest rates soared, housing starts plummeted nationwide. The demand for lumber dropped sharply. First cutbacks, then a closure led to the end of an era. The Edward Hines Lumber Company closed. In June 1981, the company's plywood plant and millwork factory machinery was put on the auction block. Over 500 registered bidders from various sections of the U. S. bid on the inventory. Some machines went at bargain prices. Two saw lines in the stud mill, each worth $500,000, went for $30,000 and $22,500 respectively. A log sorter that cost $200,000 new in 1979 was auctioned for $11,000. The mill's old-timers watched silently and nervously as the gavel banged down on machine after machine that they had come to know and operate.

Economic woes that followed the closure of the mill led to many social problems. By late 1980, some 300 people had left the Burns-Hines area. In

the following year, the unemployment rate in Harney County jumped to an alarming 16.5 percent. As people left the area seeking work elsewhere, real estate values plunged drastically. In an interview with *The Oregonian*, November 8, 1981, Gary George, a mental health counselor, succinctly stated: "The man here is a man of times past; hard-working men who pride themselves on strength and individuality." With the Hines mill closed, other businesses in the Burns-Hines area felt the economic crunch. Advertising revenue for the *Burns Times-Herald* dropped 18 percent. An auto agency closed its doors. Other business owners stubbornly hung on. "The worst is over" was the optimistic philosphy of many. It was during this same time period that the flooding of Malheur and Harney Lakes (discussed separately) added a second unneeded blow to the economy of Harney County.

In 1983, the Snow Mountain Pine Company purchased the Hines Lumber Company mill, installed new computerized equipment, and restarted lumber operations. Today, the Snow Mountain Pine Mill dominates the cultural landscape on the western entrance to Hines. Cranes glide almost noiselessly over stacks of logs that tower over Highway 20. The hum of machinery comes from the cavernous sheds. The distinctly-

HARNEY COUNTY FAIR PARADE

Just about everyone in Harney County was there. Ranches in the far-flung parts of the county were largely deserted. Schools had closed early Wednesday in the rural areas so that children could participate in 4-H projects. All the parking lots in the downtown area were jammed mainly with pickups. This was Fair Day in Burns. The parade was scheduled to start at 9 A.M.; but in realty, it began when the participants had assembled and organized themselves in the Safeway parking lot. Harney County folks, many bedecked in traditional Western wear — Levis, Stetsons, cowboy boots — waited patiently. A group of Paiute Indians stood together, silently awaiting the parade. A loud-speaker blared country and western music.

Suddenly the wail of a siren heralded the parade leaders, a Burns ambulance and a Burns Fire Department truck with a very proud-looking Dalmatian perched on the cab. The Burns High School band, in white tops, tartan sashes, and yellow hats, deservedly won a round of applause for their rendering of "The Star Spangled Banner." Then came the horses — horses and more horses! Representatives of other fairs, rodeo queens and princesses from Vale, Lakeview, Deschutes County, were well received. A variety of floats, some manned by those seeking political offices, some by local civic clubs and organizations (4-H, Elks, for example), followed and preceded more horses. Reflecting the economy of Harney County was the convoy of farm machinery which brought the parade to an end. One parade slogan aptly depicted Harney County's social character: "Pioneer Days Are Still OUR Modern Days."

designed office building that bore the name Edward Hines Lumber Company for half a century has basically changed only in name. However, the Snow Mountain Pine Company employs only a fraction of the previous work force.

The Burns-Hines area today reflects its heritage, its regional economy, and its hope for better times. In Hines the modest homes, laid out on circular streets as Mrs. Hines intended, are now partially obscured by deciduous trees which have matured over the years. Highway 20, the "main drag" between Hines and Burns, slices between typical American fast-food outlets, old and new motels, and gas stations. Empty lots await the next economic expansion in the Burns-Hines area. Highway 20 doglegs through downtown Burns. Brick buildings that have weathered the heat of many summers and the icy blasts of many winters line the main street. The names of businesses such as "The Ponderosa," "The Silver Sage" and "The Silver Spur" depict the historical character of the region. The cityscape is typical of small towns in the American West. In adjacent blocks the Burns Public Library, the Chamber of Commerce building, the Harney County Museum, and the Harney County Courthouse, among other new buildings, reflect the progress and growth of more prosperous years. The economic heritage of Harney County is artistically displayed in the Harney County Courthouse. Here a giant mural painted by E. B. Quigley, originally done for a Harney County booth at the Pacific Livestock Exposition in the early 1950s, colorfully portrays the roundup of cattle on the Alvord Desert with the rugged eastern face of Steens Mountain as a scenic backdrop.

CRANE HIGH SCHOOL

The school bell rings, signaling the end of another school day. However, there is no fleet of yellow buses or convoy of parents' cars waiting to transport the students home. "Home" to virtually the entire student body of Crane High School, at least from Sunday evening to Friday afternoon, is the on-campus dormitories. Crane High School is the only public boarding school in Oregon and one of only two tax-supported boarding high schools in the nation. (The other one is in Montana.) In the mid-1980s the cost of education and boarding at Crane was about $10,000 per student. The map of Southeastern Oregon, in particular Harney County, reveals the concept of place and space for Crane students. The 80 or so students come from within a school district that is larger in area than Delaware and Connecticut combined. Furthermore, there are no expressways or paved arterials serving most of the sprawling desert lands and vast cattle ranches. It is nearly 200 miles (320 km.) from the northern to the southern borders of the district, which includes 7,233 square miles (18,805 km²) of Harney County and 468 square miles (1,217 km²) of adjacent Malheur County. The total population of the district is around 2,000, or 0.26 people per square mile (2.6 km²). Because school board members have to drive so far, board meetings may last six hours!

The Crane Union High School was established in 1918 at the nearby community of Lawen but two years later was relocated at Crane. In its early years, Crane (named after the sandhill cranes that were once abundant in the area) was the railroad terminus before the line from Ontario was extended to Burns. At one time the lively community included four hotels, three pool halls, four restaurants, a theater, a livery stable, a lumber yard, and a post office, among other businesses. The *Crane American* was the weekly news source for the community. The dormitory for boys was constructed in 1931, the girls' dormitory added in the 1940s. Previously, the students who didn't reside in Crane boarded with local families or lived in the hotels in town. Fire destroyed the original classroom and dormitory facilities on January 25, 1967. The new facilities, modern metal structures, are located against the base of a barren-looking butte, the flanks of which are embellished with a large white "C".

Bill Thew, the school superintendent, discussed some of the unique educational aspects of Crane. "The students are largely independent and responsible. Growing up on an isolated cattle ranch, you become that way. If the new students, being away from home for the first time, make it past the first week, they survive. We have tremendous participation in sports — eight-man football, volleyball, wrestling, basketball, tennis, track, baseball, and rodeo. We don't consider sports extra-curricular; typically nearly 90 percent of the student body participates in one or more sports. One of the problems we face is retaining young women teachers. It's 28 miles (45 km.) to the nearest grocery store, and three hours drive to

Crane High School, one of the very few public boarding schools in the nation. Students attend Crane from as far away as 100 miles (160 km.) or more. The mechanical bull in the foreground is used for rodeo practice. Photo by Ray Hatton.

any serious shopping. There's little for single teachers to do in this vicinity.''

Louis Ash and Bertha Robinson, who look after the dormitories, proudly showed me the spotless kitchen and dining room. Ash, an ex-Marine who spent his early years in Frenchglen and graduated from Crane in 1944, seemed well capable of taking care of any discipline problems.

Outside the dormitories, ''El Toro'', the mechanical bucking bull, silently awaited its next challenger. In 1983, a Crane graduate, John Opie, was a national collegiate rodeo champion, competing for Blue Mountain Community College. Small as the school is, Crane's vocational classes, a handful of college-prep courses, and a variety of sports events help provide a well-rounded education for the district's high school students.

MALHEUR NATIONAL WILDLIFE REFUGE

It was on August 18, 1908, by order of President Theodore Roosevelt, that all lands within the meander lines of Malheur, Harney, and Mud Lakes became a designated federal bird refuge: the Lake Malheur Reservation. Previously, William L. Finley, a naturalist who had studied and photographed the wildlife of the area, drew attention to the importance of Malheur Lake as a breeding and resting ground for migratory waterfowl and other birds. As early as the 1870s, Captain Charles Bendire, a young ornithologist who had been stationed at nearby Camp Harney from November 1875, to January 1877, gave accounts of the Malheur Lake bird life.

For over a quarter of a century following the creation of the reservation in 1908, little was accomplished other than attempts to protect the wildlife from hunters killing birds for their feathers or for food. Indeed, during that period there were proposals by local farmers to drain Malheur Lake into Harney Lake and the South Fork of the Malheur River. In June 1913, the *Burns Times-Herald*, which favored the drainage, placed a price tag of $245,124 on the drainage proposal.

As it turned out, Mother Nature took care of the drainage of the Harney Basin lakes. The dry period began in 1908, when diminished snowpack in the mountains resulted in a shrinking volume of waters in the Harney Basin lakes. Old-timers recalled the year 1889, when Malheur Lake went dry except for water from a spring near the Sod House Ranch. There have been several indications that the lake bed has been dry previously. In 1889, sagebrush stumps were visible all over the dry lake bed. Drilling of the lake bed in September 1934 brought up a section of a willow tree from 50 feet (15.5 m.), evidence that the lake bed was once at a level well below that of 1934.

By August 1918, Malheur Lake was dry. Farmers were cutting hay so far into the middle of the lake bed that they took lunch with them. The land rights of the exposed lake bed then became a legal battle. In the 1920s, the continued drought was having a serious effect upon the bird life of the refuge. In addition, the tules left by the receding waters became parched, and the soil became like peat once the vegetation had decomposed. In April 1924 a tule fire that raged in the Malheur Lake bed for several weeks covered a 160-square mile (416 km²) area, burning pasture, stored hay, and several ranch homes.

In 1926 and again in 1930 the remnants of buffalo herds were discovered in the bed of Malheur Lake. Back in 1826, Peter Skene Ogden who had visited Malheur Lake reported finding carcasses of buffalo. The *Burns Times-Herald*, November 20, 1916, reported that an old Paiute Indian, Captain Louie, told a story in which his father had witnessed a large buffalo herd come to Harney Lake during a period of long drought. Hundreds of the animals died of thirst. Then in late December 1930, the remains of hundreds of buffalo and other mammals including grizzly bear were discovered in the lake bed. Several theories as to the cause of the animals' death were suggested. One seemingly plausible explanation was that the buffalo suffered the same fate as thousands of head of cattle in the early 1900s. Cattle had wintered in the marsh grasses; rain and melting snow caused a sudden rising of waters and stranded the cattle, who ultimately perished.

In the spring of 1934, with the lake dry, farmers seeded several thousand acres of the bed with grain. In order to protect their crops from thousands of roaming cattle, farmers fenced and patrolled 4,500 acres (1,845 ha.) of grain. That summer, the value of the grains, which included wheat, oats, and barley, was $75,000, with yields up to 100 bu./acre (35 hl./.41 ha.). However, questions of land ownership of the lake bed arose; traditionally, stockmen had grazed their livestock on the lake bed grasses.

Once again, Nature rendered a verdict as to the lake's ownership. Heavy rains in June of 1934 caused a rapid inflow of water from the Blitzen River into Malheur Lake and threatened grain stacks. In late August 1935, heavy rains caused waters to flow in large amounts into Malheur Lake once again, and within weeks birds were returning to the refuge. It was in the summer of 1935 that evidences of Indian occupancy near Harney and Malheur Lakes were discovered. In August 1935, a rancher discovered Indian relics including a stone mortar and pestle in a sand pile north of Harney Lake near the OO Ranch. In September that year, the skeleton of an Indian brave with his head resting on a flat grinding stone was found in a grave near the Sod House Springs Civilian Conservation Corps Camp. A skinning knife was also found in the grave. In May 1935, Stanley M. Jewett became the first superintendent of the refuge. He was succeeded in

The Sod House Civilian Conservation Corps (CCC) Camp located at the Malheur National Wildlife Refuge in 1935. Workers from the CCC camps did considerable work in constructing bridges, canals, barns and fencing. Photo courtesy of Marcus Haines, Burns.

1936 by John C. Scharff, who remained superintendent until his retirement in 1971. During that time Scharff, assisted by Civilian Conservation Corps workers, developed the refuge. A building program was initiated and many of the bridges, canals barns, and miles of fences were constructed by CCC people. Local sedimentary rock was used to build the refuge's headquarters. Stated John Scharff, "The refuge is a monument to what the CCC boys did."

In 1939, water began flowing into Malheur Lake from the north for the first time in 13 years. In time, Mud Lake was filled and water spilled into Harney Lake, breaking open a sand barrier that had drifted across the spillway during the period of drought. The OO Ranch, 14,751 acres (6,048 ha.) south of Harney Lake, was acquired for $116,143 from the Hanley estate in 1941 and added to the refuge holdings. The bird museum at the refuge was dedicated on October 16, 1954, in memory of George M. Benson, whose hobby was taxidermy and who assembled a wide variety of wildlife species which are now part of the museum's exhibits.

The refuge, which lies at an elevation of 4,100 feet (1,171 m.), includes irrigated meadows, alkali flats, grass and sagebrush plains, and in dry periods, large marshes supporting bulrushes, cattails and vast quantities of submerged plants that help provide the favorable waterfowl habitat. An arm of the refuge extends south for 32 miles (52 km.) into the flat Blitzen Valley. Here the landscape is one of irrigated meadows, small ponds, and willow-lined sloughs, which make the best waterfowl nesting area of the refuge. The refuge is a breeding area for all kinds of water birds; in the spring and fall, it serves as a stopover for migratory birds on the Pacific Flyway between their breeding grounds in Canada and Alaska and their wintering areas in California and Mexico. The refuge is also home to marsh and shore birds, which may number in the hundreds of thousands, and upland game birds — a total of well over 200 species of birds.

The changing of the seasons brings different bird activities to the refuge. The spring waterfowl migration between mid-March and early April brings huge flocks of white snow geese and a lesser number of Canada geese, Ross' geese, whistling swans, and the tall, ungainly sandhill cranes. Estimates of the migrant bird population at the Malheur Refuge in the late 1970s included

Snow geese pause on waters south of Burns before continuing their migratory flight. Photo by Michael Clapp, Bend.

400,000 ducks, 75,000 geese, and 3,500 swans. By late April, most of the snow geese and other migratory birds have departed, but a variety of marsh and water birds arrive at their breeding areas. The nesting colonies of marsh and water birds include the great blue herons and black-crowned night herons, common and snowy egrets, western, eared, and pied-billed grebes, bitterns, and coots. Nesting shorebirds include killdeer, avocet, willet, long-billed curlew, and common snipe. The songbird migration is at its peak about mid-May. The refuge headquarters and the upper end of the Blitzen Valley are considered the best areas for bird watchers and wildlife photographers. During this time, the marshes are alive with rustling of birds. In late May and early June, many species begin nesting in the willows and grasslands. As the meadows become dry during late July, the refuge grain-fields and ponds attract more and more birds.

With the onset of fall, a southward migration begins and reaches a peak during October. By November, the migratory birds have departed. As the shallow waters of the refuge become frozen, the marshes become silent. Every now and then an air hole in the ice reveals the presence of a muskrat. These animals, by cutting growing vegetation for their food supply, inadvertently create a more desirable habitat for waterfowl. In addition, the muskrat lodges provide potential nest sites for trumpeter swans and Canada geese.

Educational facilities at the Malheur Refuge include a small museum that houses mounted specimens of birds and mammals and provides informational pamphlets on the refuge. The Malheur Field Station, operated by several Pacific Northwest colleges, offers a variety of college credit field courses as well as research facilities. Today the Malheur Wildlife Refuge, which encompasses 181,000 acres (74,210 ha.), is a major tourist attraction in Harney County.

HARNEY COUNTY FLOODING

There was no sudden deluge or prolonged period with copious rains. Instead, a tormenting inch-by-inch rise in water slowly encroached on hay fields, lapped at ranch houses, then mercilessly inundated homes, barns and other structures. Such was the Harney Basin flood of the 1980s. Ironically, during the 1970s ranches in eastern Oregon, especially those not dependent on irrigation looked in vain to the skies for moisture. Harney Lake was a giant alkali dust bowl. Malheur Lake in October 1977 covered a relatively meager 16,000 acres (6,560 ha.) and, as seen from the Malheur Refuge headquarters, looked more like a marsh.

Beginning in 1981, the climate changed. In the three-year period 1981-1983, the Burns weather station recorded 46.77 inches (1,188 mm.) of precipitation — some 154 percent above normal. Considerable snows had piled up in the mountains. Spring runoff down the Silvies River and Silver Creek brought snowmelt waters southward from the Blue Mountains. The Blitzen River, flowing northward from Steens Mountain, did likewise. With an enclosed basin and low summer evaporation rates, the water levels of the Harney County lakes steadily rose each spring. Because the lake basin is so shallow, each one-inch (25 mm.) rise in the level of the lakes meant that an additional 8,500 acres (3,485 ha.) of land were covered by water.

By 1985, Malheur Lake had expanded to 89,000 acres (36,490 ha.). Normally dry Harney Lake to the west had 20 feet (6.2 m.) of water in its lake basin. Tiny Mud Lake, sandwiched between the two big lakes just west of what is called the Narrows, contained four feet (1.2 m.) of water. The Dunn family ranch at the Narrows, which had grown alfalfa and grains for over 80 years, was threatened. Altogether, the three lakes covered 170,000 acres (69,700 ha.) — 265 square miles (1,689 km²), perhaps the largest extent in 150 years.

The impact of the flood on individual ranches and on the Harney County economy was devastating. Ranchers first diked against the rising waters in the hope that the flood would peak before damaging their homes. One by one the ranches yielded to the inevitable. By 1985, thirty ranchers had been flooded out, their livelihoods, their lands, and in many instances their homes gone. Land values in the Harney Basin plummeted by over $12 million. Two state highways, Highway 78 southeast of Burns and Route 205, Burns-Frenchglen, were flooded. The latter highway was raised at the Narrows at a cost of $3 million. The Union Pacific rail line that connected Burns with southern Idaho was submerged for several miles, forcing the Snow Mountain Pine Company in Hines to ship its lumber by road to Meridian, Idaho, where it was transferred from truck to rail.

Irrigation systems and fences were destroyed by the high waters. The tiny community of Sod House next to the Malheur Refuge was seriously affected by the flood, and the one-room school

The Narrows, where a narrow channel connects Malheur Lake with Mud Lake and Harney Lake in wet periods, was first settled in 1889. Early in the twentieth century the Narrows had two hotels, three saloons, a school, post office, restaurant, dance hall, two livery stables, doctor's office and a large general store, the latter operated by Charles Haines. Following the abandonment of the homesteads, the Narrows declined in importance and by 1940 was abandoned. Left, view of the Narrows 1912. Right, remnants of the Narrows as seen from a similar viewpoint in the late 1960s. Photos by Marcus Haines, Burns.

was moved to higher ground. Ranches in the vicinity were completely under water. At Lawen, 17 miles southeast of Burns, flood waters advancing to within a few feet of the store and post office forced closure of the grade school. By 1984, the negative economic impact on Harney County was estimated at $36 million. During the winter of 1984-85, additional weather-related damage was done when shifting ice on the lakes snapped power poles and smashed houses and barns that had been partially submerged. The flood waters changed the ecology of the Malheur Refuge. Nests of waterfowl and song birds were flooded and many feeding sources, some of which had been established by the refuge staff, were flooded; however, new habitats were created and new species appeared.

Historically, Malheur and Harney Lakes like other lakes in the Great Basin, have periodically fluctuated widely in depth and extent. Wave-cut terraces and other geomorphic features over 200 feet (62 m.) higher than the present level of many of the lakes in Southeastern Oregon are evidence of more pluvial periods. Tree rings in the region are yet another indicator of climatic variations. According to tree ring growth, the periods 1790-92, 1802-25, and 1907-13 were exceptionally wet. It was during the latter period that homesteading of many of the valleys of Southeastern Oregon took place. The smallest growth of tree rings, a good indicator of drought, was in the years 1842-49 (a time when Goose Lake near Lakeview was crossed by immigrant wagons) and in the period 1918-34, when most of the basin lakes were completely dry. University of Oregon geographers Pat Bartlein and Patricia McDowell, in studying Harney Basin, noted ancient shorelines well above and several miles from the 1985 high-water mark. Along these old shorelines were discovered ancient campsites containing fish bones discarded 3,000 years ago by Indians living in the basin.

The first written record of the Harney Lakes was by Peter Skene Ogden of the Hudson's Bay Company. In October 1826 Ogden discovered Harney Lake, which he noted as being a "salt lake." On the last day of October he discovered Malheur Lake. His journal read: "A small ridge of land, an acre in width, divides the fresh water [Malheur Lake], from the salt lakes [Harney Lake]." Ogden estimated Harney Lake to have been 10 miles (16 km.) wide, Malheur Lake one mile (1.6 km.) wide and nine miles (14.4 km.) long. Later, emigrants traveling in wagon trains knew Harney and Malheur Lakes as the "Bitter Lakes."

In November 1931, ownership of parts of the Harney Basin was contested in the Supreme Court case *U.S. v. State of Oregon* at hearings conducted in Burns. At those lengthy hearings well over 100 people, many of them old-timers, testified their recollections of the geographical extent of the lakes and their navigability. If it could be proven that the lakes were navigable in 1859, when Oregon was admitted to the Union, then they were legally state property. Witnesses included D. W. Smyth and Chauncey Cummins (both 87 years old), members of the 1853 emigrant party heading for the Willamette Valley; William Colvig, who had been stationed at Camp Alvord in 1864; and John H. Neal, surveyor of the lakes in 1895. Mr. Neal stated that in 1895, Malheur Lake covered 60,000 acres (24,600 ha.) — two-thirds the 1985 size. Practically every witness spoke of the open waters on Malheur Lake and the fluctuating levels of both lakes.

Some of those testifying had established residence on the dry lake bed as early as 1888 and had lived there continuously except in cases of extreme high water. At that time, the settlers moved out household goods and stock, then returned when the waters had receded. In early 1890 the spring runoff flooded a large area of the Harney Basin, marooning people for weeks. Pioneer stockman William Hanley recounted in court how a sudden spring rise inundated an island near the west shore of Malheur Lake, where he had wintered cattle on the island's tules and grasses. Hanley lost thousands of cattle in the flood.[30] Several old-timers recollected using a boat to travel from Malheur Lake to Harney Lake through the Narrows and Mud Lake in the years 1889-1901.

In late 1931, following many years of drought, Malheur Lake covered a scant 400 acres (164 ha.). The *Burns Times-Herald*, December 12, 1937, stated in an editorial, "Old timers are hoping to again witness snow storms and the filling of the sloughs that lead from the Silvies River and the streams. They'd like to see the Lawen country again flooded and brought back to the production days when hundreds of livestock were pastured then and fed from wild hay out where it is now dry and grown up with sagebrush. And they may

Offices of the Snow Mountain Pine Company at Hines. The company purchased the Edward Hines Lumber Company sawmill in 1983 and extensively modernized the mill. Photo By Charles A. Blakeslee, Bend.

The common egret is a summer visitor to the marshlands and shallow water bodies in the Blitzen Valley. Photo by Charles A. Blakeslee, Bend.

see it again.''

In sum, the Harney Basin lakes have advanced and receded and, in the case of Harney and Mud Lakes, temporarily disappeared entirely. While the floods of the 1980s were the greatest recorded, by paleoclimatological standards they were not significant in extent. That, of course, was no comfort to the affected ranchers and to the Harney County economy.

The plight facing Harney Basin ranches was brought to the attention of public officials at the county, state, and national levels. Harney County officials appealed to the state for assistance. Oregon's governor Vic Atiyeh in 1984 sought emergency funds from the federal government. These were denied because the flooding directly involved so few people. Harney County appealed to Senator Mark Hatfield and U.S. Representative Bob Smith for aid. A study conducted by the Army Corps of Engineers, completed in 1985, indicated that a $45 million canal to drain floodwaters from the Harney Basin could be economically feasible if the value of hydroelectricity — $3 million per year — produced by draining the additional waters into the Malheur River, which feeds the Snake River, was taken into consideration. The plan called for a 17-mile-long (27.2 km.) canal to connect the southeast part of Malheur Lake to the South Fork of the Malheur River, using an ancient drainway that once carried floodwaters from Harney Basin to the Snake River system. This ancient outlet was eventually dammed by volcanic action. Actually, the Malheur Gap Drainage Canal had been proposed early in the twentieth century. The canal would have necessitated removing five million cubic yards of material at a total cost (1916) of $1.25 million. The plan was not considered feasible.

The 1980s concept of a canal was not without opposition. Fish and wildlife biologists were concerned about roach and carp from Malheur Lake escaping into the Malheur River, a quality trout river. Residents and ranchers living along the Malheur River, who experienced their own flooding in the early 1980s, were not enthusiastic about more potential flooding. Alkalinity of the waters from Malheur Lake was a concern expressed by farmers using irrigation water from the Malheur River in the Treasure Valley area around Ontario. Malheur Refuge officials indicated that the level of Malheur Lake should be no lower

than the meander line of 4,093 feet (1,269 m.) — nine feet (2.79 m.) below the 1985 flood mark — to protect the ecology of the refuge. By early 1987, the Corps of Engineers had decided against construction of the canal and was considering an alternate option to purchase the flooded farmland and relocate the railway that runs east of Burns.

The winter of 1986-87 was relatively mild, and snowfall in the Harney Basin watershed was below normal. Indeed, by the spring of 1987, Harney County rancher Buck Taylor, whose land in Sod House Lane had been under water since 1983 and whose ranch had been destroyed by the rising water of Malheur Lake, was further concerned about the economic future. A drought, while not rivaling that of 1976-77, threatened to reduce range grasses used for grazing. Said Taylor, "What will the ASCS (Agricultural Stabilization and Conservation Service) people say when the same people that have been asking for flood relief come in asking for relief from the drought?"

BUCHANAN

Tiny Buchanan! I had sped by it many, many times. Not surprising. It takes longer to say the name than it takes to drive past it! Finally, my curiosity got the better of me, and one day I stopped. The sign outside the store, garage, and gas station proclaimed "Indian Gifts. Free Museum." The museum is a room of modest size packed with antiques, many of the Western Americana type.

Several things immediately attracted my attention. I wondered how a Jackson and Paine piano, manufactured in London sometime between 1780 and 1820, wound up in Harney County. A buffalo skull found in Malheur Lake when it went dry in 1930 was of special interest. Then there were the clocks! Grandfather clocks, mantelpiece chime clocks, wall clocks. I stopped counting at 25 in this one room. "We have 113," said Mavis Oard, owner of the Buchanan store-museum. Then there were antique dolls, windup gramophones, balance scales, Indian basketwork, colored glassware, branding irons — the list would go on and on.

Also of particular interest was the display of different types of barbed wire, arranged by name and manufacturer in chronological order for the period 1874-1895. For example, there was Glidden twisted oval (1874); Crandal zig-zag (1879);

"Downtown" Buchanan. The museum houses many Western Americana antiques. The gift shop includes a large variety of Indian-made handicrafts, some by local Paiute Indians. Photo by Ray Hatton.

Brinkerhoff (1881); in all, 112 different kinds. It seems that following the Desert Land Act (1877) there was a tremendous demand for barbed wire — "the Devil's rope" or "thorny fence," as it was called. Although hundreds of patents were taken out, only 300-400 manufacturers, making 750 brands of barbed wire, were successful. Today, collectors of barbed wire (the International Barbed Wire Collectors Association, based in Ponder, Texas, is 10,000 strong) hunt, sell, buy, and trade "cuts" (18-inch lengths) of barbed wire. Prices for old-style barbed wire range from $75 to $5,000 a cut. And I always thought that barbed wire was, well, barbed wire.

I signed the guest book in the museum room, then flipped back to look at previous entries. There were names from all over the United States plus several from European countries. "Yes," said Mavis, "we get visitors from all over the world." Mavis, whose great-grandparents, the Dunns, settled in Harney County in 1872, provided me with a little background on Buchanan. Buchanan was an old stagecoach stop; some of the old buildings are behind the store. The Buchanan post office, named after Hattie E. Buchanan, established in 1911 and operated for eight years. A store at the site of the existing one was built in 1932 but burned down in the 1940s. The present store was built in 1948 and has been added on to several times since.

Mavis gave me a tour of the Indian handicraft section. "We have the largest Indian cradleboard collection I know of." The beautifully-crafted cradleboards, constructed with willow, handmade leather, and beadwork and made by Paiute Indians of nearby Burns, sell for $500 to $1,000. The Indian section also included turquoise jewel-ry, agates of all kinds, woodcarvings, arrowheads, blankets, and rugs. "This one," said Mavis, proudly spreading a beautiful 110-by-60-inch (279-by-152 cm.) handwoven Navajo rug across the floor, "won a blue ribbon [still attached] at the Intertribal Indian Ceremonial at Gallup, New Mexico. It sells for $9,000." The Indian sand paintings were impressive for their artistic beauty and meaning; sand paintings, using five sacred colors, are done in a precise manner by the *hatathli* (medicine man) to remove sicknesses from patients.

There was more! However, nearly two hours had slipped by, and now time was pressing. Outside, dark storm clouds had obscured the hot desert sun of earlier. Wind gusts swept across the flat Harney Basin and buffeted the rimrocks abutting the scattering of buildings that make up Buchanan. Cars and trucks zipped by on Highway 20, heading west to Burns or east towards Vale. I doubt that those motorists even notice the sign, "Free Museum. Indian Gifts."

FRENCHGLEN

Frenchglen, backed against the eastern scarp of Jackass ("Jack") Mountain at the upper end of the Blitzen Valley, is a little oasis, bustling with activity during summer and early fall, quiet and peaceful during the long cold winter months. In summer, tall poplars and patches of grass bring greenery to an otherwise yellow and brown landscape. The tiny community consists of a handful of residences, a one-room school, the

Diamond Hotel (circa 1910). Diamond is now a small quiet community on Kiger Creek. However, around 1900, Diamond was a lively settlement with a post office, merchandise store and hotel. The hotel, constructed about 1898, provided lodging, meals, and a social gathering place. In 1919, meals were 25 cents; rooms $1 a night. In later years the hotel was used as a residence. Diamond Hotel was remodeled in the late 1980s. Photo Courtesy of Marcus Haines, Burns.

A new day begins at Malheur Lake. Wisps of fog hover over the tranquil waters. Cattail (foreground) is an emergent plant and, along with other emergent vegetation, provides nesting areas for egrets, cormorants and herons. Photo by Charles A. Blakeslee, Bend.

The Harney Basin flood in the 1980s covered 170,000 acres (69,700 ha.) of land, reducing the assessed value of Harney County by $12 million. In 1983 the water in the Harney lakes stood at 4,102 feet (1,272 m.), compared to the meander line (average line in late 1800s) of 4,093 feet (1,269 m.). The flood had far-reaching impact on many Harney County ranchers. Photo by Marcus Haines, Burns.

The Malheur Lake flood in the early 1980s encroached on the headquarters of the Malheur National Wildlife Refuge. Direct access to the headquarters from the west past the Sod House Springs Ranch was severed by the flood. Photo by Marcus Haines, Burns.

The Frenchglen Hotel, which is usually open from March to November, provides accommodations and meals. During the summer and early fall months, reservations for rooms and dinners are usually necessary. Breakfasts and dinners are family style. Photo by Ray Hatton.

well-known Frenchglen Hotel, and a store that includes a post office and gas station. Travelers destined for the Catlow Valley and beyond can find gasoline and provisions at the mercantile store. The eight-room historical hotel is a focal point for those wishing to explore the southern end of the Malheur Wildlife Refuge or, in summer, Steens Mountain. The nearest town to Frenchglen is Burns 60 miles (96 km.) to the north. Limited motel facilities are at Fields in the Alvord Basin, 52 miles (83 km.) south of Frenchglen.

The *Burns Times-Herald*, June 26, 1920, reported the erection of "a fine little hotel at the P Ranch hill." The hotel was used as a stopping place by wagon trains heading to and from the Catlow Valley and by those who had business at the P Ranch, headquarters for the Eastern Oregon Livestock Company. The hotel was sold in 1935 to the U.S. Bureau of Sports, Fisheries, and Wildlife as part of the P Ranch holdings, then leased to individuals. The Frenchglen Hotel was enlarged and interior improvements — a heating plant, running water, and bath facilities — were made in 1937. In October 1972, title of the hotel was deeded to the Oregon Highway Department. The hotel reopened for business in June 1976, with Malena Konek, Manager. In 1985, Judy and Terry Santillie assumed management of the Frenchglen Hotel. During much of the summer and early fall, reservations for rooms and dinner are almost a must.

During the 1930s, the Fourth of July celebrations at Frenchglen brought people from near and far, including the Crane and Diamond country. Hundreds attended the celebrations to watch bronco riding and baseball competition during the day and to dance to the music of the Frenchglen orchestra, led by Marcus Haines. By 1933, as many as 21 students attended the Frenchglen school, reflecting the greater population in the area than at present.

The store and post office at Frenchglen were established in 1924. Jess Bradeen moved his store from Blitzen in the Catlow Valley and brother Robert operated the post office in Frenchglen until 1946. The Frenchglen store, or mercantile as it is known, has just about everything anyone could request — and more! In one nook is the post office. It looks very official, with some two dozen slots for mail pickup. There are the usual "Wanted by the F.B.I." posters tacked on the

wall. The store merchandise includes a well-stocked food section, a variety of hardware, scenic post cards, books on Southeastern Oregon, pickles, candy, handwoven Indian blankets, sheepskin rugs, a cooler with (at last count) 11 kinds of beer and—-whew! much more. Perhaps more interesting, but not for sale, is the assortment of collectibles, some Western antiques, old bottles in one-gallon sizes (empty!) of Early Times Kentucky Straight Whiskey, Platte Valley Straight Corn Whiskey, different kinds of old boots, kettles, pans, harnesses, lanterns and, again, much more.

Where the Blitzen tumbles out of the foothills of the Steens, just east of Frenchglen, the river is diverted into the West Canal and the East Canal. The canals were dug by Bill Hanley to drain and reclaim the swamp lands in the upper Blitzen Valley. The dredger he used to dig the canal was hauled in pieces by mule teams from the railhead at Winnemucca, Nevada. After assembly, the machine was fueled by cords of juniper cut on nearby Jackass Mountain. Bill Hanley recollected that when the dredger was near the base of Jackass Mountain, it would scoop up arrow points, indicating that the area was used extensively by Indians to hunt birds in the swamp lands.

Drainage of the swamp lands was completed in 1913. Between 1935 and 1942 Civilian Conservation Corps workers, stationed at the Five Mile CCC Camp north of Frenchglen, made improvements to irrigation ditches, fences, and culverts, planted trees, and remodeled the P Ranch White House and the Frenchglen Hotel.

Those seeking campsites in the Upper Blitzen Valley can use the BLM Page Springs Campground or camp at Steens Mountain Resort, located on the Steens Mountain Loop road, three miles (5 km.) from Frenchglen. While the Page Springs facilities are sparse, the Steens Mountain Resort (Camper Corral) offers hookups for trailers, trailers for rent, and has laundry and shower facilities. A small store at the resort sells ice, groceries, and a selection of books on Southeastern Oregon. The campground site and meadow to the west were originally homesteaded by Fred Brown. In 1950, Jack and Catherine Fine purchased the land and established a cattle ranch. Jim and Marilyn Taylor took over ownership in 1979 and developed the campground.

An old windmill, wagon and stock pond are reminders of the ranching activities on the Brown Ranch, which later became the Fine Ranch (near Frenchglen). The ranch property is now part of the Camper Corral Campground that includes campsites, hookups, laundry, showers, and a small store. In the background are the Upper Blitzen Valley and "Jack" Mountain. Photo by Ray Hatton.

P RANCH

Tall poplars, planted by Peter French in the 1870s, and a 100-foot (31 m.) lookout tower, built by Civilian Conservation Corps workers in the 1930s identify the site of the historic P Ranch. Although it is part of the Malheur National Wildlife Refuge, to historians the P Ranch is synonymous with the legends of Peter French. However, tangible evidences of French's ranch headquarters are rather scant. The 150-by-50-foot (46-by-16 m.) weather-worn long barn, built with native materials in the 1880s, is the only original Peter French building that remains intact. It was here that buckaroos fed horses, and where stock wandered in to feed. Also remaining is the large, square-shaped beef wheel, once used to hang beef.

Gone is the pine-board store that French had built in 1876. Supplies such as clothing, footwear, tobacco, and dry goods were hauled in from Canyon City or Fort Bidwell and sold to Peter French's employees and neighboring settlers. In the 1920s the store was dismantled and moved to Frenchglen, where it is now the main part of the mercantile store. Gone are the harness shop, meathouse, machine shed, and round barn. The bunkhouse, cookhouse, and blacksmith's shop are no longer standing, although as late as the 1970s the old brick-and-cement forge remained, near what is now the Center Patrol Road. Altogether, the P Ranch complex consisted of 21 buildings. Fire consumed some of them; others were torn down as they deteriorated. Part of the old bunkhouse was moved to the Roaring Springs Ranch.

It was in 1872 that Peter French (christened John William French), working for Dr. Hugh J. Glenn of northern California, drove 1,000 cattle into Oregon with a half dozen vaqueros and a Chinese cook. The tall green grasses in the southern end of the Blitzen Valley attracted French. A prospector named Porter, discouraged by the lack of gold in the Blitzen Valley, gladly sold his dozen cattle to French, along with a branding iron giving French ownership of any cattle branded "P". In the late 1870s Peter

The Peter French Round Barn was constructed around 1880. The barn, which is 100 feet (31 m.) in diameter, was part of French's vast cattle empire. It was donated to the Oregon Historical Society in the late 1960s by T. E. and R. J. Jenkins. The barn is a major historical landmark in Harney County. Photo by Marcus Haines, Burns.

The White House at the P Ranch. Following Peter French's death, John South and later Bill Hanley reconstructed Peter French's single-story house into an imposing 22-foot (6.8 m.) by 84-foot (26 m.) house that was used for entertaining important visitors. The White House was destroyed by fire in 1948. Photo courtesy of Marcus Haines.

Buckaroos drive cattle across the sage-studded High Desert country. The word "buckaroo" is derived from the Spanish word "Vaquero" — cattlemen who drove cattle into Southeastern Oregon in the late 1800s. Buckaroos are noted for their horsemanship, roping skills, fine silver work (bits, spurs) and clothing as shown in the Maynard Dixon drawing in this volume. Photo by Stuart G. Garrett, M.D., Bend.

French established his residence by the Blitzen River, near where it enters the flat Blitzen Valley. French lived in a modest one-story structure. Here French kept records of his cattle transactions, and devised engineering plans for irrigation and drainage of the upper Blitzen Valley.

Over the years, French amassed quite a cattle empire. Although drought in the late 1880s and a severe winter 1889-90 killed approximately half of the cattle in Harney County, French survived the hard years with wise management, skilled buckaroos, able ranch hands, and a storage of feed.

French purchased land from settlers in several different valleys, including the Diamond and Happy Valleys. At one time, French had over a dozen outlying ranches in five large divisions: P Ranch, Catlow Valley, Diamond, Happy Valley, and Sod House Divisions. French acquired 1,409,000 acres (57,400 ha.) of deeded land and, in addition, used vast acreages of public domain. Here French ran 45,000 cattle and 3,000 horses. Cattle were first driven to Winnemucca, Nevada, a three-to- six weeks drive, then shipped by rail to San Francisco. After the railroad reached Ontario

The Frenchglen Mercantile offers motorists and local residents a wide array of goods. The store includes a post office and is the only retailer of gasoline between Burns and Fields, a distance of 110 miles (176 km.). Photo by Charles A. Blakeslee, Bend.

(1903), the cattle were then driven to that eastern Oregon city. French employed hundreds of men. Then on December 26, 1897, following an altercation, Peter French was murdered by Ed Oliver, a Harney County settler. Following French's death, French's successor at the P Ranch, John South, and, later yet, Bill Hanley each added a wing to Peter French's house. The large house that graced the meadows just south of Blitzen River became known as the White House.

In 1905, the French-Glenn holdings were subsequently sold to the Blitzen Valley Land Co. who, under the management of Bill Hanley, not only maintained the work of the P Ranch but developed the water resources of the Blitzen Valley by dredging canals, building dikes, and draining the marshlands. Hanley, who used the Bell A Ranch (Burns) as a home base, had a new wing added to the White House. Here he entertained important visitors to the P Ranch. In 1916, the Blitzen Valley Land Co. was reorganized and the properties then came under the management of the Eastern Oregon Livestock Co., with the Swift meat packing company the major shareholder. From then until 1935, when the U. S. government purchased the ranch for $675,000, the P Ranch operations alternately declined and prospered. The sale to the U. S. government was noted with some regret by many Harney County residents, fearing a sizeable loss to their tax base.

Following the sale, CCC workers remodeled the White House, and it was then used as a residence for refuge biologists and maintenance people. On August 10, 1947, fire destroyed the White House. Today, the stone-and-cement foundation of the original house and its additions marks where they stood. The only vertical structure left standing from the fire is the vine-covered brick chimney. Despite the loss of many buildings, visitors to the P Ranch can, with imagination, turn the clock back a century or more and "see" buckaroos saddling their horses. Freight wagons arrive with lumber, machinery, or supplies. In the blacksmith's shop, the smithy is busily repairing wagon wheel rims or fashioning branding irons. The towering Lombardy and Norwegian poplars planted for shade and as windbreaks by Peter French in the 1870s have witnessed the fascinating history of the P Ranch.

WILD RANGE-HORSES IN THE CORRAL

Illustrations by Maynard Dixon following a horseback trip to Harney County in 1901. Dixon reflects the image of the buckaroos who worked for the big cattle ranches in Southeastern Oregon. Each spring several hundred wild horses were caught, broken, and used for cattle operations. Buckaroos shown here used California style saddles, riatas (braided rawhide ropes), angora chaps, leather cuffs, quirts (short whips) and fine silverwork (silver bits and spurs). Corrals were built of juniper wood. From the collection of the High Desert Museum, Bend.

Steens Mountain

Frenchglen is the most commonly used gateway to the Steens. From this small hamlet Steens Mountain looks unimpressive and belies its 9,670 feet (2,998 m.) elevation. The western slopes of the Steens rise in what looks like a series of gently-tilted grassy slopes. The highest ridges are, however, 20 miles (32 km.) east of Frenchglen and 4,500 feet (1,355 m.) higher.

Steens Mountain was named after Major Enoch Steen, lst U.S. Dragoons, who was sent to the area in 1860 to determine the feasibility of routes from the Willamette Valley to Southeastern Oregon. Steen's historical fame came from his pursuit of Paiute Indians up the Donner and Blitzen River to the summit of the mountain and down the rough Wildhorse Canyon to the Alvord country. As if that were not enough, Steen continued the chase south into Nevada, only to lose track of the Paiutes near Disaster Peak. It would seem logical that the mountain be correctly termed Steen's Mountain. However, through common usage, the accepted name of the mountain is "Steens."

Perhaps the first white man to describe the

HARPER'S WEEKLY

NEW YORK, MARCH 22, 1902

THE TRIALS OF A "BRONCO-BUSTER"

ing of the mustang, or bronco, while not without danger, is generally attended with considerable fun, for the spectators at st. The animal's fore legs are strapped together, and the lariat around his neck is used as an additional means of coercion. The term "bronco-busting" is plains vernacular for horse-breaking, which is particularly active just now, for the mustangs are being trained for sale in the Eastern markets as polo-ponies

HARPER'S WEEKLY

NEW YORK, APRIL 19, 1902

"STAY WITH HIM! STAY WITH HIM!"

Whorehouse Meadows on the Steens Mountain Loop. The area was a camp area for sheepherders in the days when many bands of sheep grazed the Steens. What was once a shallow lake has, over the years, been filled in. A variety of plant life now occupies the site. Photo by Charles A. Blakeslee, Bend.

An early summer view looking up the length of Big Indian Gorge. The Steens Mountain Loop enables motorists to see the spectacular glaciated gorges on the Steens. Many backpackers and hikers explore the less accessible areas of Steens Mountain, seeking their favorite places. Photo by Charles A. Blakeslee, Bend.

Steens was John Work, trapper for the Hudson's Bay Company who, in his journal June 29, 1831, wrote, "We crossed a valley [Alvord Basin], part of which had the appearance of a bed of a lake, but is quite dry, and encamped near the foot of a mountain covered with snow." (Steens Mountain was at one time known as Snow Mountains).

Steens Mountain has special meanings to different people. It attracts hunters of upland birds including sage grouse, quail, and chukars. Big game hunters stalk deer, antelope and, by special permit, bighorn sheep. Fish Lake, located high on the western slope of the mountain, is a popular spot for anglers and campers. Geology students use the Steens for a variety of field studies of faulting, volcanism, and alpine glaciation. However, most of the summer visitors are attracted to the mountain for sightseeing, photo-

graphy, and hiking. Formerly, the Steens was used (more correctly, overused) by thousands of sheep for summer grazing pastures. Early in the twentieth century as many as 180,000 sheep grazed 450 square miles (1,170 km²) of Steens during the summer months.

Ecologically, Steens Mountain is unique. In his research on the Steens (1956), Charles G. Hansen identified 506 different species of plants and 591 species of animals, including 484 mammals and 43 reptiles. Ecological zones on the western slope of the Steens are readily discernible to those ascending the Steens Loop road. The tall sagebrush belt at elevations of 4,200-5,500 feet (1,302-1,705 m.) gives way to a zone of western juniper. Between 6,500 and 8,000 feet (2,015-2,480 m.), clusters of aspens occupy areas where more moisture is available. It is these aspen groves that in early fall

Lily Lake is a small, shallow lake near the Steens Mountain Loop. As the lake shrivels in size and depth, a succession of plants (water lilies, rushes, willows, different species of grasses and in the background, aspen) invade the area. Photo by Charles A. Blakeslee, Bend.

turn shades of yellow and orange, bringing late season visitors and photographers to the mountain. Above 8,000 feet (2,480 m.), in the subalpine zone, bunchgrasses once prevailed, but excessive grazing by sheep has exposed bare soil. The summit area of the Steens is subjected to high winds, which reduce the accumulation of snow. Less protected soils dry out more rapidly and become vulnerable to wind erosion. With a very brief growing season, revegetation is extremely slow. Any illegal vehicular use compounds the problem, and vehicles are restricted to the Steens Loop road.

The changing of the seasons on the Steens depends on elevation and exposure to sun or shade. Wild flowers such as clarkia, white

wyethia, blue camas, yellow evening primrose, and wild phlox may bloom among the sage during the late spring while upper zones on the mountain are still buried by snow. In late August, after the snows have melted from upper meadows, alpine wild flowers show their colors, especially where small creeks are spring-fed or are fed from melting snows. It is the changing seasonal landscapes on the Steens that bring back visitors time and time again.

Late spring and early fall snows are not uncommon on the Steens, and snowfalls of a foot or more at the elevation of Fish Lake in late May and early June, or in mid-September may stop travel on the mountain. In summer, when humid subtropical air sweeps up from the south, the massive mountain can trigger violent thunderstorms.

Cultural landscapes on the Steens are few and widely scattered. Old homestead cabins, mostly on private lands, are tucked away in aspen groves or in valleys. On the eastern slopes of the Steens are small mining ventures. The focal point for many visitors to the Steens is Fish Lake, by the Steens Loop road at an elevation of 7,371 feet (2,285 m.). The lake has attracted anglers since the 1920s. In August 1927, the *Burns Times-Herald* reported on fishing excursions to Eldon Johnson's homestead at Fish Lake, with successful anglers snagging 22-to-30-inch Eastern brook trout.

Cabins were constructed at Fish Lake in 1928, and resort owner Charles Johnson rented boats and sold merchandise. During World War II, gasoline rationing greatly curtailed recreational use at the Fish Lake Resort. In an effort to sell war bonds in August 1942, Steens Mountain sheepmen sponsored a lamb barbecue at Fish Lake. Over 200 people participated in the event. A speedily-built stage was used for dancing. The orchestra was a piano that was hauled up the mountain from the Frenchglen school. In 1956 the Fish Lake Resort was sold for $20,000 to the Oregon State Game Commission.

One of Oregon's highest flower gardens was cultivated by Mrs. Glenn Brown who, according to the *Burns Times-Herald*, August 15, 1941, raised gladioli, irises, rambler roses, pink oriental poppies, and pansies at her summer cabin located north of Fish Lake, near 9,000 feet (2,790 m.) in elevation.

Historically, the Steens has been synonymous with the sheep industry. For many years, thousands of sheep grazed the upland meadows. The sheepherder's life was a lonely existence. Bert Huffman, writing for the *East Oregonian* (reprinted in *The Burns Times-Herald*, August 8, 1908), reported that after coming across a sheepherder's tent, "my heart went out in sympathy for him in his alleged loneliness." Huffman visited the sheepherder's camp that evening and then changed his mind:

"In the corner of his tent was a good phonograph and near it several choice records. For my delight he rendered two or three choice selections from Patti, Caruso, Schumann-Heink and other singers, a speech by Bryan, a vaudeville selection and an act from Shakespeare's *Julius Caesar*.

"Under the head of his bed were half a dozen of the best late magazines (some of which I had not found time to read) and at the foot of the bed lay well-thumbed copies of the latest novels.

"I looked at this bronzed son of the hills in genuine envy. Here he may read, write, think, commune with nature or be carried to the great conservatories of the artists, while the driven slaves of the city must bend over a desk day and night to meet the tariffed competition of this soulless commercial age."

Between 1923 and 1926, supplies for the sheepherders were purchased from a supply camp named Somerage, and later from the store at Frenchglen. Sheep that wintered in the Alvord Basin were driven up the steep eastern flank of the Steens to summer pastures, a four-day trek for the 5,000-foot (1,550 m.) climb over a four-mile (6.5 km.) distance. Leaving the sheep with the herders, the foremen traveled down the western slope and around the mountain to the Alvord, 115 miles (185 km.) in less than a day. In 1936, which was ironically the best grazing year in ages, the Taylor Grazing Act forced many sheepherders to leave the Steens, with the loss of business hurting Frenchglen. What was Frenchglen's loss was Steens Mountain's gain. John Scharff, long-time superintendent of the Malheur Wildlife Refuge, described the impact of grazing on the Steens and of the recovery of the vegetation:

"I first saw the mountain [Steens] in 1935, and at that time there were thousands of acres of rock showing that are now covered with a stand of grass. After the Taylor Act became law there was a marked reduction in the number of sheep, cattle and horses that grazed on the Steens. The *big* thing that helped the mountain was the P Ranch being sold to the Refuge, which made a substantial reduction of some 60,000 AUMs (animal units per month), mostly being on some part of the mountain from Long Hollow to Diamond Valley."

John observed and reported that within three years, in both a controlled plot and elsewhere, vegetation of different types returned to the Steens. John added, "It has been my experience that a range can be brought back with limited grazing faster than with no grazing."

The completion of the Steens Mountain Loop has had tremendous impact on the mountain in terms of recreational use. The road from

The start of the race at Jackman Park is at an elevation of 7,835 feet (2,429 m.) Nothing like a little hill to test the lungs early!

The Steens Mountain Chris Miller Memorial Run. This is an annual 10 km (6.2 miles) race held in conjunction with the Steens Mountain Days at Frenchglen in August. Chris Miller, who lost his life in a hunting accident, had been an avid runner and participant in the race. The race is undoubtedly the highest ''road'' race in Oregon.

The scenery along the race route is spectacular. If only one had energy to look at it!

The rewards! Runners admire the view from the rim of the Kiger Gorge.

Photos by Ruth Miller, Burns.

The finish. Nick Miller (8 years old) of Hines seems unperturbed by the altitude of 9,700 feet (3,007 m.).

Yellow aspens and a light covering of a mid-September snowfall signal the end of summer on the Steens. A view of Big Indian Gorge, one of the glaciated valleys on Steens Mountain. Photo by Ray Hatton.

Frenchglen to Fish Lake had already been built by Civilian Conservation Corps workers in the 1930s. In the summer of 1941, civic leaders were looking forward to construction of an eight-mile (13 km.) road to the summit. The *Burns Times-Herald*, August 15, 1941, headlined the story "Tourist Lure Seen In New Steens Road."

The onset of World War II delayed plans for the Steens Loop road. It was not until the early 1960s that the road was completed. The graded road climbs the gentle western slopes and comes within a half mile of the spectacular Kiger Gorge. A bumpy side road, sign posted, leads to the gorge overlook, elevation 8,800 feet (2,728 m.). What a view! The ground drops almost vertically 1,200 feet (372 m.) to the valley floor. Kiger Creek, which originates as a spring halfway up the gorge wall, meanders northward towards the Diamond Valley. The dark ribs of Steens Mountain, layer after layer of uplifted basaltic lava flows, contrast sharply with the deep green carpeted floor of the U-shaped valley. The Kiger Gorge is one of the most photographed spots on the Steens. Its valley is a textbook example of alpine glaciation.

The road then clings tenaciously to the narrow divide that separates the steep eastern flank and the head of glaciated Little Blitzen Gorge before descending the divide between Big Indian and Little Blitzen Gorges. From there, the road drops sharply to the High Desert country around the Blitzen Crossing. Environmentalists contend that

Opposite:

Kiger Gorge is a valley carved by glaciers on Steens Mountain. During cooler and wetter climatic periods of the Pleistocene, glaciers were extensive in the High Cascades, but rare in Southeastern Oregon. Steens Mountain is one of the few mountain areas in southeastern Oregon that is high enough to have supported glaciers. The valley glacier here flowed northwestward toward the valley of the Donner and Blitzen River. The valley has the classic U-shape of a glacial trough. The Steens basalt of Late Miocene age is exposed in the high sides of the gorge. Rock slides have scoured the steep walls. Photo by Charles A. Blakeslee, Bend.

THE KIGERS

It was in 1874 that the Kigers, Reuben Christopher (known as R.C.) and Minerva Jane (known as Dolly), who had been married in Corvallis, November 18, 1866, moved from the Willamette Valley to establish a cattle ranch in Harney County. Following a severe winter in which the Kigers were nearly starved out, R.C. investigated a gap in the Steens Mountain, "an entrance a quarter of a mile wide with high cliffs on either side — a deep valley, shaped like a huge cupped hand. In its palm meandered a willow-fringed creek while fertile grazing land curved upwards like fringes to high rimrocks that arose straight up hundreds of feet into the sky."[31]

The Kigers moved their stock and built a cabin near a silver stream, which Dolly named Kiger Creek. Naturally, the gorge was called Kiger Gorge. During the four years that the Kigers lived in the gorge, two children, John and Dick, were born (a third son was later born at Fort Harney). There were always dangers. Rattlesnakes crawled down from the rimrock where they holed up in the winter months, and "the valley was alive with them." Then there were the Indians, sometimes entering the cabin but usually standing or crouching at the cabin door, "their black beady eyes following Dolly's every move."

R.C. made the acquaintance of Peter French, the Blitzen Valley cattle baron. Neighbors to the Kigers were the Smyths, Riddles, and McCoys, who had settled on other creeks that flowed northward from the Steens.

Indians "on the warpath" forced the settlers to flee to Fort Harney for safety and protection as the Indians raided, plundered, and killed throughout the region. Although peace was restored to Harney County, Dolly's plea to return to the Willamette Valley was heeded by R.C. In 1878, the Kigers sold their land and cattle to Peter French for $80,000. Before leaving for the last time, R.C. "traversed every familiar trail, looked nostalgically at the high bunch grass. Lolling cattle raised their heads, gold-tinged horses raced from the lacy shade of the willows, their manes waving a farewell." Dolly never returned to the Kiger Gorge from Fort Harney. Reuben Kiger died in 1907, his wife in Corvallis in 1928.

---

the fragile alpine environment suffers from overuse, and such a road invites destruction of the wilderness experience. Advocates of the Steens Mountain Loop claim that it enables the young, old, and handicapped a chance to enjoy the magnificent panorama from the summit area, over 9,000 feet (2,790 m.) in elevation.

The abruptness of the eastern slopes of the Steens markedly contrasts with the relatively gentle western slopes. To be sure, the U-shaped valleys of the western side, Kiger and Little Blitzen, Big Indian and Little Indian, are spectacular sights. However, the intricate detailing of the eastern scarp face is equally fascinating. Half a dozen serrated ridges at right angles to the mountain mass seem to form buttresses to the escarpment as if to help support it. In swales, pockets of soil cling to the precipitous face, and where moisture is available, patches of bright green stand out against the black and gray

basaltic walls. Water tumbling hundreds of feet down the steep slopes has carved deep V-shaped canyons. Far, far below, the waters have discharged their cargo of rocks and silt onto the desert edge.

The Alvord Ranch complex 5,000 feet (1,550 m.) below, as seen from the summit of the Steens, appears like a miniature oasis of green, its buildings hidden amid clumps of trees. Beyond the snow-white alkali of the Alvord Desert and the shrinking waters of Alvord Lake, barren inhospitable mountains such as the Sheepsheads stretch to the eastern horizon. The valley to the north of the Alvord Basin cradles four lakes, Mann, Tudor, Juniper, and Ten Cent. Cultural impact on the desert is evidenced by swatches of green where sprinklers irrigate the parched soils, but it is not difficult to visualize the days when cavalry pursued Indians in the Alvord and stockmen trekked their cattle to distant markets.

Catlow Valley

From Dick and Pat Raney's living room picture window at the historic Roaring Springs Ranch, the view extends westward across the flat Catlow Valley. In the distance the gentle slopes of Hart Mountain and Poker Jim Ridge mark the horizon. To the southwest, Beatys Butte rises more than 3,000 feet (900 m.) above the valley floor, its pyramidal shape indicating origin as an ancient volcano. Pat surveys the landscape and turns: "I love this view, the open spaces, the beautiful sunsets and especially the springs when everything is green."[32]

The Catlow Valley, or Catlow Basin as geologists would prefer it be called, is a flat expanse of land some 30 miles (48 km.) long and 10-15 miles (16-24 km.) wide. Catlow Rim, a fault scarp rising as much as 1,500 feet (465 m.) over the valley, borders the eastern margins. In other directions the valley merges with gentle juniper-studded slopes. Rock Creek, an intermittent flowing stream, winds its way northeast from Hart Mountain. However, most of the drainage into Catlow Valley is from the east, off the southern block of the Steens. A number of relatively short creeks such as Three Mile Creek and Home Creek (both of which lend their names to ranches located on the creeks) cut steep-walled canyons into the sharp western edge of Catlow Rim. Conspicuous wave-cut terraces along the lower slopes of Catlow Rim indicate that the valley was once occupied by an extensive body of water. Small sand dunes along the east side of the valley date from the time when the waters of Pleistocene Lake Catlow shaped beaches from sediments on its shore. Evidence of Indian occupancy in the Catlow Valley was found by University of Oregon anthropologist Luther S. Cressman, who excavated the floor of the Roaring Springs Cave in the 1930s. Among other things, Cressman's crew unearthed mats woven from sagebrush, an arrowhead shaft (atlatl) with feathers still in it, and human remains, all of which helped Cressman reconstruct Indian lifestyles along the shores of Lake Catlow.

Catlow Valley was named by the Shirk family, one of the pioneer cattle families in the valley, after John Catlow, an Englishman who settled in the Alvord Basin but who ran cattle in the valley

Aerial view of the Catlow Rim, a fault scarp that marks the western edge of the Steens. At one time, Catlow Valley was a large expanse of water. Old shorelines are evident from the Frenchglen-Fields road that parallels the base of Catlow Rim. Photo by Tim Townsend, Eugene.

that bears his name. Describing the Catlow Valley when he first filed a claim on Home Creek in 1876, David Shirk wrote, "It was then as now one of the most beautiful valleys in Southeastern Oregon. Bunch grass was waving over the broad stretches like a grain field." Early in the twentieth century only five cattle ranches dotted the entire valley. Surface water was used to irrigate hay pastures.

Following the 1909 Homestead Act, settlers flocked to the Catlow Valley, and within the space of a few years a number of small settlements became established. In the spring of 1913 newly-arrived settlers to the Catlow Valley established the community known as Ragtown, so named because homesteaders, lacking nearby lumber, fastened tents over pits dug seven or eight feet into the earth. Within a year Catlow Valley boasted three schools, and optimism for successful crops ran high. By late 1914 the population of Catlow Valley had grown to 500. The *Burns Times-Herald*, December 5, 1914, reported that the entire valley was thickly populated "with all sorts of habitations — tents, cabins, houses and stores from Clover Swale in the north to Skull Creek to the south, although lumber had to be hauled 80-100 miles and rock seven to fifteen miles."

In January 1914, the Beckley post office was receiving 1,000 pounds (746 kg.) of mail per week. By spring that year, with a high demand for seeds for planting, mail delivery increased to 5,000 pounds (3,732 kg.) per week. For a few years Catlow Valley hummed with activity. Community events such as socials, baseball games, and dances were common. The Fourth of July

Early fall is a special time on the Steens. Usually by late September or early October, leaves on quaking aspen turn fluorescent shades of yellow or orange. Trees that change color at the same time come from the same root system. Exposure to sun, wind, rain and elevation make a difference when the leaves on separate groves of aspens change color. Photo by Stuart G. Garrett, M.D., Bend.

Opposite:
Summer thunderstorm moves over the southern end of the Steens and Alvord Basin. Wildhorse Lake occupies a glacial cirque just south of the highest point on the Steens. Photo by Charles A. Blakeslee, Bend.

The Steens takes on a different mood and personality during the winter months. Despite big snowfalls, south-facing slopes lose their snow much more rapidly than the north-facing slopes. Hart Mountain and Poker Jim Ridge show on the horizon. Photo by Marcus Haines, Burns.

Homesteads!   HOMESTEADS!   Homesteads!

·-. BEAUTIFUL CATLOW VALLEY .-·

100,000 acres of choice sage brush land in one of the greatest valleys in Eastern Oregon. We start excursions to settle this rich valley on April 1, 1910. We can settle 500 families on choice rich land. It will all be gone by Sept. 1, 1910. Will you join us?

Address Southern Oregon Realty Co., Lakeview, Oregon.

Advertisement in the *Lake County Examiner*, March 3, 1910, regarding the opening for homestead entry lands in the Catlow Valley. Such ads were typical of the promotion of desert lands in Southeastern Oregon between 1910 and 1915.

celebrations in 1914 attracted 400 people to the Three Mile Ranch where, following foot races and a baseball game, dancing continued to 5 A.M. At one time seven schools operated in the Catlow Valley including a branch of the Harney County High School, offering courses in agriculture and domestic science.

Within a few years drought, which plagued the entire High Desert, left its mark on the Catlow Valley. One homesteader, F.C. Kelley, was quoted in the *Burns Times-Herald*, November 8, 1919: "To depend upon the elements alone to furnish necessary moisture to make crops grow is too much of a gamble. The past few seasons have been so dry that many [of the homesteaders] have become discouraged and have left for other parts where they find employment. They would like to return to their homesteads and be independent but the moisture is not dependable." By 1920 the census report for North and South Catlow Valley showed only 178 people.

Two years later Stanley G. Power, who conducted a biological survey of Catlow Valley, wrote in the *Portland Telegram*, August 25, 1922, "The faith of the settlers, believing water must come to break the death grip of dryness, is almost pitiful. Only 50 settlers and two post offices remain. Blitzen, the biggest town, has four families and a general store-post office. Relics of the brief age of prosperity are to be seen through the whole length of the valley — abandoned buildings, some of considerable size, deserted houses, and rusting implements. Artesian water is the only remedy. The land is fertile when irrigated and wonderful

crops can be grown. Water for drinking is hauled 10-20 miles."

By the 1920s all of the settlements except Blitzen had been abandoned. Blitzen lingered as the "capital of the Catlow Valley", serving sheepherders, stockmen and summer tourists. In the summer of 1928 a motorist described his stop at Blitzen, then population 12: "We spent the night at the Blitzen Hotel, operated by Mr. and Mrs. Duval. The charge for dinner, breakfast and bed was $1.50, the most reasonable rate your auto editor discovered in all of his travels in Oregon." The Duvals also operated the post office and general store in Blitzen.

By 1930 enrollment at the school at Blitzen was seven; by 1933 it dropped to one. Those who stayed had faith that the dry spell would end. For example, when deep snows covered the valley in February 1932, the report from the Catlow Valley was not a complaint on the isolation caused by the snows but enthusiasm for summer crops and ranges. The Catlow Valley correspondent to the *Burns Times-Herald* often noted the floral beauty of the Catlow Valley and the magnificent sunsets — "colors of crimson, purples, mauves, reds, and blues with golden lighting." One report in 1938 noted that the valley was "looking beautiful with waving fields of wheat, oats, and rye."

At its height, Blitzen had two stores, a hotel, a saloon, and a school; an official U.S. weather station was operated at Blitzen from 1914 to 1933. The store at Blitzen closed in November 1942. Today the skeletal remains of the town line the main street, now bypassed, since the north-south highway through the valley hugs the base of Catlow Rim.

One September evening I visited Blitzen. Ominous clouds gathered over Beatys Butte to the south. To the west a broken cloud cover gave a hint of a spectacular sunset to come. The decaying buildings were hauntingly silhouetted against the darkening southern horizon. Loose boards rattled in the desert wind. I lingered alone in the quiet of the evening, absorbing the unseen energy and mystique of the desert. It was not difficult to imagine Blitzen in its days of glory, the hotel catering to thirsty motorists, its store supplying provisions to sheepherders driving their flocks to summer pastures on Hart Mountain, or the post office distributing mail to the valley homesteaders. As dusk approached, the western sky put on a symphony of colors — oranges, reds, ochres — all set against a background of pale blue. For a few moments Blitzen suddenly became "alive" as the setting sun seemed to bring a flush to its structures. As darkness approached I headed towards Frenchglen. Behind me the gathering darkness and the curvature of the flat Catlow Valley combined to hide Blitzen from my view. The desert experience, however, lingered long with me.

The landscape of Catlow Valley today reflects the human imprint and nature's control over the environment. Electricity, irrigation systems and the comforts of mobile home living reflect the role of modern technology. In summer, the valley is a checkerboard of greens, where irrigated, and tans where the desert prevails. Thousands of cattle that graze the Catlow Valley in the winter are moved to the Steens for summer pasturing. Tucked under or near the walls of Catlow Rim are the legacies of earlier years, Home Creek, Three Mile, and Roaring Springs Ranches.

Mature poplar trees almost hide the historic Roaring Springs Ranch, which backs against the rimrock. Water from the springs which give the ranch its name tumbles down the steep hillside. Indeed one of the creeks was once used to generate 7.5 kilowatts of electricity for the ranch. "It would be neat to resurrect the old power plant," Pat Raney stated. Although modernization at the Roaring Springs Ranch has inevitably caught up with the operations, the bunkhouse, smokehouse, kitchen, and dining facilities reflect an earlier time. And the seasonal routine of calving, branding, driving the cattle to the desert

pastures, and the fall roundup are still part of the Catlow Valley scene.

Alvord Basin

The gravel road from the Catlow Valley climbs up Long Hollow, twists a little, then plunges into the Alvord Basin. The Alvord is an area rich in history and scenic geology. The Steens towers up to 5,000 feet (1,550 m.) over the gravel road that hugs the western edge of the basin. During the spring, creeks such as Indian, Pike, Wildhorse, and Big Alvord tumble down the steep escarpment of the Steens, bringing debris to the basin floor. There is no surface outlet from the Alvord, and the water balance of the bodies of water in the basin is determined by the inflow from the surrounding mountains, principally the Steens, and by summer evaporation, which is considerable. In humid years the Alvord Desert and Alvord Lake become shallow bodies of water. During extended arid conditions the water evaporates, leaving dazzling white salt flats. Relic shorelines in the valley indicate that a lake 400 feet (124 m.) deep existed at one time. Alvord, Mann and Juniper Lakes are all that is left of the once large lake. Stream- and wind-deposited sediments fill part of the valley.

The name "Alvord" was given by Captain George B. Currey of the lst Oregon Cavalry at the time of the 1864 Snake War to honor his commander, Brigadier General Benjamin Alvord. In 1864 Currey established Camp Alvord near the mouth of Wildhorse Creek at the foot of the Steens. Currey noted that Camp Alvord was located "in the midst of the finest grass valley I have seen since I left the broad prairie of the Mississippi Valley. Undoubtedly, stock raising from California and Nevada will locate here next summer."[33]

With peace restored to the region, ranches were indeed located in the Alvord Basin, and the cultural landscape today reflects the legacy of over a century of cattle raising. The Alvord and Whitehorse Ranches were established in the 1860s, and the names Devine, Todhunter, and Miller and Lux became synonymous with the large-scale cattle industry in Harney County. Irrigated meadows between the lower slopes of the Steens and the basin floor now produce

View from the Roaring Springs Cave located in the western flank of Catlow Rim. In the 1930s Professor Luther S. Cressman and his students from the University of Oregon excavated the cave and discovered a variety of Indian artifacts. Photo by Stuart G. Garrett, M.D., Bend.

The ''ghost town'' of Blitzen at sunset. Blitzen, named after the Donner and Blitzen River, was at one time, on the main north-south route through the Catlow Valley. The settlement had a hotel, school, post office and store. Drought forced homesteaders from the Catlow Valley. The post office closed February 2, 1943. Photo by Ray Hatton.

The Steens rises over 5,000 feet (1,550 m.) above the Alvord Valley floor. Photo by Marcus Haines, Burns.

The Steens provides a scenic background to the historic Alvord Ranch. The ranch, which celebrated its centennial in June 1971, is still a working ranch. Although the original large white ranch house used by John Devine in the nineteenth century burned down, some of the original buildings (rock store house and granary) are still being used. Photo by Marcus Haines, Burns.

alfalfa for winter feed for the thousands of cattle that spread out over juniper, grassland and desert scrub from Juniper Lake in the north to the Nevada state line in the south.

Despite the 4,100-foot (1,270 m.) elevation, several of the ranches raise some of their own vegetables and fruit. The geologist Israel C. Russell, in his travels through the basin in 1908, noted that all kinds of vegetables and hardy fruits were doing well. In 1915 a Winnemucca attorney, C.E. Robins, stated that with irrigation waters, he could make the Alvord the "Italy of Southeastern Oregon", growing grapes in the valley. The *Burns Times-Herald*, July 24, 1920, reported that George Smyth of Andrews was successfully growing raspberries, gooseberries, grapes, watermelons, apricots, peaches, peas, and plums.

The Alvord Ranch, secluded amid tall poplars, weeping willows, locusts, and cottonwoods, is located at the base of the Steens, which rises dramatically to the west. The ranch still reflects the historical heritage of the old Harney County cattle empires, although the storehouse and the granary built in the 1870s by original owner John Devine are the only original buildings in use. Let's turn the clock back and look at the Alvord Ranch as it was early in the twentieth century, as described by Evelyn Gilcrest. [34]

Following the death of John Devine, Evelyn's father John Gilcrest, who worked for Henry Miller's vast Pacific Livestock Company, was appointed manager of the Alvord Ranch. In 1902, Mrs. Gilcrest and her three children left their comfortable Oakland home to join Mr. Gilcrest at the isolated ranch. Evelyn described the four-day wagon trek northward from the railhead at Winnemucca: "One is overwhelmed by the immensity of the surrounding space and the engulfing quiet. The twisting, dusty track extends out and away over the next ridge in the distance, and once that ridge is topped, over another beyond.... The ranch was like an oasis, a desert with green alfalfa fields, rich meadow grasses with cattle and horses grazing. The house itself, a comfortable eight-room one including five bedrooms, was set in a beautiful grove of poplar with its back to the mountains and front to the [Alvord] desert...."

Evelyn Gilcrest remembers the wonderful fruit and vegetable garden — carrots, beets, lettuce, cauliflower, corn, strawberries and several kinds of fruit. Freight wagons with supplies came to the ranch twice a year. Burns, where the nearest physician was located, was three days distance. Mail came twice a week if weather conditions permitted (today it is delivered three times a week). Water for domestic use was carried into the house. Kerosene lamps provided lighting and stoves fueled by sagebrush supplied heat for cooking.

In 1933 a visitor to the Alvord Ranch described it as being self-sufficient — no phone, no electricity. In 1930, Senator J.D. Billingsley of Ontario proposed purchasing the Alvord Ranch and developing it into a hunting and fishing lodge. Billingsley, who had lived at both the Whitehorse and Alvord Ranches for many years, also planned on using the Alvord Desert as a race track for autos and improving access to the Alvord from Burns and Winnemucca.

On June 20, 1971, the Alvord Ranch celebrated its centennial. Ed Davis, owner of the Alvord, recollected the occasion: "Yes, on that day we had an estimated 2,000 people, some coming from as far away as Maine. We barbecued three cows and went through 40 kegs of beer. By 6 P.M. we had run out of the 20,000 paper cups we had ordered. Dancing continued until the early hours of the next day to a country and western band from Vale. It was quite a celebration!"

A narrow road climbs sharply from the Alvord Desert, twisting, turning, and climbing some more. Except for the phone lines that run straight up the mountain, there is little to indicate that the road leads anywhere but smack into the Steens. In reality, it leads to the home of the Weston brothers, Mike and Jim, both near 80 years old in 1986. These two prospectors, who work their cinnabar (mercury) claim, live in a Quonset hut embedded into the side of the mountain and covered with dirt and rock.

On the occasion of my visit, Jim was heading down the mountain to pick up the mail and drive to Fields. Mike was at home, and he extended a welcome. A wood stove emitted a cheery heat to ward off the December cold. The cavernous room, perhaps 50 feet (15 m.) in length, functioned as kitchen, dining room, living room, bedroom, and library. The brothers cook on an old cast-iron wood-fueled stove, a propane range, or a modern electric range. A microwave oven stood by to supplement the other three cooking devices! A dishwasher, a refrigerator, and a freezer lined the wall next to the stoves. Across the room an afternoon soap opera beamed into the living area. "All we can get is from Boise, Idaho," said Mike.

At the back of the hut was a wall-to-wall library. "We do a lot of reading in the winter," added Mike. The stacks of books included several large reference books. Books were everywhere! A short tunnel at the back of the hut opened to a bathroom, to a walk-in refrigerator, and to another storage area. A longer tunnel, which served as a workshop, led to a narrow shaft. Here a fixed wooden ladder climbed upward to their greenhouses, heated by warm air rising from the ground. Mike nimbly clambered up the ladder, then proceeded to explain how he grew yams.

Back down and along the tunnel, Mike proudly pointed out the hot water system. "We burn sagebrush in 100-gallon barrels. The burning sagebrush heats our water in just minutes." Telephone links the Westons with the outside world. Shopping is done in Burns monthly. Mike, who first established the mining claim in 1951, moved to the property in 1958, when sections of the Quonset hut were hauled up the steep road and reassembled against the mountainside. When asked about pets, Mike said, "We had a dog once. He didn't last long — got hold of the wrong snake. We've seen large bobcats prowling around." Obviously, pets would not last long!

Outside the hut, an official U.S. weather station has been operated by the Westons since 1969. Day-to-day data is relayed to the Weather Service by amateur radio; monthly records are sent to Asheville, North Carolina.

Some 15 miles (24 km.) south of the Alvord Ranch is the tiny settlement of Andrews. Although Oregon state highway maps shows Andrews, and indeed, a collection of buildings crowd the gravel highway that skirts the Steens, the community has declined from its early years. The settlement was originally named Wildhorse by the Smyths, who relocated in the Alvord Basin from Diamond in 1897. Evelyn Gilcrest wrote of the community, "Sometimes in the summer...we went on picnics down the valley towards the little settlement of Wild Horse [sic], which consisted of post office [officially known as Andrews], store, two saloons and a few houses." Subsequently, the community itself was renamed Andrews, after postal authorities modified the spelling of the name of Pietre Andrievs who had settled in the vicinity in 1890. Later the Smyth Hotel, built

The Andrews Hotel, also known as the Smyth Hotel after its original owners was, according to the *Harney County Historical Inventory,* the scene of much socializing and "revelry." In 1924 the hotel caught fire and was destroyed. Photo courtesy of Marcus Haines, Burns.

about 1910, operated at Andrews. The hotel included a pool hall, dining room, kitchen and living quarters in addition to the bedrooms. By 1920 the census of the Andrews precinct was listed at 135.

Andrews was a lively place at that time. Buckaroos and sheepherders gathered in the saloon to drink, argue, or play poker. During the Prohibition era the saloon, used for dances and parties, remained a social center for the Alvord Valley. On Christmas Eve, 1924, fire destroyed the Andrews Hotel. With the decline of the sheep industry in the Steens and with faster travel time to larger service towns, Andrews declined in population. The saloon with its false front still stands, but any mementos of the building's boisterous past are locked behind boarded-up doors and windows.

Andrews still operates a compact stone-built grade school. In the 1986-87 school year, the enrollment was down to two. Bonnie Weter, the teacher, introduced me to the entire student body, Shawn Blair in 6th grade and brother Shannon in kindergarten. Bonnie, who was in her last year of teaching before retirement, had previously lived in western Oregon and in Chicago. What a contrast to the Alvord Desert country! Apart from having to adjust her shopping habits ("It is over two hours to the Burns stores!"), Bonnie found the desert a fascinating place with its quality of light, the colors of the sunrise, and the rapid weather changes as winds suddenly sweep down the Steens.

Shannon proudly demonstrated his computer skills as he slipped software disks into the disk

The old saloon at Andrews. The saloon was built by the Smyth brothers in the late 1890s. For years the saloon was patronized by travelers and Basque sheepherders and Alvord Valley residents. It was also used for community activities, periodically for church services, or as a photograph studio. One of its five small rooms had a wall-length mirror and a copper railing. Photo by Ray Hatton.

The Andrews one-classroom school and (left) teacher's residence. The Steens towers over 5,000 feet (1,550 m.) above the school grounds. Photo by Ray Hatton.

drive, then proceeded to match objects shown on the screen. Shannon, who rode his horse to school in fine weather, excitedly discussed the artifacts he had discovered on the nearby desert. When cleaning up was to be done at the school, Shawn and Shannon became janitors and earned a little pocket money for their work.

In 1987 only four people lived in Andrews. Standing watch over Andrews, the Steens remains as a silent witness to the community's brief but lively history.

A few miles southeast of Andrews lies Alvord Lake. In extended periods of dry weather the lake evaporates, leaving a large area of white alkali salts. Borax was mined as early as 1897. Charles Taylor and John Fulton, who had previously mined borax in Nevada, purchased 3,000 acres (1,230 ha.) of "worthless desert" for $7,000 and established the Rose Valley Borax Co. The company's Chinese laborers lived in "sod houses" built of bricks made from the boras residue and thatched with sod and tules; they were paid $1.50 a day. The borax was processed in 6,000-gallon (22,700 l.) vats, using water from nearby hot springs, then taken 150 miles (240 km.) by 16-mule-team wagons to the railhead at Winnemucca, Nevada.

Increased operating costs, decreasing availability of fuel (sagebrush), reduced quality of the salts, and cheaper deposits in California combined to terminate operations in 1907. However, in 1960 the Boron Products and Mineral Production Co. stated that it intended to mine borax salts at the site and to bring trailers for 80 families to nearby Fields. Nothing materialized from those plans, and in the late 1980s only the mounds of debris, rusty boiling vats, and the ruins of one of the sod houses remain of the early-day Alvord mining venture.

Throughout the Alvord Basin are several hot springs. Earthquake activity was felt in the region in the 1920s. Then on August 9 and 10, 1943, at least a dozen shocks were felt in Fields, and in September 1961, other shocks occurred over a wider area. The steepness of the fault scarp along the west side of the valley is further testimony to the recent geologic activity in the area.

Fields, established as a stagecoach and freighting station in 1881 and named after early settler Charles Fields, has neither grown nor shrunk in over a century. In November 1945, fire destroyed the general merchandise store and dance hall. A

Old stone schoolhouse on the Defenbaugh Ranch near the Trout Creek Mountains, in the southern section of Harney County. Photo by Lyn Jensen, Moonbeam Graphics, Bend.

Hikers Larry Asmussen, Jim Alger, and Howard Bay, members of the Desert Trail Association, pause on their hike across the Alvord Desert. The D.T.A., with headquarters in Burns, was the creation of Russ Pengelly of Burns. The D.T.A. has established hiking trails in the Steens, Alvord Desert, and Pueblos. It schedules several annual hikes. Photo by Russ Pengelly, Burns.

The small community of Fields, located in the southern end of the Alvord Valley, includes a schoolhouse and Fields Station. The original Fields Station, established in 1881 as a stagecoach and freighting place, was destroyed by fire in 1945. Today Fields Station consists of a store, post office, cafe, and small motel. Photo by Ray Hatton.

The Whitehorse Ranch barn, with a white wooden horse atop the cupola. Although the barn has undergone modifications, it has been well maintained since it was built during the time cattleman John Devine established his cattle empire in Harney County (1868-1889). On August 23, 1969, over 800 guests joined the Naftzger family, owners, in celebrating the 100th anniversary of the Whitehorse Ranch. Photo courtesy of Marcus Haines, Burns.

rebuilt store, post office, and restaurant caters to area residents and travelers through the Alvord Basin. A tiny motel offers overnight accommodations. The Fields schoolhouse, which boasts an outdoor covered play area, has an enrollment of four. West and southwest of Fields the Pueblo Mountains dominate the landscape.

The highway south of Fields parallels the eastern base of the Pueblo Mountains, from which tumble a half dozen fast-flowing creeks during wet periods or times of snowmelt. South of Alvord Lake the depression is known as the Pueblo Valley. East of the upper end of the Pueblo Valley stand the barren, bulky Trout Creek Mountains.

Straddling the Oregon-Nevada border is Denio.

Until December 31, 1950, the Denio post office was situated (barely) in Oregon. According to an old-timer, when no one in Oregon wanted the postmaster's job, "they moved the thing [post office] into Nevada." In the frontier days, about 1900, the population of the Denio Station area, which included borax miners, sheepherders, and drifters, was estimated to be 1,000. Denio at that time supported three saloons and four hotels. Today it is a small community serving local ranches and motorists entering the Pueblo-Alvord Basin from the south.

TREASURE VALLEY AND THE OWYHEE COUNTRY

Treasure Valley

Ross Butler, long-time resident of the Treasure Valley area and local historian, said it well: "The Snake River and its tributaries are the lifeblood of this area." Salmon runs on the Snake River provided food for Indians, who called the region "the Valley of the Rivers."

A detailed topographical map of eastern Oregon and southern Idaho supports this statement. Upstream from Marsing, Idaho, the Snake River is mostly incised into a plateau and for several miles it receives no major tributaries. Downstream from Weiser, Idaho, the Snake River carves the deepest gorge in North American, Hells Canyon. Between Marsing and Weiser, some 50 miles (80 km.), the Snake sluggishly makes its way across the Treasure Valley, receiving tributaries such as the Owyhee and Malheur from the Oregon side and the Boise, Payette, and Weiser from the Idaho side. In addition, the Treasure Valley is crisscrossed by canals, both in Oregon and in Idaho.

The landscape of the Treasure Valley reflects the impact of water and of a climate that is conducive for the growth of a variety of crops. Topography and soil types, to a large extent, help direct what is grown and where. While row crops are grown in the deep silt loams of the Owyhee-Greenleaf soils close to the Snake River, the moderate deep loams of the bench-lands are better suited to wheat and corn. The green and golden fields where slopes, water, and soils are favorable for farming contrast markedly with the untamed sagebrush of the adjacent desert. In sum, the treasure of the valley is not gold but the agricultural bounty in the form of sweet Spanish onions, potatoes, corn, sugar beets, wheat, and other crops, plus livestock.

In parts of the Treasure Valley, the Snake River forms the border between Idaho and Oregon. The Treasure Valley country was visited by the white man as early as 1811, when the Wilson Price Hunt company of the Astor expedition passed through the region. Oregon Trail pioneers converged on the Treasure Valley in the 1840s. Fort Boise, an important Hudson Bay outpost, was located on the Snake River where the Boise River entered the Snake, a few miles south of Nyssa.

Today, the Treasure Valley is a geographical region that encompasses agricultural lands located in both Oregon and Idaho. Oregonians from Ontario and Nyssa shop in Nampa and Boise for a better selection of goods. Idahoans from Payette, Parma, Caldwell, and other Idaho communities shop in Ontario to avoid Idaho sales tax. Residents of the Idaho cities of Payette, Fruitland, New Plymouth, and Caldwell work in Ontario. An informal survey of customers at the opening of the Ontario branch of the Emporium department store revealed that 43 percent of the shoppers were from Ontario; 11 percent from Vale; over 36 percent were Idaho residents. Ontario is the trade center for 50,000 to 60,000 people.

The social ties between residents of eastern Oregon and southern Idaho are strong. Residents of Ontario, Nyssa, and Vale watch Idaho news on any of five television channels and often listen to Idaho radio stations. The Sunday newspaper for many Oregonians in the Treasure Valley is the *Idaho Statesman*, although the Ontario *Daily Argus-Observer* publishes a Sunday edition. Many of the Treasure Valley residents in both Oregon and Idaho are members of the Church of

The canyonlands of the Owyhee country are very different from the Basin and Range landforms found elsewhere in Southeastern Oregon. Outcrops of multi-colored volcanic tuffs, sculptured by weathering and erosion, appear in many scenic geological features such as Leslie Gulch. Leslie Gulch was named after a Silver City cattleman, Hiram E. Leslie, who was killed by a bolt of lighting May 31, 1882. Photo by Ron Cornmesser, Ontario.

Jesus Christ of Latter Day Saints. Students at Treasure Valley Community College in Ontario mostly come from Treasure Valley towns, whether in Oregon or Idaho. Idaho students are not charged out-of-state tuition.

The entire area is on Mountain Standard Time. Said Bob Kindschy, resident of Vale since 1957, "When I pick up *The Oregonian*, I read about strange towns and strange people."

ONTARIO

While some of the migrants on the Oregon Trail "dropped out" along the Snake River area, most of the Ontario area was settled by migrants who had reached their goal, the lush Willamette Valley, but who retraced their steps to the

In summer the green farm fields of the Treasure Valley (southwest of Ontario) contrast with the nearby parched hills. Photo by Ray Hatton.

Treasure Valley, for whatever reason, and established homesteads along the Snake and lower Malheur Rivers. One of the first settlers, James W. Virtue, named the new community of Ontario after his place of birth, Ontario, Canada. By the early 1880s Ontario was considered a "cow town", but even then crops were grown on the fertile lands in the vicinity. The arrival of the railroad in Ontario in 1884 enabled the city to become a shipping point for cattle from both Malheur and Harney County rangelands. The town was laid out by railroad builder Robert E. Strahorn in the early 1880s, who at that same time laid out Caldwell, Idaho. In 1886, some 673 cars of livestock were shipped from Ontario. Eleven years later the shipments of livestock totaled nearly 2,000 cars. In 1899, during a six-week period, $1.5 million worth of cattle were shipped. In addition, large quantities of wool were moved.

Reclamation of the sagebrush lands west of Ontario started around 1880, when families (originally from Nevada) diverted water from the Malheur River. By the turn of the century, several thousand acres of land around Ontario were under irrigation. It was, however, the completion of dams on the Malheur and its tributaries and on the Owyhee that "made the desert bloom." By 1902, Ontario was "the metropolis of Malheur County", with all lines of business well represented. It was described as a very desirable place of residence, with planted trees on the main street. Stage lines ran daily to Vale and Burns. Trains stopped in the city; two ferryboats operated on the Snake River.

In 1911 a wagon bridge was built across the Snake River at a cost of $30,000. *The Oregonian*, November 9, 1913, reported: "The road leading across the bridge has a steady stream of teams going and coming. Practically half the trade of Ontario comes across from Idaho. So you can see what sort of a stroke the Ontario people made when they built this bridge and road and annexed this slice of Idaho's territory." The newspaper added how Ontario had grown — new buildings, two fine hotels including the five-story Hotel Moore, two banks, and two good weekly newspapers. Across the river from Ontario, added the newspaper, was one of the best fruit districts in Idaho or Oregon.

Ontario's early economic base was agricultural. Today, the economy of not only Ontario but also of Malheur County is still predominately related to some type of agriculture. While many farms in the Midwest were suffering economically in the

GEOLOGY: OWYHEE UPLANDS
By Bruce Nolf

The Owyhee bedrock, like that of most Southeastern Oregon, is comprised of young (mid-Cenozoic) volcanic and volcanically derived materials, including tuffs, tuffaceous sediments, and lava flows. The thick sequences of basalt flows so conspicuous west of the Owyhee country, in such ranges as Steens Mountain, are thinner and less prominent in the Owyhee Uplands. However, large-volume explosive silicic volcanism is well recorded in the Owyhee area by thick sequences of ashflow tuffs, many of them notably welded and thus forming high cliffs in outcrop. Alteration by fluids escaping from the cooling ashflows, by younger hydrothermal activity, and by weathering, has produced a variety of colors on these cliffs. A number of isolated buttes represent the dissected roots of ancient volcanoes. Some very recent basaltic flows occur where the Brothers Fault Zone crosses the Owyhee area. The Cow Lake-Jordan Craters flows are the most notable of these. Old, pre-Cenozoic basement crops out just east of the Oregon line, in southwestern Idaho, and has been the site of considerable mining activity in the past. Bedrock on the northeast end of the Owyhee area is young sedimentary and volcanic deposits associated with the Snake River Plain, a site of considerable subsidence and volcanism in late Cenozoic time.

The Owyhee landscape differs from that of most of Southeastern Oregon for two principal reasons. First, Basin-Range faulting is much less prominent in the Owyhee country, and the terrain is not broken by faults into the high, north-south-trending ranges so conspicuous in the landscape to the west. Second, the Snake River, the major tributary to the great Columbia River drainage system, has a route (southwest and west along the Snake River downwarp, and north across the Blue Mountains) that takes it very close to the Owyhee Uplands. The seaward flow in the Snake and Columbia drainages has been of such magnitude as to cut and maintain canyons and valleys close to sea level across many major ranges of the North American Cordillera. In turn, streams tributary to the Snake, such as the Owyhee River, have cut deeply into lands adjacent to the Snake River, and have dissected these areas greatly. Thus the Owyhee area, although not in a region of particularly high precipitation, bears the imprint of stream erosion much more conspicuously than any other part of Southeastern Oregon. The effectiveness of stream erosion is directly related to the steepness of stream flow, among other factors. The Owyhee River, which joins the Snake River at an elevation of only 2,200 feet (670 m.), has been able to cut deeply into uplands that are mostly between 4,000 and 5,000 feet (1,200-1,500 m.) in elevation. The canyon formed by the Owyhee River and some of its tributaries (Leslie Gulch, as an example), with steep walls of multicolored tuffs and other volcanic units, is one of the most notable features of the Owyhee landscape.

As a result of the well-developed external drainage to lower elevations, and the absence of strongly developed Basin-Range faulting, the flat-floored, sediment-filled basins so prominent west of the Owyhee Uplands (Alvord, Catlow, Warner, etc.) are missing from the Owyhee landscape.

Irrigated fields south of Malheur Butte (background-left) contrast with the rugged hills that border the Treasure Valley west of Ontario. Pipeline (right) carries irrigation water across the valley. Photo by Ron Cornmesser, Ontario.

1980s, according to Malheur County extension agent Ben Simko, "The diversity [of agriculture] has helped Malheur County farms." This diversity includes not only the chief crops and livestock (1986 sales in millions of dollars) — cattle ($32.6m), Spanish onions ($25m), sugar beets (13.8m), milk ($11.6m), and potatoes ($9.5m) — but also quite a variety of other agricultural products including corn, alfalfa, wheat, barley, peppermint, spearmint, beans, and various kinds of fruit. The total agricultural income for Malheur County in 1986 was $125 million, down from 1980 ($137 million) but a substantial increase from $82 million in 1974.

The processing of agricultural crops is one of the major industries in the Treasure Valley, the biggest concerns being Ore-Ida Foods in Ontario, the largest diversified frozen foods company in the U.S., and the Amalgamated Sugar Company plant at Nyssa. Ore-Ida Foods contracts with local farmers for the corn, onions and potatoes that the plant processes and freezes. The company has its own research kitchens and laboratories and employs its own agronomists. Much of the labor is seasonal at the processing plant. The company's payroll is a big contribution to the economy of the Treasure Valley. About half of the workers at the Ontario plant live in Idaho, reflecting once again the strong bi-state regionalism of the Treasure Valley.

Harvesting of Spanish onions in the Treasure Valley. In the mid-1980s, the sale of onions in Malheur Country was valued at $25 million. Photo by Ron Cornmesser, Ontario.

Right: **Most of the residents of Malheur County live in the Treasure Valley area. Rugged topography in the Owyhee country and arid High Desert lands in the southern part of Malheur County result in a sparse population and limited travel routes.** Source: Official Highway Map of Oregon.

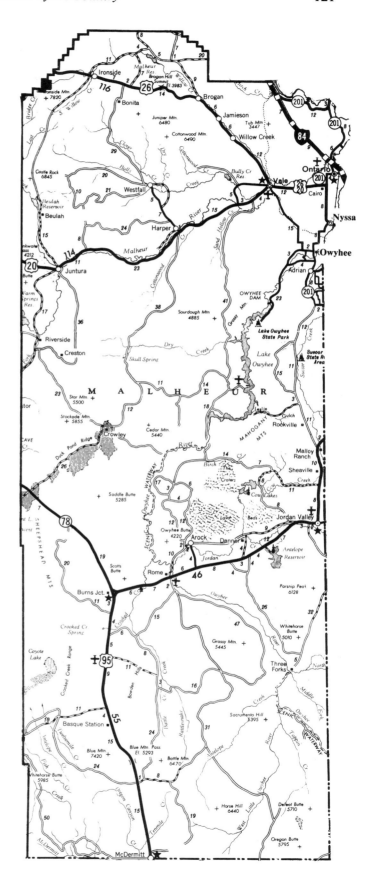

One interesting aspect of the geography of Malheur County is the cultural diversity. In addition to the Basques, discussed in the section on Jordan Valley, the Ontario area has strong ethnic minorities in the Japanese and Hispanics. The first Japanese family arrived in the Treasure Valley in the 1930s. During World War II, Japanese internees were sent to the Ontario area. Many Japanese became involved in farming and have become especially successful in intensive row crops, potatoes, sugar beets, and onions in particular. Ross Butler of Ontario stated, "The Japanese have become some of the finest citizens of the county. Their children have assimilated well into the public schools."

Each summer, usually in July, the Japanese in Ontario stage the Obon Festival, the "Festival of Joy" celebrating an ancient Buddhist legend. The Buddhist temple in Ontario has an open house,

Left:

The Obon Festival in Ontario is an annual event staged by the Japanese in Malheur County. The festival includes dancing, flower arranging, and dinner in the Buddhist Temple. Photo by Ron Cornmesser, Ontario.

Below:

Basque children participate in native dances, part of celebrations by the many Basques living in eastern Oregon and southern Idaho. The festivities are held in both Boise and Ontario. Photo by Ron Cornmesser, Ontario.

Succor Creek is a unique area, one noted for its wildlife, scenic geology, and relict Miocene flora. Within the area are herds of wild horses and bighorn sheep. Succor Creek is a favorite area for photographers drawn to the massive, colorful castle-like formations. Photo by Ron Cornmesser, Ontario.

with displays of crafts and a performance of the traditional Obon Odori dance. Also in Ontario is a food store, Kobayashi's, which retails a wide variety of Japanese foods.

The first Mexican to work in Malheur County came in 1918. However, it was not until the 1930s and 1940s that Hispanics came in large numbers, as intensive agriculture (especially the growing of sugar beets which was very labor-intensive) expanded in the Treasure Valley. During the summer, workers from the lower Rio Grande Valley migrated to the area. Many subsequently established residency in Malheur County, in particular in the Nyssa area. Like the Japanese, the Mexican-Americans preserve their own culture. The Cinco de Mayo Fiesta, with Mexican dancing and food, is held every year in Ontario, as it is in every Mexican community, to celebrate the defeat of the French army on May 5, 1862, in Pueblo, Mexico.

The Buddhist Temple in Ontario is one of the few such temples in Oregon. It is the site of the annual Obon Festival in July. Photo by Ron Cornmesser, Ontario.

Another aspect of the cultural diversity in the Treasure Valley is the strong membership in the Church of Jesus Christ of Latter Day Saints — the Mormons. Many Mormons moved to the Treasure Valley and purchased land in the 1930s, when irrigation of farmlands was expanded. Today, Mormons make up 15-17 percent of the population of Malheur County.

The most distinctive natural landmark in the Ontario-Vale area is Malheur Butte. The butte, once known as Kennedy Butte after a pioneer who homesteaded at its base, is a weathered volcanic plug that rises abruptly above the lush farmlands along the banks of the Malheur River. Malheur Butte was used by Indians as a vantage point to observe approaching wagon trains on the Oregon Trail in the 1840s. In my travels to eastern Oregon and Idaho, I look for Malheur Butte as a landmark: not far to Ontario, now! The butte seems to change its personality with the season. One December, when a persistent damp fog shrouded the Treasure Valley, Malheur Butte suddenly loomed from the mist as if it were a white apparition. It looked cold and forbidding, with snow draping its craggy pinnacles. In spring, a deep green skirt dresses the lower grassy slope. By summer, a scorching sun has long since parched the grass, and its landscape reveals the true nature of the region — desert.

ADRIAN

Adrian is a small, quiet farming community located on the Snake River, 12 miles (19 km.) south of Nyssa. The forerunner of Adrian was Riverview, established 1911, a community that was located on the eastern side of the Snake River. When the Oregon Short Line Railroad was extended in 1912 from Nyssa to a point opposite Riverview, on the west side of the river, the railroad named the place "Adrian" in recognition of James Adrian, a local sheepman. In 1915 the Riverview post office was moved across the river to Adrian. The completion of a highway bridge over the Snake River in 1914 ended the old ferry that shuttled across the river.

By 1919, Adrian was a thriving little village with several businesses and homes. Small-scale irrigation in the Adrian area had begun in 1914. The *Vale Enterprise*, January 8, 1914, reported, "Only 12 years ago the land was vast sagebrush. Now that it is cleared, two canals bring water from the Boise River. Alfalfa, clover hay, corn, clover seed, potatoes, cherries and apples are grown." The Owyhee project brought people to Adrian and other Treasure Valley towns to settle the newly irrigated lands.

NYSSA

From a distance, the skyline of Nyssa is more typical of a Plains State farm town, with the tall Amalgamated Sugar Companny silos rising above the flat Treasure Valley plains. As with Adrian, the railroad and the Owyhee irrigation waters helped create Nyssa. Both towns are on the Snake River, directly opposite Idaho. The Oregon Short Line came to Nyssa in 1883, and by the turn of the century Nyssa was a trading center amid rich and productive lands. Although a variety of crops such as potatoes, Spanish onions, and corn are grown, Nyssa has become better known as "Oregon's sugar bowl." The Amalgamated Sugar Company processing plant is located in Nyssa, on the western bank of the Snake River. The factory, built in 1938 and subsequently expanded, is Oregon's only sugar-producing plant and is the fourth largest beet sugar factory in the United States. The company employs agronomists to assist Treasure Valley growers with their various farm operations. Up-to-date information on growing techniques and proper application of chemicals and fertililzers is provided by the specialists. At Nyssa's agricultural research and development facilities, scientists and technicians are continually involved in attempting to produce new and better varieties of sugar beet seeds through genetic studies of the plant. Of critical importance to both the growers and the processors are the sugar content of the beet, the yield, and the plant's resistance to disease. The company has its own farm for growing and testing sugar beets. A quality-control laboratory helps ensure the finished product has met required standards. Dried molasses beet pulp, residue from the processing of sugar, a high-protein livestock feed, is sold to farmers and livestock feeders throughout the West and in several foreign countries. The sugar, granulated, powdered, and brown, is marketed under the White Satin label. Sugar beets are harvested in the fall, and convoys of beet-laden trucks converge on the Nyssa plant.

VALE

When Malheur County was carved from Baker County in 1887, a vote was taken to determine the county seat of the newly-created county. Vale edged Jordan Valley, 215 to 202. Ontario, Paris (a townsite optimistically laid out by Upper Malheur

The Rinehart "Stone House" at Vale. This historic building, built in 1872, served travelers and was a place of refuge during the Bannock Indian Wars of 1878. Photo by Bob Kindschy, Vale.

Succor Creek arises in Idaho but mainly flows through Malheur County before joining the Snake River back in Idaho. The Succor Creek area includes a variety of landscapes — escarpments, deep, narrow canyons and gulches, rolling hills and confined pasturelands along the valley floor. Oregon Economic Development Photo.

River ranchmen), Grove City, and Baxterville also received votes. In a runoff election, Vale won the majority support. By 1902 Vale, then population 200, was described as a thriving county seat with wooden sidewalks, feed barns, and the only flour mill in the county. The Ontario-Burns stage line, with one stage in each direction daily, stopped at Vale. Just outside of town are hot springs "possessing highly valuable medicinal properties . . superior of any mineral water on the Pacific Coast." Today, despite being dwarfed in size and population by Ontario, Vale is still the Malheur County seat. It lies astride Highway 20, the main artery that runs from Bend to Burns, Ontario, and Boise.

Vale's start was related to gold mining in the Mormon Basin, located north of Vale. Accommodations for miners and travelers passing through the Malheur Valley were established at Vale in 1864. The old "stone house," built in 1872 by L.B. Rinehart using stone blocks carved from nearby cliffs, was long an important station for travelers and for social events, and a place of refuge during the Bannock Indian Wars (1878). A century or so later, the Rinehart "stone house" was declared a historic landmark.

With the completion of the Vale and Owyhee irrigation projects, the county around Vale grew. The city itself, which had a population of about 1,000 in 1940, climbed to 1,500 by 1950 and reached its peak, 1,750, in the mid-1970s.

In the 1840s, Oregon Trail migrants crossed the Malheur River at Vale and welcomed the use of the hot springs there for bathing and for laundry use. In the mid-1980s the hot springs were used in the growing of mushrooms. Paul Ruthen, a Dutch authority on mushrooms, established the appropriately-named Oregon Trail Mushroom Company at Vale in 1984. In the controlled growing environment, air temperature, carbon dioxide levels, ventilation, and water requirements are monitored by computers. Employees at the plant are engaged in preparing the synthetic compost, sterilizing it, and establishing the mushroom beds. By their third week, the already-sprouted mushrooms are doubling their weight every 24 hours. Pickers are able to gather three crops from one bed of mushrooms. The mushrooms are sorted and packaged under the "Le Champignon" brand. Some of the mushrooms are sold in the Treasure Valley area, but over half are shipped to distant markets such as Spokane,

The Owyhee Dam, dedicated in 1932, rises 417 feet (129 m.) above the bed of the Owyhee River. At the time of its completion it was the highest dam in the world. The Owyhee Reservoir, over 50 miles (80 km.) long, provides water for recreation and irrigation for the fertile Treasure Valley. Photo by Ray Hatton.

Owyhee River Canyon Viewpoint on the Three Forks Road, 15 miles (24 km.) southeast of Rome, Malheur County. Photo by Lyn Jensen, Moonbeam Graphics, Bend.

Seattle, and Salt Lake City.

The main employers in Vale are the Bureau of Land Management and the Malheur County offices. Vale has the third largest livestock auction in the Pacific Northwest, with buyers coming from as far away as California and the Midwest.

Around Vale, each valley contains isolated ranches. The commercial area of Vale, its 15 farm machine repair shops, farm equipment and fertilizer sales, reflects the agrarian nature of the Vale district.

The Owyhee Country

THE OWYHEE PROJECT

The Owyhee Project started with a dream by visionary Malheur County residents. Although the Owyhee Ditch, a private undertaking, was irrigating some 30,000 acres (12,300 ha.) of land as early as 1896, the Owyhee Irrigation District made plans that would change the landscape of the Vale-Ontario area. Government surveys for a dam site on the Owyhee River had been made in 1905, and one private company attempted to construct a dam on the Owyhee but went broke in 1909.

On December 5, 1924, Congress authorized the Owyhee Project. At that time Dr. Elwood Mead, U.S. reclamation commissioner, saw the magnitude of the project and laid plans for the settlement of the lands to be irrigated. After a survey of the site and the drilling of test holes, construction started in July 1928. During the period when the dam was built, the town of Owyhee became the construction camp. Dedication of the Owyhee Dam was held July 17, 1932. A special train, then busses, carried visitors from Dunaway, four miles (6.4 km.) west of Nyssa, to the dedication site. The railroad was later removed and the railbed converted to highway. The

Above:
A water wheel, used for irrigating a small area of flat land adjacent to the Owyhee River above the slack water of Owyhee Reservoir. The river turns buckets, which rise and tip water into an irrigation flume. Photo by Bob Kindschy, Vale.

Below:
The Rome "Coliseums" are located near the community of Rome (on the Owyhee River). The geological formations, tuffaceous deposits capped by a thin layer of basalt, are several hundred feet high. Differential erosion helped shape the formations. Photo by Bob Kindschy, Vale.

Oregonian, July 17, 1932, in reporting the dedication, noted, "Today hundreds of new homes blossom on the productive land that was desert from Harper to Vale in 1929." The curving concrete dam rises 405 feet (126 m.) and backs up the Owyhee River for over 30 miles (48 km.). Miles of tunnels, siphons, and canals take the water from the Owyhee to irrigate 119,000 acres (48,790 ha.) of fertile land throughout the Treasure Valley. The project cost $18 million.

The economic return on the project and the impact on the land by the irrigation waters have been impressive. Farmland, which was sold for under 75 cents per acre before the project, in time sold for $3,500 an acre. The annual value of the crops using Owyhee water is over $80 million. Desert land has been reclaimed. Farm families have been settled. Farm payroll is spent in Ontario and adjacent towns, thus creating serv-

The Old Basque Inn, Jordan Valley, once known as the Madariaga Boarding House after the Basque family that operated it, provided rooms and meals for travelers along what is now known as Highway 95. The original house dates back to the early 1900s. Photo by Ray Hatton.

Jordan Craters, located about 30 miles (48 km.) west of Jordan Valley, is a 28-square-mile (72 km2) area of relatively young volcanic features. Within the Jordan Craters area are examples of pahoehoe lava flows, lava blisters, lava tubes and spatter cones. Photo shows Coffeepot Crater with spatter cones in foreground. Jordan Craters, designated a Federal Reserve Natural Area because of its unique flora and geology, is managed by the Vale District of the BLM. Photo by Bob Kindschy, Vale.

ice-type employment. In 1929 there were only 278 acres (114 ha.) of farmland in the Ontario area that were planted with row crops. By 1946 row crops covered 10,000 acres (4,100 ha.). In turn, these crops have formed the basis for the two large food processing plants in the Treasure Valley. Francis McClean, publisher of the *Daily Argus-Observer*, Ontario's newspaper, in 1986 informed me, "Other dams helped, but this one [the Owyhee] is what made this country."

JORDAN VALLEY

It was mid-December and late at night. We had groped our way through a cold, thick fog since leaving the Alvord Basin. The warning light on my gas gauge flickered red. Burns Junction back down the road had appeared closed for the night. Suddenly ahead, bright lights — Texaco, Union 76, Shell, Chevron. Welcome, Jordan Valley!

The next morning was crisp, cold but clear. A heavy sparkling frost coated everything. Truck engines idled along Main Street. The JV Club Cafe did a brisk business, catering to truck drivers, other motorists, and local ranchers. I explored the town. Gas station signs towered over Main Street. Two motels and three cafes gave further evidence of the role of Jordan Valley, servicing truckers and motorists on Highway 95, which links the Snake River Plain with Winnemucca and the metropolitan areas of northern California. A number of abandoned business buildings, many built of durable stone, gave testimony to the time when Jordan Valley offered a wider range of services. The homey old-world atmosphere of the Old Basque Inn reminded me of the town's most unique cultural and historical aspect — its Basque population. I saw a large number of trailers and mobile homes parked on trailer pads, the solution to the housing shortage created by the opening of the DeLamar silver mines (located just across the border in Idaho) in 1977. To the north of town, Pharmacy Butte, a prominent natural landmark, looked down on the small community.

It was in 1863 that gold and silver were discovered in Idaho's section of the Owyhee Mountains. Within a few years, cities such as Ruby, Silver City, Dewey, DeLamar, and Bullion were thriving mining towns. In the late 1860s, the population of Bullion was pegged at 2,500; that of Silver City 5,000. Close on the heels of the miners came merchants, blacksmiths, carpenters,

and gamblers. Along the stream that flowed westward out of the Owyhee Mountains — Jordan Creek, named after the first mining party's leader, Michael Jordan — were hundreds of acres of tall, wild hay meadows, ideal for stock raising. Indians were a constant threat at that time, and settlers suffered heavy losses in cattle and horses. Military forts, Camp Lyons and Camp Three Forks, were established to protect miners and settlers. Hay was in great demand for both the military and the mining camps. In the winter of 1864, hay was packed to Silver City by mules and sold for an astronomical $300 a ton.

One of the early settlers on Jordan Creek was John Baxter. Baxter built a small stone residence and a larger building that functioned as a store, a post office, and a hotel for travelers. Thus Baxterville (also nicknamed Dog Town) was established. About the time Malheur County was formed, the settlement was renamed Jordan Valley. In 1888, in a vote for the county seat, Vale edged Jordan Valley by a scant 215-202 margin.

As mining in the Owyhee Mountains declined, the Jordan Valley economic base became cattle and hay. In 1901 the town had a bank, two stores, three hotels, two livery stables, several saloons, and a newspaper. Jordan Valley had no railroad, although a line joining Winnemucca, Nevada, with Caldwell, Idaho, was proposed. By the early twentieth century the sheep population in Oregon was estimated to be over three million. As the demand for sheepherders increased, Basques migrated to the Owyhee country beginning in 1889. Many of the Basques were young unmarried males, mostly from small villages in the northern Spanish province of Vizcaya. The Basques brought with them their distinctive culture, including their language (Euskara), dress, and customs. Thus the Basques of Jordan Valley developed a strong sense of community, one ethnically different from the Anglos. Marriages within the Basque population strengthened this community. Even in the early years, Basques were buried in a separate section of the Jordan Valley cemetery.

The Basques staged their own festivals. Social events included Sunday evening dances. The pelota court, built of sandstone quarried near Jordan Valley and completed in 1917, was used for years for the Basque game of pelota, also known as jai-alai. Basques helped with money and labor in the building of the Catholic church in

Farm dogs join Robert Aja, Jr. with his chores on the Hanley Ranch at Jordan Valley. Mike Hanley, author of the book *Owyhee Trails*, still uses horse teams on his ranch. Photo by Charles A. Blakeslee, Bend.

Jordan Valley. Sandstone was used in the construction of several buildings in Jordan Valley; Basques are skilled stonemasons. Several of these buildings display the characteristics of Basque houses in the Pyrenees — square, thick walls and pyramidal roofs.

In the 1920s, some 300,000 sheep grazed the hills and valleys around Jordan Valley. Basque herders moved the sheep from their winter pastures in the valleys to the new spring feed in the mountains. Seasonal and daily routine marked the life of the sheepherder. Lambing in late winter was followed by shearing in May, by transient shearers. At the end of summer, at least until 1937, sheep were moved to Murphy, a rail town in Idaho. From Murphy the sheep were shipped by rail to Nampa before moving to processing plants in Ogden, Kansas City, or Chicago. In the 1930s, trucks conveyed the sheep from the Jordan Valley area directly to Nampa.

In 1920 Jordan Valley's population was estimated at 350. From then, a steady decline in population set in until 1970, when the population was a little over 200. The sheep industry declined markedly after World War I. In January 1925 the Bank of Jordan Valley, which depended heavily on the local sheep industry failed. The collapse of the sheep market forced many Basques into bankruptcy. Many moved to Idaho. The 1934 Taylor Grazing Act, which curtailed grazing on the public domain, further hastened the decline of the number of sheep.

When the main Nevada-Idaho highway, later Highway 95, was completed and graveled in the 1930s and then paved in the 1940s, Jordan Valley became less isolated. Daily traffic in Jordan Valley in the mid-1940s averaged less than 200 vehicles a day. By 1980, it was 1,100 vehicles a day. The character of Jordan Valley was similarly changed. Gone are the Basque sheepherders. Gone are the Basque-owned and-operated boarding houses. The pelota game was abandoned in favor of American sports. Gone are the pool halls and Basque-owned mercantiles. Instead, Jordan Valley caters to local cattle ranchers, miners, and those traveling between Idaho and California.

Like cities in the Treasure Valley, Jordan Valley's economic and cultural ties are in many ways more with Idaho than with Oregon. The *Idaho Statesman* is read more than the *Oregonian*. Boise radio stations are easily picked up. Television news comes from Boise. The closest major shopping center is Nampa or Boise. Jordan Valley has become a truck stop. Giant multi-trailer trucks line the main street, their drivers pausing for coffee and meals before continuing their journeys.

In the mid-1970s, the DeLamar mine, an open pit extracting silver and gold, reopened. The population of Jordan Valley, which had dropped below 200 in 1975, doubled to 400 only two years

Burns Junction is located on a windswept plateau at the junction of Highways 78 and 95, some 92 miles (147 km.) southeast of Burns and 46 miles (74 km.) west of Jordan Valley. Services at Burns Junction include a cafe, store, gift section, gas station and four-unit motel. The settlement, established in the 1950s, caters mainly to motorists and, in the fall, to bird and big game hunters. Photo by Ray Hatton.

later. As a consequence, the grade school was overcrowded. Many bartenders, ranch hands, cashiers, waitresses, and dishwashers quit their jobs in Jordan Valley to work at the mines. Trailers and mobile homes were brought in to provide instant homes for the influx of workers. By the mid-1980s, half of the residences of Jordan Valley were mobile homes. The mine's tax dollars go to Idaho, but services for the employees are provided by the Oregon community in which the workers live.

EPILOGUE

It is time to reflect on our journey through Oregon's Big Country. As I stated in my introductory chapter, my first impression of the region was one of space. I still feel that way. Furthermore, with 38 percent of the people in this region clustered in Lakeview, Burns-Hines, and Ontario, I calculate that outside these three urban areas, the density of population within Southeastern Oregon averages only a little over one person per square mile (2.6 km²).

Thus small settlements like Brothers, Hampton, Plush, and Valley Falls often assume importance far beyond what their size would indicate. They serve local residents from a wide geographical area. They provide more than staple groceries, coffee, beer, and other supplies. The small towns function as places to socialize and exchange news. Major shopping excursions and medical, dental, and legal services that are not locally available mean long drives to Lakeview, Ontario, Bend or Boise. Whatever the destination, space has to be bridged by auto or pickup. To motorists traversing Oregon's Big Country, the small settlements are little oases, providing fuel, refreshment, or emergency supplies.

Between these small communities are wide-open places — Oregon's Big Country. Here, vistas are far-reaching. The many different forces of nature are well evident. Spectacular, elongated fault-block mountains such as Abert Rim, Hart Mountain, and the Steens tower over enclosed basins. Our time on earth is so brief, it is hard for us to picture the tectonic forces that created these fault scarps. It is difficult to envision the time when dry lake basins once cradled 200 feet (62 m.) or more of water. We see the results of the erosive power of glaciers on Steens Mountain or of running water in the Owyhee canyons, or wind on sand dunes, but we must imagine the long, slow processes that helped shape the landscapes.

The basins between the fault-block mountains, such as the Chewaucan, Catlow, and Alvord, have become the avenues for travel and settlement. Where irrigation waters have been brought to the surface, as in Christmas Valley, or carried by canals or aqueducts as in the Treasure Valley, there is a tamed look to the landscape. The summer green of alfalfa fields contrasts with the beiges and tans of the adjacent desert. But the desert has only been tamed in a few favored locations.

One of my former geography students, Carolee Thurman, summed up her perception of Oregon's Big Country, its nature and its mystique:

"Nature: impetuous, willful, headstrong, temperamental, passionate, fickle. The high desert country of Southeastern is Nature — wild and free, harsh and cold, warm and inviting, hot and searing; often, all in the space of a few hours of man-time. The desert seduces; lures with wild flower jewels of amethyst and ruby; teases with tiny surprises, the glint of obsidian, the flash of a pronghorn; the desert caresses with the splendor of a crimson sunset; it kisses with the tingling fresh chill of a sparkling morn; it wraps and enfolds in the silent embrace of a starlit night."

Go, venture, experience this part of Oregon.

END NOTES

1. *An Illustrated History of Baker, Grant, Malheur and Harney Counties* (1902), p. 742.

2. Clark and Tiller (1966).

3. *Cascades*. Vol. 12 (No. 1) Feb., 1971.

4. *Silver Lake Leader*, Feb. 16, 1912.

5. *The Burns Times-Herald* (Burns), March 7, 1914.

6. *Oregon Historical Quarterly*, December, 1902.

7. *An Illustrated History of Baker, Grant, Malheur and Harney Counties* (1902), P. 741.

8. On March 8, 1988, Bill Mellin was shot and killed at his Millican Store. Many of his collectibles over the years were auctioned off on May 7, 1988.

9. See Cressman (1964) and Bedwell (1973).

10. Bowman (1931), p. 106.

11. *The Oregon Journal*, November 20, 1960.

12. Allen (1980), p. 53.

13. Hedges (1930), p. 65.

14. Parks (N.D.), p. 1.

15. *The Bulletin*. May 27, 1986.

16. Allison, Ira S. (1979). *Pluvial Fort Rock Lake, Lake County, Oregon.*

17. E. D. Cope, (1889), The *American Naturalist*, p. 982.

18. *An Illustrated History of Central Oregon* (1905), p. 807

19. *Lake County Examiner*, March 25, 1915

Water cascades down the precipitous slopes of Big Indian Gorge, Steens Mountain. Several springs discharge into Big Indian Creek. Glaciated Big Indian Gorge is 1,600 feet (496 m.) deep. Photo by Jack Schwartz, Bend.

Even in late summer, patches of snow cling to some upper slopes of the eastern escarpment on Steens Mountain. The photo shows the basaltic layers that have been uplifted and then subjected to erosional forces. A small glacial cirque can be seen (left). In the background is Mann Lake, a popular fishing spot in the northern end of the graben geographically known as the Alvord Valley. Photo by Ray Hatton.

20. "The Journal of John Work." *California Historical Society Quarterly*, September 1943, p. 195.

21. *Lake County Examiner*, August 13, 1929.

22. *An Illustrated History of Central Oregon* (1905), p. 815.

23. The New Camp Warner, located on Honey Creek site was the original site for Camp Warner, having been selected by a small party of soldiers sent from Fort Vancouver. However, the 23rd Infantry sent out from Fort Harney could not cross the string of lakes and swamps of Warner Valley and set up what is now called Post Meadows on Hart Mountain.

24. *An Illustrated History of Central Oregon* (1905). p. 815.

25. *Lake County Examiner*, April 24, 1969.

26. Monroe (1930), P. 71.

27. Written by Alma Dell Campbell Reprinted in *The Burns Times-Herald*, January 31, 1960.

28. Monroe (1930), p. 75.

29. An interesting account of McGowan's life in Australia, in the Civil War and travels in the West, his marriage and settlement in Burns is included in the *Eastern Oregon Herald*, December 21, 1897.

30. *Burns Times-Herald*, November 13, 1931.

31. *Kiger Gorge* (unpublished manuscript) N.D.

32. The Raneys left the Roaring Spring Ranch in 1987 when the ranch was put up for auction

33. *Harney Country Inventory* 1978), p. 107.

34. Gilcrest, Evelyn (1962). *Oregon Historical Quarterly*, Vol. 63.

BIBLIOGRAPHY

Allen, Barbara. *Talking about the Past: A Folkloristic Study of Orally Communicated History.* Ph.D. Dissertation, University of California. Los Angeles, 1980.

Allen, Barbara. *Homesteading the High Desert.* Salt Lake City, University of Utah Press, 1987.

Allison, Ira S. *Fossil Lake, Oregon.* Corvallis, Oregon State University Press, 1966.

Allison, Ira S. *Geology of Pluvial Lake Chewaucan.* Corvallis, Oregon State University Press, 1982.

Beers, Christian. *Basque Settlement in Jordan Valley, Oregon.* M.A. Thesis, University of Oregon, 1982.

Bedwell, Stephen F. *Fort Rock: Prehistory and Environment.* Eugene: University of Oregon, 1973.

Bowman, Isaiah. *The Pioneer Fringe,* New York: The American Geographical Society, 1921.

Brimlow, George Francis. 1951. *Harney County Oregon and Its Range Land.* Portland: Binford & Mort Publishing, 1964.

Brogan, Phil F., and L. K. Phillips. *East of the Cascades,* Portland: Binford & Mort Publishing, 1964.

Buckles, James S. *The Historical Geography of the Fort Rock Valley. 1900-1941.* M.A. Thesis, University of Oregon, 1959.

Clark, Keith, and Lowell Tiller. *Terrible Trail: The Meek Cutoff, 1845.* Caldwell, Idaho: The Caxton Printers, Ltd., 1966.

Cressman, L. S. *The Sandal and the Cave.* Portland: Beaver Books, 1964.

Crow, Rankin. *Rankin Crow and the Oregon Country.* Ironside, Oregon, 1970.

Daubenmire, R. "Ecologic Plant Geography of the Pacific Northwest, *Madrono* Vol. 20, 1969.

Dicken, Sam and Emily. *Oregon Divided.* Portland: Oregon Historical Society, 1982.

Ferguson, Denzel and Nancy. *Oregon's Great Basin Country.* Burns: Gail Graphics, 1978.

Franklin J. and C. Dyrness, *Natural Vegetation of Oregon and Washington.* U. S. Forest Service, 1973.

French, Giles. *Cattle Country of Peter French.* Portland: Binfords and Mort, Publishers, 1964.

Gilcrest, Evelyn. "Alvord Ranch Interlude: Life on a Celebrated Range." *Oregon Historical Quarter.* Vol 63, 1962.

Hanley, Mike, and Ellis Lucia. *Owyhee Trails: The West's Forgotten Corner,* Caldwell, Idaho: Caxton Printers, 1973.

Hanson, Charles G. *Ecological Survey of the Vertebrate Animals on Steens Mountain, Harney County, Oregon.* Ph.D. dissertation. Oregon State University, 1956.

Hatton, Raymond R. *High Desert of Central Oregon.* Portland: Binford & Mort Publishing, 1977.

Hatton, Raymond R. *Pioneer Homesteaders of the Fort Rock Valley.* Portland: Binford & Mort Publishing, 1982.

Hedges, Ada Hastings. *Desert Poems.* Portland: Metropolitan Press, 1930.

Illustrated History of Baker, Grant, Malheur and Harney Counties. Spokane: Western Historical Publishing Co., 1902.

Illustrated History of Central Oregon. Spokane: Western Historical Publishing Co., 1905.

Jackman, E. R., and John Scharff, photography by Charles Conkling. *Steens Mountain in Oregon's High Desert Country.* Caldwell, Idaho: Caxton Printers, 1967.

Johnson, Daniel M. et al. *Atlas of Oregon Lakes.* Corvallis, Oregon State University Press, 1985.

Loy, William. *Atlas of Oregon,* Eugene, University of Oregon, 1976.

McArthur, Lewis A. *Oregon Geographic Names,* Fourth Edition. Portland: Oregon Historical Society, 1974.

Monroe, Anne S. *Feelin' Fine!* New York: Doubleday & Co., 1930.

Nielsen, Lawrence. *In the Ruts of the Wagon Wheels.* Bend, Oregon: Maverick Publications, 1987.

Otto, Bruce R. and Dana A. Hutchison. "The Geology of Jordan Craters, Malheur County, Oregon." *The Ore Bin.* Vol. 39, No.8, August, 1977.

Parks, Merritt Y. (Bud). *History of the Parks Family.* Unpublished Ms. N.P.

Preston, R. N. *Historical Early Oregon.* Corvallis, Oregon: Western Guide Publishers, 1972.

Shirk, David. *The Cattle Drives of David Shirk from Texas to the Idaho Mines. Portland: Champoeg Press, 1956.*

Talbot, Caryn. *P. Ranch, History and Preservation and Interpretive Development.* Burns: Malheur Wildlife Refuge, 1976.

INDEX